Hygiene Movement, which has since become a world-wide effort for the reduction, control, and prevention of mental disorders and the protection and promotion of mental health.

As the work developed, the preventive aspects of the movement came to the fore, and it is now widely recognized that mental hygiene is for the benefit of all of us since its objective is not merely freedom from mental disease, but the positive possession of mental health.

A MIND THAT FOUND ITSELF contains also the best and most concise account of the mental-hygiene movement—the early history, 1909–33, by Dr. C. E. A. Winslow, later developments, 1934–48, by Luther E. Woodward, Ph.D., and a new account of the most recent and current trends by Nina Ridenour, Ph.D.

A MIND THAT FOUND ITSELF

Pirie MacDonald

A MIND THAT FOUND ITSELF

An Autobiography

BY

CLIFFORD WHITTINGHAM BEERS

GARDEN CITY, NEW YORK

DOUBLEDAY & COMPANY, INC.

The printings listed in *Italics* were published by Longmans, Green & Company and those in CAPS by Doubleday & Company, Inc.

First edition, March, 1908
Second edition, with additions, June, 1910
Reprinted, November, 1912
Third edition revised, March, 1913
Reprinted, September, 1913
Reprinted, July, 1914
Fourth edition revised, March, 1917
Reprinted, February, 1920
Fifth edition revised, October, 1921

REPRINTED, JULY, 1923
REPRINTED, MARCH, 1924
REPRINTED, FEBRUARY, 1925
REPRINTED, APRIL, 1927
REPRINTED, MAY, 1928
REPRINTED, MAY, 1929, WITH ADDITIONS
REPRINTED, MARCH, 1930
REPRINTED, AUGUST, 1930
REPRINTED, FEBRUARY, 1931
REPRINTED, NOVEMBER, 1932
REPRINTED, OCTOBER, 1933
REPRINTED, JUNE, 1934
25TH ANNIVERSARY EDITION, ISSUED
MARCH, 1935, WITH ADDITIONS
REPRINTED, JUNE, 1937
REPRINTED, MAY, 1939
REPRINTED, AUGUST, 1940
REPRINTED, MAY, 1942
REPRINTED, FEBRUARY, 1944
REPRINTED, MARCH, 1945
REPRINTED, APRIL, 1948, WITH ADDITIONS
REPRINTED, JANUARY, 1950
REPRINTED, NOVEMBER, 1952
REPRINTED, AUGUST, 1953, WITH ADDITIONS
REPRINTED, JUNE, 1956
REPRINTED, APRIL, 1960
REPRINTED, DECEMBER, 1962

IN order that this book may be used more widely in the interests of the mental hygiene movement, the author, the sole owner of it, has assigned "absolutely and forever" to The American Foundation for Mental Hygiene, Inc., the copyright and all future profits accruing from the sale of the book.

EDITOR'S PREFACE TO 29TH PRINTING

THE death of Clifford Beers, which occurred on July 9, 1943, brought to a close one of the most remarkable careers in modern philanthropy. It is not the editor's purpose to recount here the unique achievements of Beers's life and work, which have been admirably summarized in the tributes to him that have since appeared in the press, and are reflected also, to an extent, in the concluding pages of this book, which contain a partial account of the growth and development of the movement he started. The editor ventures, however, to mention one or two less well-known aspects of Beers's vivid personality, from a more or less intimate knowledge of him as a friend and associate of many years, and to comment briefly on the meaning and significance of his self-imposed mission.

Upon his recovery from mental illness in 1904, Beers returned to business, the field he had always looked to as his life work after leaving college. It was characteristic of the man, however, that he did not hesitate to give up his aspirations to a business career and its material promise for the sake of the higher vocation to which, it became plain to him, he was being called. He did not choose his career, he said, it was thrust upon him. Beers had a profound admiration for many of our outstanding businessmen and he sometimes seemed to

regret the turn of fate that led him away from his youth-
ful ambition to succeed in business and into a totally
different career. But he sublimated his instincts for
material success and, as his friend, Dr. C.-E. A. Winslow
of Yale University, points out, "by his vision, energy
and organizing ability promoted an enterprise that
produced profits in the form of increased health and
happiness for the men, women and children of the
nation." If he was not a captain of industry, as Dr.
Winslow further expressed it, he was certainly a captain
courageous, because of his daring in publishing the
story of his experiences while mentally ill and his willingness to exploit his story—and himself—for the benefit
of others. "Thanks to the great moral courage of
Beers in, literally, making his life an open book, sufferers
from mental ills, and their families, encouraged by the
wholesome change that is taking place in the public
attitude toward diseases of the mind, are shedding their
wonted reticence in discussing their afflictions." He
breached the barriers of public reticence and the false
sense of shame and stigma hitherto attached to the
subject.

Just as it was his courage and vision that started the
mental hygiene movement, so it was Beers's faith and
sureness of purpose that helped to carry it through
stressful periods that are bound to occur in every pioneering enterprise. The National Committee for Mental Hygiene, which he organized in 1909, faced a difficult
task from the outset, for its work always loomed
mountain high beside funds all too limited for its needs.

Starting the work on borrowed money, Beers was subsequently instrumental in securing for it many large gifts which, with substantial grants from Funds and Foundations, kept the work going. His was a dynamic, energetic personality. He has been called a supersalesman of philanthropy, the dynamo of the mental hygiene movement. Withal, he was blessed with a sparkling sense of humor that served him well in many a moment of discouragement and defeat. He would remark, facetiously, when the National Committee was confronted with financial crises—and there were many of them— that a crisis "stimulated and refreshed" him, and he would forthwith go into action and raise the necessary funds to meet it. These crises, however, were a constant source of worry and harassment to him in later years and finally took their toll, becoming too burdensome for even his abounding energy and vitality. Undoubtedly they were a factor in the breakdown of his health that forced him to retire from active work four years ago, and it is not inaccurate to say that he not only dedicated his life to the cause of mental hygiene but ultimately gave it to that cause.

In an effort to solve the problem of recurring deficits, Beers established, in 1928, the American Foundation for Mental Hygiene, as a mechanism to raise funds not only for the National Committee but for state societies and other agencies working in the wide field of mental health. It was a unique "Foundation," starting, unlike other Foundations, with no great funds in its coffers but with hope and faith in its future as an instrumen-

tality for the financial stabilization of organized work
in mental hygiene.   Beers visualized it as a sort of
"community trust" of the people for the purpose of
securing and administering gifts and bequests for use in
protecting and promoting their mental health.   He obtained gifts and conditional pledges amounting to several
hundred thousand dollars but never realized his larger
hope of adequate financing of the Foundation com-
mensurate with the great work waiting to be done, and
this was a keen disappointment to him.   But Beers
builded better than he knew and he laid the groundwork
for big objectives in relation to human welfare that may
not be realized this year or next but will be in years
to come.

Four years ago the Central Hanover Bank and Trust
Company of New York, attracted by the possibilities
and promise of the mental hygiene movement, issued,
as a public service, a brochure for the information and
guidance of the philanthropically inclined, in which are
described the aims and activities of the National Committee for Mental Hygiene and of other organizations
and agencies working in its field. This interesting and
illuminating account of mental health progress urges
widespread support of the work, to extend the gains
that have been made, and "to crystallize and bring into
the present, possibilities of mental hygiene that now lie
largely in the future." It concludes: "We face a
troubled world, its unhappy difficulties due in great,
perhaps greatest part, to the mental, physical and moral
maladjustments of its peoples . . .   But mental hy-

giene has not as yet been far enough advanced to play
its essential part. When it has been, and the co-
ordinated efforts of those who heal the mind, of those
who heal the body, and of those who heal the soul are
brought to bear upon our world problems, shall we not
see the beginnings of a brighter day—the rise of a finer
and more stable civilization?" What better memorial
to Clifford Beers than to nourish, vitalize and carry
forward the noble work he started!

PAUL O. KOMORA

December 1943

INTRODUCTORY

From a letter to the author from William James that appeared in the 1st Edition:

You have handled a difficult theme with great skill, and produced a narrative of absorbing interest to scientist as well as layman. It reads like fiction, but it is not fiction; and this I state emphatically, knowing how prone the uninitiated are to doubt the truthfulness of descriptions of abnormal mental processes.

A letter to the author from Booth Tarkington, on the publication of the 25th Anniversary Edition:

"Seawood"
Kennebunkport, Maine.
September 29th, 1934.

MY DEAR MR. BEERS:

I am delighted to learn that the 25th Anniversary year of The National Committee for Mental Hygiene is to be marked by the publication of a 25th Anniversary Edition of A MIND THAT FOUND ITSELF—the book with which you launched the movement for mental health that has now become world-wide.

To be the author of a book that on its own merits and value—and without any formal advertising—has been reprinted almost every year for a quarter of a century

is a rare distinction, indeed.   It seems to me inevitable
that A MIND THAT FOUND ITSELF must be kept always
in print, for, after twenty-five years, it is already a
"classic", so to speak.

Your book is a unique human record of inner experience as well as a poignantly moving and inspiring tale
of truly adventurous achievement.   In addition, it pos-
sesses the sustained and climactic interest that novel
readers hope to find in novels.   The great William
James said that "It reads like fiction, but it is not fiction—" and the immense number of readers it has
already won prove Dr. James to have been right.
Readers of fiction as well as readers who prefer "non-
fiction" are bound to find A MIND THAT FOUND ITSELF
excitingly absorbing and to be interested not only in
your biography but in the Epilogue that is in this Anniversary Edition.

All of us who know your book admiringly of old, and
also those of us who are now introduced to it for the
first time, must find its value enhanced by the new material, which tells of the immense accomplishment in the
battle to win mental health.

Your book and the work that has grown out of its
publication have already saved many lives and added
incalculably to human happiness.   I am more than ever
convinced that none of us can *afford* to miss reading it
or to remain ignorant of the ways and means and the
agencies for protecting mental health.

Faithfully yours,
BOOTH TARKINGTON

FOREWORD TO SEVENTH EDITION

"A MIND THAT FOUND ITSELF" is a chronicle of the experiences of Clifford W. Beers with our culture of the early twentieth century and its instruments—called hospitals—for the care of the "insane." The story reflects ignorance, callousness, and irresponsibility of a sort that can be matched, and in many places more than matched, today in the middle of that century. But bad as conditions are at worst, there has been distinct progress at the top as a result of Beers's effort. The existence of low spots makes Beers's story as timely today as when written.

But this story also tells us through one example about an era in the history of social progress. If we look upon what happened to Mr. Beers in the psychiatric field as one facet of our culture at that time, we learn a great deal about that culture beyond the specific field of psychiatry. We are shown its processes in dealing with social problems. We dare to hope that this era is drawing to a close.

Prominent among the processes of that era is righteous indignation and blind and artless opposition to social evils. It all seemed so simple. If people lacked food, we fed them. If they lacked shelter, we housed them. If they behaved wrong, we told them not to, and if they did it again, we incarcerated them. We didn't waste money on minute studies that dealt with sequences and causes. We could not easily sell playgrounds, but we could sell courts and hospitals.

If under this principle society itself misbehaved; if, for example, inhumanities cropped up, we used the same technique. We ranted and blamed anybody conveniently situated who could be vulnerable to blame. We did not analyze the problem. We did not even imply that the public had failed in allowing that vulnerable person to be in a position of authority. And, of course, we did not reach beyond blame toward a realization that civilization itself was merely maturing and not fully matured.

It was this immaturity in our cultural development which Beers faced at every turn both as a patient and as a prophet. The explosive pressure within the mental hygiene field was so great that when he and his collaborators succeeded in correcting an irregularity at one point, and the record is filled with achievements, there appeared a bulge somewhere else. We have now, we dare to hope, arrived at a point where this kind of blind and artless effort may be supplanted by patient analysis and planning, skill and strategy. With the development of scientific medicine, careful diagnosis before treatment has become the key to progress in treating the ills of man. Possibly it will open up opportunities for progress similarly in treating the ills of mankind.

If the mentally ill are not dealt with humanely the first step is not a hue and cry, the one-time signal used in the pursuit of a felon, but rather a series of questions.

Can we cite chapter and verse? In what way is this inhumanity expressed? Then one becomes more specific. The mentally ill are housed badly, fed badly, injured bodily, and stigmatized. And still one must continue his query and ask "Why is this so?" Why are they housed badly? Study will show that, as a rule, it is because legislatures have been stingy and yet, as a rule, one finds that legislators know more about these problems than the average man. Then why does the legislature continue to be stingy? Because legislatures respond primarily to the will of the average man. If they go further than this, as they sometimes do under great pressure and embarrassment, the result is ephemeral. Have we then reached the ultimate in the conclusion that the culprit is the average citizen? Is it now time to be indignant? Only if we have no faith in the intelligence and good will of the average citizen. But let us, first of all, before righteous indignation, try an approach that admits that the average good citizen is capable of acting in good faith. Let us organize such citizens. Give them knowledge. Give them leadership. Give them sound solutions to the problem. Let the citizen in this way learn a type of citizenship which will eventually reach far beyond his responsibility to the mentally ill and affect his full obligations as a citizen.

Let us realize that the ills of the mental hospitals are not his evil intent, but the heritage of an outworn system which is wasting his money and opportunity. Under this system the mentally ill are "put away," so far away that they cease to be a part of his life. It is as though they no longer existed, as if putting them away had solved the problem. Under this system, which is so devoid of spirit, personnel of the best training and scientific inquisitiveness are not attracted and this adds further to the isolation. The precursors and early stages of mental illness are left without attention in the communities in which they developed and those patients who have recovered in the hospitals are returned home without the guidance that convalescent patients should have.

In this way the evil by-products of the neglect by society are constantly burdening it further : humanity and scientific treatment within the institutions are neglected and prevention of mental illness and the promotion of a higher level of mental health within the community are stunted.

In informing the average citizen our first task is to broaden his vision in order that he may see that the threat lies not in the mentally ill, however fractious they may be, but in the hiding from society of the evidences of its own shortcomings. In full perspective he will then see that the problem in its entirety includes :

1. The public needs protection from mentally ill and defective offenders.

2. Mentally ill and defective patients for whom treatment offers little promise need humane custodial care, both in institutions and in the community.

3. Patients with mental diseases need curative treatment and convalescent care, and mental defectives need

training and protection in the institution and in the community.

4. People need treatment for lesser mental deviations not requiring hospital service. These people include most of those with neuroses and those who are seriously maladjusted because of personality handicaps.

5. Clients of social agencies, physically ill patients, school children and college students, probationers of courts, and prisoners, all are the concern of non-psychiatric agencies, and others often require psychiatric diagnoses, consultation, and advice for known or suspected mental abnormality.

6. The personnel of these other community agencies need psychiatric instruction or orientation, in order to have a foundation for collaboration with psychiatrists and for understanding and treating the simpler mental health problems encountered in their work.

7. The community needs psychiatric consultation in planning and operating its various services and agencies in order to insure mentally hygienic conditions in schools, recreation, industry, etc., and in order to modify those conditions that are threats to mental health.

His vision may also be broadened so that he may understand that in the performance of his responsibilities as a citizen he can use the same devices to solve problems as scientific medicine uses to solve bodily ills—deliberate observation, analysis, diagnosis, planning, and treatment. He will then realize that he is not only serving better the mental hygiene needs of the mentally ill, of his neighbors and himself, but is maturing out of an era of feudalism in which he could delegate his responsibilities to a higher authority and in return be dependent upon it.   He is evolving out of such dependency and into a government by himself—the people.

That this progress is actually taking place is documented in the first chapter supplement to this edition of Beers's book, "The Mental Hygiene Movement from 1908 to 1933 and Its Founder" by Dr. Winslow and others.   This was included in recent previous editions, but it is brought up to date by a second chapter supplement in this edition, "The Mental Hygiene Movement —More Recent Developments," by Dr. Woodward. Dr. Woodward's experience in the mental hygiene field has run the full range and out of this he is appropriately equipped to bring our perspective to date.

Seen beneath its surface then "A Mind That Found Itself" is not merely a chronicle of one mind which had wandered, but also a prophecy that a larger mind, the citizen mind, is discovering itself in fulfillment of its role in a democracy.

GEORGE S. STEVENSON, M.D.
Medical Director,
National Committee for Mental Hygiene.

January 2, 1948.

A Mind That Found Itself

I

THIS story is derived from as human a document as
ever existed; and, because of its uncommon nature, perhaps no one thing contributes so much to its value as its
authenticity.   It is an autobiography, and more: in part
it is a biography; for, in telling the story of my life, I must
relate the history of another self—a self which was dominant from my twenty-fourth to my twenty-sixth year.
During that period I was unlike what I had been, or
what I have been since.   The biographical part of my
autobiography might be called the history of a mental civil war, which I fought single-handed on a battle-
field that lay within the compass of my skull.   An Army
of Unreason, composed of the cunning and treacherous
thoughts of an unfair foe, attacked my bewildered consciousness with cruel persistency, and would have destroyed me, had not a triumphant Reason finally interposed a superior strategy that saved me from my unnatural self.

I am not telling the story of my life just to write a book.
I tell it because it seems my plain duty to do so.   A nar-

row escape from death and a seemingly miraculous return to health after an apparently fatal illness are enough
to make a man ask himself: For what purpose was my
life spared?   That question I have asked myself, and
this book is, in part, an answer.

I was born shortly after sunset about thirty years ago.
My ancestors, natives of England, settled in this country
not long after the *Mayflower* first sailed into Plymouth
Harbor.   And the blood of these ancestors, by time and
the happy union of a Northern man and a Southern
woman—my parents—has perforce been blended into
blood truly American.

The first years of my life were, in most ways, not unlike those of other American boys, except as a tendency
to worry made them so.   Though the fact is now
difficult for me to believe, I was painfully shy.   When
first I put on short trousers, I felt that the eyes of the
world were on me; and to escape them I hid behind
convenient pieces of furniture while in the house and,
so I am told, even sidled close to fences when I walked
along the street.   With my shyness there was a degree
of self-consciousness which put me at a disadvantage
in any family or social gathering.   I talked little and
was ill at ease when others spoke to me.

Like many other sensitive and somewhat introspect-
ive children, I passed through a brief period of morbid
righteousness.   In a game of "one-old-cat," the side on
which I played was defeated.   On a piece of scantling

which lay in the lot where the contest took place, I scratched the score. Afterwards it occurred to me that my inscription was perhaps misleading and would make my side appear to be the winner. I went back and corrected the ambiguity. On finding in an old tool chest at home a coin or medal, on which there appeared the text, "Put away the works of darkness and put on the armour of light," my sense of religious propriety was offended. It seemed a sacrilege to use in this way such a high sentiment, so I destroyed the coin.

I early took upon myself, mentally at least, many of the cares and worries of those about me. Whether in this I was different from other youngsters who develop a ludicrous, though pathetic, sense of responsibility for the universe, I do not know. But in my case the most extreme instance occurred during a business depression, when the family resources were endangered. I began to fear that my father (than whom a more hopeful man never lived) might commit suicide.

After all, I am not sure that the other side of my nature —the natural, healthy, boyish side—did not develop equally with these timid and morbid tendencies, which are not so very uncommon in childhood. Certainly the natural, boyish side was more in evidence on the surface. I was as good a sport as any of my playfellows in such games as appealed to me, and I went a-fishing when the chance offered. None of my associates thought of me as being shy or morose. But this was because I masked my troubles, though quite unconsciously, under a camouflage of sarcasm and sallies of wit, or, at least, what seemed to pass for wit among my immature acquaintances. With grown-ups, I was at times inclined to be pert, my degree of impudence depending no doubt upon how ill at ease I was and how perfectly at ease I wished to appear. Because of the constant need for appearing happier than I really was, I developed a knack for saying things in an amusing, sometimes an epigrammatic, way. I recall one remark made long before I could possibly have heard of Malthus or have understood his theory regarding birth rate and food supply. Ours being a large family of limited means and, among the five boys of the family, unlimited appetites, we often used the cheaper, though equally nutritious, cuts of meat. On one occasion when the steak was tougher than usual, I epitomized the Malthusian theory by remarking: "I believe in fewer children and better beefsteak!"

One more incident of my boyhood days may assist the reader to make my acquaintance. In my early teens I was, for one year, a member of a boy choir. Barring my voice, I was a good chorister, and, like all good choir-boys, I was distinguished by that seraphic passiveness from which a reaction of some kind is to be expected immediately after a service or rehearsal. On one occasion this reaction in me manifested itself in a fist fight with a fellow choir-boy. Though I cannot recall the time when I have not relished verbal encounters, physical encounters had never been to my taste, and I did not seek this fight. My assailant really goaded me into it. If the honors were not mine, at least I must have acquitted myself creditably, for an interested passer-by made a remark which I have never forgotten. "That boy is all right after he gets started," he said. About twelve years later I did get started, and could that passer-by have seen me on any one of several occasions, he would have had the satisfaction of knowing that his was a prophetic eye.

At the usual age, I entered a public grammar school in New Haven, Connecticut, where I graduated in 1891. In the fall of that year I entered the High School of the same city. My school courses were completed with as little trouble as scholastic distinction. I always managed to gain promotion, however, when it was due; and, though few of my teachers credited me with real ability, they were always able to detect a certain latent capacity, which they evidently believed would one day develop sufficiently to prevent me from disgracing them.

Upon entering the High School I had such ambitions as any schoolboy is apt to have. I wished to secure an election to a given secret society; that gained, I wished to become business manager of a monthly magazine published by that society. In these ambitions I suc- ceeded. For one of my age I had more than an average love of business. Indeed, I deliberately set about learn- ing to play the guitar well enough to become elig- ible for membership in the Banjo Club—and this for no more æsthetic purpose than to place myself in line for the position of manager, to which I was later elected.

In athletics there was but one game, tennis, in which I was actively interested. Its quick give-and-take suited my temperament, and so fond was I of it that during one summer I played not fewer than four thousand games. As I had an aptitude for tennis and devoted more time to it than did any of my schoolmates, it was not surprising that I acquired skill enough to win the school championship during my senior year. But that success was not due entirely to my superiority as a player. It was due in part to what I considered unfair treatment; and the fact well illustrates a certain trait of character which has often stood me in good stead. Among the spectators at the final match of the tournament were several girls. These schoolmates, who lived in my neighborhood, had mistaken for snobbishness a certain boyish diffidence for which few people gave me credit. When we passed each other, almost daily, this group of girls and I, our mutual sign of recognition was a look in an opposite direction. Now my opponent was well liked by these same girls and was entitled to their support. Accordingly they applauded his good plays, which was fair. They did not applaud my good plays, which was also fair. But what was not fair was that they should applaud my bad plays. Their doing so roiled my blood, and thanks to those who would have had me lose, I won.

In June, 1894, I received a high school diploma. Shortly afterwards I took my examinations for Yale, and the following September entered the Sheffield Scientific School, in a non-technical course.

The last week of June, 1894, was an important one in my life. An event then occurred which undoubtedly changed my career completely. It was the direct cause of my mental collapse six years later, and of the distressing and, in some instances, strange and delightful experiences on which this book is based. The event was the illness of an older brother, who, late in June, 1894, was stricken with what was thought to be epilepsy. Few diseases can so disorganize a household and distress its members. My brother had enjoyed perfect health up to the time he was stricken; and, as there had never been a suggestion of epilepsy, or any like disease, in either branch of the family, the affliction came as a bolt from a clear sky. Everything possible was done to effect a cure, but without avail. On July 4th, 1900, he died, after a six years' illness, two years of which were spent at home, one year in a trip around the world in a sailing vessel, and most of the remainder on a farm near Hartford. The doctors finally decided that a tumor at the base of the brain had caused his malady and his death.

As I was in college when my brother was first stricken, I had more time at my disposal than the other members of the family, and for that reason spent much of it with him. Though his attacks during the first year occurred only at night, the fear that they might occur during the day, in public, affected my nerves from the beginning.

Now, if a brother who had enjoyed perfect health all his life could be stricken with epilepsy, what was to prevent my being similarly afflicted? This was the thought that soon got possession of my mind. The more I considered it and him, the more nervous I became; and the more nervous, the more convinced that my own breakdown was only a matter of time. Doomed to what I then considered a living death, I thought of epilepsy, I dreamed epilepsy, until thousands of times during the six years that this disquieting idea persisted, my over-wrought imagination seemed to drag me to the very verge of an attack. Yet at no time during my life have these early fears been realized.

For the fourteen months succeeding the time my brother was first stricken, I was greatly harassed with fear; but not until later did my nerves really conquer me. I remember distinctly when the break came. It happened in November, 1895, during a recitation in German. That hour in the class room was one of the most dis-agreeable I ever experienced. It seemed as if my nerves had snapped, like so many minute bands of rub-ber stretched beyond their elastic limit. Had I had the courage to leave the room, I should have done so; but I sat as if paralyzed until the class was dismissed.

That term I did not again attend recitations. Con-tinuing my studies at home, I passed satisfactory ex-aminations, which enabled me to resume my place in the class room the following January. During the remain-der of my college years I seldom entered a recitation room with any other feeling than that of dread, though the absolute assurance that I should not be called upon to recite did somewhat relieve my anxiety in some classes. The professors, whom I had told about my state of health and the cause of it, invariably treated me with consideration; but, though I believe they never doubted the genuineness of my excuse, it was no easy matter to keep them convinced for almost two-thirds of my college course. My inability to recite was not due usually to any lack of preparation. However well prepared I might be, the moment I was called upon, a mingling of a thousand disconcerting sensations, and the distinct thought that at last the dread attack was at hand, would suddenly intervene and deprive me of all but the power to say, "Not prepared." Weeks would pass without any other record being placed opposite my name than a zero, or a blank indicating that I had not been called upon at all. Occasionally, however, a professor, in justice to himself and to the other students, would insist that I recite, and at such times I managed to make enough of a recitation to hold my place in the class.

When I entered Yale, I had four definite ambitions: first, to secure an election to a coveted secret society; second, to become one of the editors of the *Yale Record*, an illustrated humorous bi-weekly; third (granting that I should succeed in this latter ambition), to convince my associates that I should have the position of business manager—an office which I sought, not for the honor, but because I believed it would enable me to earn an amount of money at least equal to the cost of tuition for my years at Yale; fourth (and this was my chief ambition), to win my diploma within the prescribed time. These four ambitions I fortunately achieved.

A man's college days, collectively, are usually his happiest. Most of mine were not happy. Yet I look

back upon them with great satisfaction, for I feel that I
was fortunate enough to absorb some of that intangible,
but very real, element known as the "Yale spirit." This
has helped to keep Hope alive within me during my most
discouraged moments, and has ever since made the accomplishment of my purposes seem easy and sure.

II

On the thirtieth day of June, 1897, I graduated at Yale. Had I then realized that I was a sick man, I could and would have taken a rest. But, in a way, I had become accustomed to the ups and downs of a nervous existence, and, as I could not really afford a rest, six days after my graduation I entered upon the duties of a clerk in the office of the Collector of Taxes in the city of New Haven. I was fortunate in securing such a position at that time, for the hours were comparatively short and the work as congenial as any could have been under the circumstances. I entered the Tax Office with the intention of staying only until such time as I might secure a position in New York. About a year later I secured the desired position. After remaining in it for eight months I left it, in order to take a position which seemed to offer a field of endeavor more to my taste. From May, 1899, till the middle of June, 1900, I was a clerk in one of the smaller life-insurance companies, whose home office was within a stone's throw of what some men consider the center of the universe. To be in the very heart of the financial district of New York appealed strongly to my imagination. As a result of the contagious ideals of Wall Street, the making of money was then a passion with me. I wished to taste the bitter-sweet of power based on wealth.

11

For the first eighteen months of my life in New York, my health seemed no worse than it had been during the preceding three years. But the old dread still possessed me. I continued to have my more and less nervous days, weeks, and months. In March, 1900, however, there came a change for the worse. At that time I had a severe attack of grippe which incapacitated me for two weeks. As was to be expected in my case, this illness seriously depleted my vitality, and left me in a frightfully depressed condition—a depression which continued to grow upon me until the final crash came, on June 23rd, 1900. The events of that day, seemingly disastrous as then viewed, but evidently all for the best as the issue proved, forced me along paths traveled by thousands, but comprehended by few.

I had continued to perform my clerical duties until June 15th. On that day I was compelled to stop, and that at once. I had reached a point where my will had to capitulate to Unreason—that unscrupulous usurper. My previous five years as a neurasthenic had led me to believe that I had experienced all the disagreeable sensations an overworked and unstrung nervous system could suffer. But on this day several new and terrifying sensations seized me and rendered me all but helpless. My condition, however, was not apparent even to those who worked with me at the same desk. I remember trying to speak and at times finding myself unable to give utterance to my thoughts. Though I was able to answer questions, that fact hardly diminished my feeling of apprehension, for a single failure in an attempt to speak will stagger any man, no matter what his state of health. I tried to copy certain records in the day's work, but my hand was too unsteady, and I found it difficult to read the words and figures presented to my tired vision in blurred confusion.

That afternoon, conscious that some terrible calamity was impending, but not knowing what would be its nature, I performed a very curious act. Certain early literary efforts which had failed of publication in the college paper, but which I had jealously cherished for several years, I utterly destroyed. Then, after a hurried arrangement of my affairs, I took an early afternoon train, and was soon in New Haven. Home life did not make me better, and, except for three or four short walks, I did not go out of the house at all until June 23d, when I went in a most unusual way. To relatives I said little about my state of health, beyond the general statement that I had never felt worse—a statement which, when made by a neurasthenic, means much, but proves little. For five years I had had my ups and downs, and both my relatives and myself had begun to look upon these as things which would probably be corrected in and by time.

The day after my home-coming I made up my mind, or that part of it which was still within my control, that the time had come to quit business entirely and take a rest of months. I even arranged with a younger brother to set out at once for some quiet place in the White Mountains, where I hoped to steady my shattered nerves. At this time I felt as though in a tremor from head to foot, and the thought that I was about to have an epileptic attack constantly recurred. On more than one occasion I said to friends that I would rather die than live an epileptic; yet, if I rightly remember, I never declared the actual fear that I was doomed to bear such an affliction. Though I held the mad belief that I should suffer epilepsy, I held the sane hope, amounting to belief, that I should escape it. This fact may account, in a measure, for my six years of endurance.

On the 18th of June I felt so much worse that I went to my bed and stayed there until the 23d. During the night of the 18th my persistent dread became a false belief—a delusion. What I had long expected I now became convinced had at last occurred. I believed myself to be a confirmed epileptic, and that conviction was stronger than any ever held by a sound intellect. The half-resolve, made before my mind was actually impaired, namely, that I would kill myself rather than live the life I dreaded, now divided my attention with the belief that the stroke had fallen. From that time my one thought was to hasten the end, for I felt that I should lose the chance to die should relatives find me in an attack of epilepsy.

Considering the state of my mind and my inability at that time to appreciate the enormity of such an end as I half contemplated, my suicidal purpose was not entirely selfish. That I had never seriously contemplated suicide is proved by the fact that I had not provided myself with the means of accomplishing it, despite my habit, which has long been remarked by my friends, of preparing even for unlikely contingencies. So far as I had the control of my faculties, it must be admitted that I deliberated; but, strictly speaking, the rash act which followed cannot correctly be called an attempt at suicide —for how can a man who is not himself kill himself?

Soon my disordered brain was busy with schemes for death. I distinctly remember one which included a row on Lake Whitney, near New Haven. This I intended to take in the most unstable boat obtainable. Such a craft could be easily upset, and I should so bequeath to relatives and friends a sufficient number of reasonable doubts to rob my death of the usual stigma. I also remember searching for some deadly drug which I hoped to find about the house. But the quantity and quality of what I found were not such as I dared to trust. I then thought of severing my jugular vein, even going so far as to test against my throat the edge of a razor which, after the deadly impulse first asserted itself, I had secreted in a convenient place. I really wished to die, but so uncertain and ghastly a method did not appeal to me. Nevertheless, had I felt sure that in my tremulous frenzy I could accomplish the act with skilful dispatch, I should at once have ended my troubles.

My imaginary attacks were now recurring with distracting frequency, and I was in constant fear of discovery. During these three or four days I slept scarcely at all — even the medicine given to induce sleep having little effect. Though inwardly frenzied, I gave no outward sign of my condition. Most of the time I remained quietly in bed. I spoke but seldom. I had practically, though not entirely, lost the power of speech; but my almost unbroken silence aroused no suspicions as to the seriousness of my condition.

By a process of elimination, all suicidal methods but one had at last been put aside. On that one my mind now centred. My room was on the fourth floor of the house—one of a block of five—in which my parents lived. The house stood several feet back from the street. The sills of my windows were a little more than thirty feet above the ground. Under one was a flag pavement, extending from the house to the front gate. Under the other was a rectangular coal-hole covered with an iron grating. This was surrounded by flagging over a foot in width; and connecting it and the pavement proper was another flag. So that all along the front of the house, stone or iron filled a space at no point less than two feet in width. It required little calculation to determine how slight the chance of surviving a fall from either of those windows.

About dawn I arose. Stealthily I approached a window, pushed open the blinds, and looked out—and down. Then I closed the blinds as noiselessly as possible and crept back to bed: I had not yet become so irresponsible that I dared to take the leap. Scarcely had I pulled up the covering when a watchful relative entered my room, drawn thither perhaps by that protecting prescience which love inspires. I thought her words revealed a suspicion that she had heard me at the window, but speechless as I was I had enough speech to deceive her.

For of what account are Truth and Love when Life itself has ceased to seem desirable?

The dawn soon hid itself in the brilliancy of a perfect June day. Never had I seen a brighter—to look at; never a darker—to live through—or a better to die upon. Its very perfection and the songs of the robins, which at that season were plentiful in the neighborhood, served but to increase my despair and make me the more willing to die. As the day wore on, my anguish became more intense, but I managed to mislead those about me by uttering a word now and then, and feigning to read a newspaper, which to me, however, appeared an unintelligible jumble of type. My brain was in a ferment. It felt as if pricked by a million needles at white heat. My whole body felt as though it would be torn apart by the terrific nervous strain under which I labored.

Shortly after noon, dinner having been served, my mother entered the room and asked me if she should bring me some dessert. I assented. It was not that I cared for the dessert; I had no appetite. I wished to get her out of the room, for I believed myself to be on the verge of another attack. She left at once. I knew that in two or three minutes she would return. The crisis seemed at hand. It was now or never for liberation. She had probably descended one of three flights of stairs when, with the mad desire to dash my brains out on the pavement below, I rushed to that window which was directly over the flag walk. Providence must have guided my movements, for in some otherwise unaccountable way, on the very point of hurling myself

out bodily, I chose to drop feet foremost instead.
With my fingers I clung for a moment to the sill.
Then I let go. In falling my body turned so as to
bring my right side toward the building. I struck
the ground a little more than two feet from the
foundation of the house, and at least three to the left of
the point from which I started. Missing the stone pavement by not more than three or four inches, I struck on
comparatively soft earth. My position must have been
almost upright, for both heels struck the ground squarely.
The concussion slightly crushed one heel bone and
broke most of the small bones in the arch of each foot,
but there was no mutilation of the flesh. As my feet
struck the ground my right hand struck hard against
the front of the house, and it is probable that these
three points of contact, dividing the force of the shock,
prevented my back from being broken. As it was, it
narrowly escaped a fracture and, for several weeks
afterward, it felt as if powdered glass had been substi-
tuted for cartilage between the vertebræ.

I did not lose consciousness even for a second, and the
demoniacal dread, which had possessed me from June,
1894, until this fall to earth just six years later, was
dispelled the instant I struck the ground. At no time
since have I experienced one of my imaginary attacks; nor has my mind even for a moment entertained
such an idea. The little demon which had tortured me
relentlessly for so many years evidently lacked the
stamina which I must have had to survive the shock of
my suddenly arrested flight through space. That the

very delusion which drove me to a death-loving desperation should so suddenly vanish would seem to indicate
that many a suicide might be averted if the person contemplating it could find the proper assistance when
such a crisis impends.

III

IT was squarely in front of the dining-room window that
I fell, and those at dinner were, of course, startled. It
took them a second or two to realize what had happened.
Then my younger brother rushed out, and with others
carried me into the house. Naturally that dinner was
permanently interrupted. A mattress was placed on
the floor of the dining room and I on that, suffering intensely. I said little, but what I said was significant.
"I thought I had epilepsy!" was my first remark; and
several times I said, "I wish it was over!" For I
believed that my death was only a question of hours.
To the doctors, who soon arrived, I said, "My back is
broken!"—raising myself slightly, however, as I said so.

An ambulance was summoned and I was placed in
it. Because of the nature of my injuries it had to
proceed slowly. The trip of a mile and a half seemed
interminable, but finally I arrived at Grace Hospital
and was placed in a room which soon became a chamber
of torture. It was on the second floor; and the first
object to engage my attention and stir my imagination
was a man who appeared outside my window and placed
in position several heavy iron bars. These were, it
seems, thought necessary for my protection, but at that
time no such idea occurred to me. My mind was in
a delusional state, ready and eager to seize upon any
external stimulus as a pretext for its wild inventions,

and that barred window started a terrible train of delusions which persisted for seven hundred and ninety-eight days. During that period my mind imprisoned both mind and body in a dungeon than which none was ever more secure.

Knowing that those who attempt suicide are usually placed under arrest, I believed myself under legal restraint. I imagined that at any moment I might be taken to court to face some charge lodged against me by the local police. Every act of those about me seemed to be a part of what, in police parlance, is commonly called the "Third Degree." The hot poultices placed upon my feet and ankles threw me into a profuse perspiration, and my very active association of mad ideas convinced me that I was being "sweated"—another police term which I had often seen in the newspapers. I inferred that this third-degree sweating process was being inflicted in order to extort some kind of a confession, though what my captors wished me to confess I could not for my life imagine. As I was really in a state of delirium, with high fever, I had an insatiable thirst. The only liquids given me were hot saline solutions. Though there was good reason for administering these, I believed they were designed for no other purpose than to increase my sufferings, as part of the same inquisitorial process. But had a confession been due, I could hardly have made it, for that part of my brain which controls the power of speech was seriously affected, and was soon to be further disabled by my ungovernable thoughts. Only an occasional word did I utter.

Certain hallucinations of hearing, or "false voices," added to my torture. Within my range of hearing, but beyond the reach of my understanding, there was a hellish vocal hum. Now and then I would recognize the subdued voice of a friend; now and then I would hear the voices of some I believed were not friends. All these referred to me and uttered what I could not clearly distinguish, but knew must be imprecations. Ghostly rappings on the walls and ceiling of my room punctuated unintelligible mumblings of invisible persecutors.

I remember distinctly my delusion of the following day—Sunday. I seemed to be no longer in the hospital. In some mysterious way I had been spirited aboard a huge ocean liner. I first discovered this when the ship was in mid-ocean. The day was clear, the sea apparently calm, but for all that the ship was slowly sinking. And it was I, of course, who had created the situation which must turn out fatally for all, unless the coast of Europe could be reached before the water in the hold should extinguish the fires. How had this peril overtaken us? Simply enough: During the night I had in some way—a way still unknown to me—opened a porthole below the water-line; and those in charge of the vessel seemed powerless to close it. Every now and then I could hear parts of the ship give way under the strain. I could hear the air hiss and whistle spitefully under the resistless impact of the invading waters; I could hear the crashing of timbers as partitions were wrecked; and as the water rushed in at one place I could see, at another, scores of helpless

passengers swept overboard into the sea—my unintended
victims. I believed that I, too, might at any moment be
swept away. That I was not thrown into the sea by
vengeful fellow-passengers was, I thought, due to their
desire to keep me alive until, if possible, land should
be reached, when a more painful death could be inflicted
upon me.

While aboard my phantom ship I managed in some
way to establish an electric railway system; and the trol-
ley cars which passed the hospital were soon running
along the deck of my ocean liner, carrying passengers
from the places of peril to what seemed places of comparative safety at the bow. Every time I heard a car
pass the hospital, one of mine went clanging along the
ship's deck.

My feverish imaginings were no less remarkable than
the external stimuli which excited them. As I have
since ascertained, there were just outside my room an
elevator and near it a speaking-tube. Whenever the
speaking-tube was used from another part of the building, the summoning whistle conveyed to my mind the
idea of the exhaustion of air in a ship-compartment, and
the opening and shutting of the elevator door completed
the illusion of a ship fast going to pieces. But the ship
my mind was on never reached any shore, nor did she
sink. Like a mirage she vanished, and again I found
myself safe in my bed at the hospital. "Safe," did I say?
Scarcely that—for deliverance from one impending dis-
aster simply meant immediate precipitation into another.

My delirium gradually subsided, and four or five days

after the 23d the doctors were able to set my broken bones. The operation suggested new delusions. Shortly before the adjustment of the plaster casts, my legs, for obvious reasons, were shaved from shin to calf. This unusual tonsorial operation I read for a sign of degradation—associating it with what I had heard of the treatment of murderers and with similar customs in barbarous countries. It was about this time also that strips of court-plaster, in the form of a cross, were placed on my forehead, which had been slightly scratched in my fall, and this, of course, I interpreted as a brand of infamy.

Had my health been good, I should at this time have been participating in the Triennial of my class at Yale. Indeed, I was a member of the Triennial Committee and though, when I left New York on June 15th, I had been feeling terribly ill, I had then hoped to take part in the celebration. The class reunions were held on Tuesday, June 26th—three days after my collapse. Those familiar with Yale customs know that the Harvard baseball game is one of the chief events of the commencement season. Headed by brass bands, all the classes whose reunions fall in the same year march to the Yale Athletic Field to see the game and renew their youth—using up as much vigor in one delirious day as would insure a ripe old age if less prodigally expended. These classes, with their bands and cheering, accompanied by thousands of other vociferating enthusiasts, march through West Chapel Street—the most direct route from the Campus to the Field. It is upon this line of march that Grace Hos-

pital is situated, and I knew that on the day of the game
the Yale thousands would pass the scene of my incarcer-
ation.

I have endured so many days of the most exquisite torture that I hesitate to distinguish among them by
degrees; each deserves its own unique place, even as a
Saint's Day in the calendar of an olden Spanish inquis-
itor. But, if the palm is to be awarded to any, June 26th,
1900, perhaps has the first claim.

My state of mind at that time might be pictured thus:
The criminal charge of attempted suicide stood against
me on June 23rd. By the 26th many other and worse
charges had accumulated. The public believed me the
most despicable member of my race. The papers were
filled with accounts of my misdeeds. The thousands of
collegians gathered in the city, many of whom I knew
personally, loathed the very thought that a Yale man
should so disgrace his Alma Mater. And when they approached the hospital on their way to the Athletic Field,
I concluded that it was their intention to take me from
my bed, drag me to the lawn, and there tear me limb from
limb. Few incidents during my unhappiest years are
more vividly or circumstantially impressed upon my
memory. The fear, to be sure, was absurd, but in the
lurid lexicon of Unreason there is no such word as "absurd." Believing, as I did, that I had dishonored Yale
and forfeited the privilege of being numbered among her
sons, it was not surprising that the college cheers which
filled the air that afternoon, and in which only a few days
earlier I had hoped to join, struck terror to my heart.

IV

NATURALLY I was suspicious of all about me, and became more so each day. But not until about a month later did I refuse to recognize my relatives. While I was at Grace Hospital, my father and eldest brother called almost every day to see me, and, though I said little, I still accepted them in their proper characters. I remember well a conversation one morning with my father. The words I uttered were few, but full of meaning. Shortly before this time my death had been momentarily expected. I still believed that I was surely about to die as a result of my injuries, and I wished in some way to let my father know that, despite my apparently ignominious end, I appreciated all that he had done for me during my life. Few men, I believe, ever had a more painful time in expressing their feelings than I had on that occasion. I had but little control over my mind, and my power of speech was impaired. My father sat beside my bed. Looking up at him, I said, "You have been a good father to me."

"I have always tried to be," was his characteristic reply.

After the broken bones had been set, and the first effects of the severe shock I had sustained had worn off, I began to gain strength. About the third week I was able to sit up and was occasionally taken out of doors.

But each day, and especially during the hours of the night, my delusions increased in force and variety. The world was fast becoming to me a stage on which every human being within the range of my senses seemed to be playing a part, and that a part which would lead not only to my destruction (for which I cared little), but also to the ruin of all with whom I had ever come in contact. In the month of July several thunder-storms occurred. To me the thunder was "stage" thunder, the lightning man-made, and the accompanying rain due to some clever contrivance of my persecutors. There was a chapel connected with the hospital—or at least a room where religious services were held every Sunday. To me the hymns were funeral dirges; and the mumbled prayers, faintly audible, were in behalf of every sufferer in the world but one.

It was my eldest brother who looked after my care and interests during my entire illness. Toward the end of July, he informed me that I was to be taken home again. I must have given him an incredulous look, for he said, "Don't you think we can take you home? Well, we can and will." Believing myself in the hands of the police, I did not see how that was possible. Nor did I have any desire to return. That a man who had disgraced his family should again enter his old home and expect his relatives to treat him as though nothing were changed, was a thought against which my soul rebelled; and, when the day came for my return, I fought my brother and the doctor feebly as they lifted me from the bed. But I soon submitted, was placed in a carriage, and driven to the house I had left a month earlier.

For a few hours my mind was calmer than it had been. But my new-found ease was soon dispelled by the appearance of a nurse—one of several who had attended me at the hospital. Though at home and surrounded by relatives, I jumped to the conclusion that I was still under police surveillance. At my request my brother had promised not to engage any nurse who had been in attendance at the hospital. The difficulty of procuring any other led him to disregard my request, which at the time he held simply as a whim. But he did not disregard it entirely, for the nurse selected had merely acted as a substitute on one occasion, and then only for about an hour. That was long enough, though, for my memory to record her image.

Finding myself still under surveillance, I soon jumped to a second conclusion, namely, that this was no brother of mine at all. He instantly appeared in the light of a sinister double, acting as a detective. After that I refused absolutely to speak to him again, and this repudiation I extended to all other relatives, friends and acquaintances. If the man I had accepted as my brother was spurious, so was everybody—that was my deduction. For more than two years I was without relatives or friends, in fact, without a world, except that one created by my own mind from the chaos that reigned within it.

While I was at Grace Hospital, it was my sense of hearing which was the most disturbed. But soon after I was placed in my room at home, *all* of my senses became perverted. I still heard the "false voices"—which were doubly false, for Truth no longer existed. The tricks played upon me by my senses of taste, touch, smell, and sight were the source of great mental anguish. None of my food had its usual flavor. This soon led to that common delusion that some of it contained poison— not deadly poison, for I knew that my enemies hated me too much to allow me the boon of death, but poison sufficient to aggravate my discomfort. At breakfast I had cantaloupe, liberally sprinkled with salt. The salt seemed to pucker my mouth, and I believed it to be powdered alum. Usually, with my supper, sliced peaches were served. Though there was sugar on the peaches, salt would have done as well. Salt, sugar, and powdered alum had become the same to me.

Familiar materials had acquired a different "feel.' In the dark, the bed sheets at times seemed like silk. As I had not been born with a golden spoon in my mouth, or other accessories of a useless luxury, I believed the detectives had provided these silken sheets for some hostile purpose of their own. What that purpose was I could not divine, and my very inability to arrive at a satisfactory conclusion stimulated my brain to the assembling of disturbing thoughts in an almost endless train.

Imaginary breezes struck my face, gentle, but not welcome, most of them from parts of the room where currents of air could not possibly originate. They seemed to come from cracks in the walls and ceiling and annoyed me exceedingly. I thought them in some way related to that ancient method of torture by which water is allowed to strike the victim's forehead, a drop at a time, until death releases him. For a while my

sense of smell added to my troubles. The odor of burning human flesh and other pestilential fumes seemed
to assail me.

My sense of sight was subjected to many weird and uncanny effects. Phantasmagoric visions made their visitations throughout the night, for a time with such regularity that I used to await their coming with a certain
restrained curiosity. I was not entirely unaware that
something was ailing with my mind. Yet these illusions
of sight I took for the work of detectives, who sat up
nights racking their brains in order to rack and utterly
wreck my own with a cruel and unfair Third Degree.

Handwriting on the wall has ever struck terror to the
hearts of even sane men. I remember as one of my most
unpleasant experiences that I began to see handwriting on
the sheets of my bed staring me in the face, and not me
alone, but also the spurious relatives who often stood or
sat near me. On each fresh sheet placed over me I would
soon begin to see words, sentences, and signatures, all in
my own handwriting. Yet I could not decipher any of
the words, and this fact dismayed me, for I firmly believed that those who stood about could read them all
and found them to be incriminating evidence.

I imagined that these visionlike effects, with few ex-
ceptions, were produced by a magic lantern controlled by
some of my myriad persecutors. The lantern was rather
a cinematographic contrivance. Moving pictures, often
brilliantly colored, were thrown on the ceiling of my
room and sometimes on the sheets of my bed. Human
bodies, dismembered and gory, were one of the most

common of these. All this may have been due to the
fact that, as a boy, I had fed my imagination on the
sensational news of the day as presented in the public
press. Despite the heavy penalty which I now paid
for thus loading my mind, I believe this unwise indulgence gave a breadth and variety to my peculiar psychological experience which it otherwise would have lacked.
For with an insane ingenuity I managed to connect
myself with almost every crime of importance of which
I had ever read.

Dismembered human bodies were not alone my bed-
fellows at this time. I remember one vision of vivid
beauty. Swarms of butterflies and large and gorgeous
moths appeared on the sheets. I wished that the usually unkind operator would continue to show these
pretty creatures. Another pleasing vision appeared
about twilight several days in succession. I can trace
it directly to impressions gained in early childhood. The
quaint pictures by Kate Greenaway—little children in
attractive dress, playing in old-fashioned gardens—
would float through space just outside my windows.
The pictures were always accompanied by the gleeful
shouts of real children in the neighborhood, who, before
being sent to bed by watchful parents, devoted the last
hour of the day to play. It doubtless was their shouts
that stirred my memories of childhood and brought forth
these pictures.

In my chamber of intermittent horrors and momentary delights, uncanny occurrences were frequent. I be-
'ieved there was some one who at fall of night secreted

himself under my bed.   That in itself was not peculiar, as
sane persons at one time or another are troubled by that
same notion.   But *my* bed-fellow—under the bed—was
a detective; and he spent most of his time during the
night pressing pieces of ice against my injured heels, to
precipitate, as I thought, my overdue confession.

The piece of ice in the pitcher of water which usually
stood on the table sometimes clinked against the
pitcher's side as its center of gravity shifted through
melting.   It was many days before I reasoned out the
cause of this sound; and until I did I supposed it was
produced by some mechanical device resorted to by the
detectives for a purpose.   Thus the most trifling occurrence assumed for me vast significance.

V

AFTER remaining at home for about a month, during which time I showed no improvement mentally, though I did gain physically, I was taken to a private sanatorium. My destination was frankly disclosed to me. But my habit of disbelief had now become fixed, and I thought myself on the way to a trial in New York City, for some one of the many crimes with which I stood charged.

My emotions on leaving New Haven were, I imagine, much the same as those of a condemned but penitent criminal who looks upon the world for the last time. The day was hot, and, as we drove to the railway station, the blinds on most of the houses in the streets through which we passed were seen to be closed. The reason for this was not then apparent to me. I thought I saw an unbroken line of deserted houses, and I imagined that their desertion had been deliberately planned as a sign of displeasure on the part of their former occupants. As citizens of New Haven, I supposed them bitterly ashamed of such a despicable townsman as myself. Because of the early hour, the streets were practically deserted. This fact, too, I interpreted to my own disadvantage. As the carriage crossed the main business thoroughfare, I took what I believed to be my last look at that part of my native city.

From the carriage I was carried to the train and placed in the smoking car in the last seat on the right-hand side.

The back of the seat next in front was reversed so that my legs might be placed in a comfortable position, and one of the boards used by card-playing travelers was placed beneath them as a support. With a consistent degree of suspicion I paid particular attention to a blue mark on the face of the railroad ticket held by my custodian. I took it to be a means of identification for use in court.

That one's memory may perform its function in the grip of Unreason itself is proved by the fact that my memory retains an impression, and an accurate one, of virtually everything that befell me, except when under the influence of an anæsthetic or in the unconscious hours of undisturbed sleep. Important events, trifling conversations, and more trifling thoughts of my own are now recalled with ease and accuracy; whereas, prior to my illness and until a strange experience to be recorded later, mine was an ordinary memory when it was not noticeably poor. At school and in college I stood lowest in those studies in which success depended largely upon this faculty. Psychiatrists inform me that it is not unusual for those suffering as I did to retain accurate impressions of their experiences while ill. To laymen this may seem almost miraculous, yet it is not so; nor is it even remarkable. Assuming that an insane person's memory is capable of recording impressions at all, remembrance for one in the torturing grip of delusions of persecution should be doubly easy. This deduction is in accord with the accepted psychological law that the retention of an impression in the memory depends largely upon the intensity of the impression itself, and the frequency of its repetition. Fear to speak, lest I should incriminate myself and others, gave to my impressions the requisite intensity, and the daily recurrence of the same general line of thought served to fix all impressions in my then supersensitive memory.

Shortly before seven in the morning, on the way to the sanatorium, the train passed through a manufacturing center. Many workmen were lounging in front of a factory, most of them reading newspapers. I believed these papers contained an account of me and my crimes, and I thought everyone along the route knew who I was and what I was, and that I was on that train. Few seemed to pay any attention to me, yet this very fact looked to be a part of some well-laid plan of the detectives.

The sanatorium to which I was going was in the country. When a certain station was reached, I was carried from the train to a carriage. At that moment I caught sight of a former college acquaintance, whose appearance I thought was designed to let me know that Yale, which I believed I had disgraced, was one of the powers behind my throne of torture.

Soon after I reached my room in the sanatorium, the supervisor entered. Drawing a table close to the bed, he placed upon it a slip of paper which he asked me to sign. I looked upon this as a trick of the detectives to get a specimen of my handwriting. I now know that the signing of the slip is a legal requirement, with which every patient is supposed to comply upon entering such an institution—private in character—unless he has been committed by some court. The exact wording of this "voluntary commitment" I do not now recall; but, it was, in substance, an agreement to abide by the rules of the institution—whatever *they* were—and to submit to such restraint as might be deemed necessary. Had I not felt the weight of the world on my shoulders, I believe my sense of humor would have caused me to laugh outright; for the signing of such an agreement by one so situated was, even to my mind, a farce. After much coaxing I was induced to go so far as to take the pen in my hand. There I again hesitated. The supervisor apparently thought I might write with more ease if the paper were placed on a book. And so I might, had he selected a book of a different title. One more likely to arouse suspicions in my mind could not have been found in a search of the Congressional Library. I had left New York on June 15th, and it was in the direction of that city that my present trip had taken me. I considered this but the first step of my return under the auspices of its Police Department. "Called Back" was the title of the book that stared me in the face. After refusing for a long time I finally weakened and signed the slip; but I did not place it on the book. To have done that would, in my mind, have been tantamount to giving consent to extradition; and I was in no mood to assist the detectives in their mean work. At what cost had I signed that commitment slip? To me it was the act of signing my own death-warrant.

VI

DURING the entire time that my delusions of persecution, as they are called, persisted, I could not but respect the mind that had laid out so comprehensive and devilishly ingenious and, at times, artistic a Third Degree as I was called upon to bear. And an innate modesty (more or less fugitive since these peculiar experiences) does not forbid my mentioning the fact that I still respect that mind.

Suffering such as I endured during the month of August in my own home continued with gradually diminishing force during the eight months I remained in this sanatorium. Nevertheless my sufferings during the first four of these eight months was intense. All my senses were still perverted. My sense of sight was the first to right itself—nearly enough, at least, to rob the detectives of their moving pictures. But before the last fitful film had run through my mind, I beheld one which I shall now describe. I can trace it directly to an impression made on my memory about two years earlier, before my breakdown.

Shortly after going to New York to live, I had explored the Eden Musée. One of the most gruesome of the spectacles which I had seen in its famed Chamber of Horrors was a representation of a gorilla, holding in its arms the gory body of a woman. It was that impression which now revived in my mind. But by a process strictly in accordance with Darwin's theory, the Eden Musée gorilla had become a man—in appearance not unlike the beast that had inspired my distorted thought. This man held a bloody dagger which he repeatedly plunged into the woman's breast. The apparition did not terrify me at all. In fact I found it interesting, for I looked upon it as a contrivance of the detectives. Its purpose I could not divine, but this fact did not trouble me, as I reasoned that no additional criminal charges could make my situation worse than it already was.

For a month or two, "false voices" continued to annoy me. And if there is a hell conducted on the principles of my temporary hell, gossippers will one day wish they had attended strictly to their own business. This is not a confession. I am no gossipper, though I cannot deny that I have occasionally gossipped—a little. And this was my punishment: persons in an adjoining room seemed to be repeating the very same things which I had said of others on these communicative occasions. I supposed that those whom I had talked about had in some way found me out, and intended now to take their revenge.

My sense of smell, too, became normal; but my sense of taste was slow in recovering. At each meal, poison was still the *pièce de résistance*, and it was not surprising that I sometimes dallied one, two, or three hours over a meal, and often ended by not eating it at all.

There was, however, another reason for my frequent refusal to take food, in my belief that the detectives had resorted to a more subtle method of detection. They now intended by each article of food to suggest a certain idea, and I was expected to recognize the idea thus suggested. Conviction or acquittal depended upon my correct interpretation of their symbols, and my interpretation was to be signified by my eating, or not eating, the several kinds of food placed before me. To have eaten a burnt crust of bread would have been a confession of arson. Why? Simply because the charred crust suggested fire; and, as bread is the staff of life, would it not be an inevitable deduction that life had been destroyed—destroyed by fire —and that I was the destroyer? On one day to eat a given article of food meant confession. The next day, or the next meal, a refusal to eat it meant confession. This complication of logic made it doubly difficult for me to keep from incriminating myself and others.

It can easily be seen that I was between several devils and the deep sea. To eat or not to eat perplexed me more than the problem conveyed by a few shorter words perplexed a certain prince, who, had he lived a few centuries later (out of a book), might have been forced to enter a kingdom where kings and princes are made and unmade on short notice. Indeed, he might have lost his principality entirely—or, at least, his subjects; for, as I later had occasion to observe, the frequency with which a dethroned reason mounts a throne and rules a world is such that self-crowned royalty receives but scant homage from the less elated members of the court.

For several weeks I ate but little. Though the desire for food was not wanting, my mind (that dog-in-the-manger) refused to let me satisfy my hunger. Coaxing by the attendants was of little avail; force was usually of less. But the threat that liquid nourishment would be administered through my nostrils sometimes prevailed, for the attribute of shrewdness was not so utterly lost that I could not choose the less of two evils.

What I looked upon as a gastronomic ruse of the detectives sometimes overcame my fear of eating. Every Sunday ice cream was served with dinner. At the beginning of the meal a large pyramid of it would be placed before me in a saucer several sizes too small. I believed that it was never to be mine unless I first partook of the more substantial fare. As I dallied over the meal, that delicious pyramid would gradually melt, slowly filling the small saucer, which I knew could not long continue to hold all of its original contents. As the melting of the ice cream progressed, I became more indifferent to my eventual fate; and, invariably, before a drop of that precious reward had dripped from the saucer, I had eaten enough of the dinner to prove my title to the seductive dessert. Moreover, during its enjoyment, I no longer cared a whit for charges or convictions of all the crimes in the calendar. This fact is less trifling than it seems; for it proves the value of strategy as opposed to brute and sometimes brutal force, of which I shall presently give some illuminating examples.

VII

CHOICE of a sanatorium by people of limited means is, unfortunately, very restricted. Though my relatives believed the one in which I was placed was at least fairly well conducted, events proved otherwise. From a modest beginning made not many years previously, it had enjoyed a mushroom growth. About two hundred and fifty patients were harbored in a dozen or more small frame buildings, suggestive of a mill settlement. Outside the limits of a city and in a state where there was lax official supervision, owing in part to faulty laws, the owner of this little settlement of woe had erected a nest of veritable fire-traps in which helpless sick people were forced to risk their lives. This was a necessary procedure if the owner was to grind out an exorbitant income on his investment.

The same spirit of economy and commercialism pervaded the entire institution. Its worst manifestation was in the employment of the meanest type of attendant —men willing to work for the paltry wage of eighteen dollars a month. Very seldom did competent attendants consent to work there, and then usually because of a scarcity of profitable employment elsewhere. Providentially for me, such an attendant came upon the scene. This young man, so long as he remained in the good graces of the owner-superintendent, was admittedly one of the best attendants he had ever had. Yet aside from a five-dollar bill which a relative had sent me at Christmas and which I had refused to accept because of my belief that it, like my relatives, was counterfeit—aside from that bill, which was turned over to the attendant by my brother, he received no additional pecuniary rewards. His chief reward lay in his consciousness of the fact that he was protecting me against injustices which surely would have been visited upon me had he quitted his position and left me to the mercies of the owner and his ignorant assistants. To-day, with deep appreciation, I contrast the treatment I received at his hands with that which I suffered during the three weeks preceding his appearance on the scene. During that period, no fewer than seven attendants contributed to my misery. Though some of them were perhaps decent enough fellows outside a sickroom, not one had the right to minister to a patient in my condition.

The two who were first put in charge of me did not strike me with their fists or even threaten to do so; but their unconscious lack of consideration for my comfort and peace of mind was torture. They were typical eighteen-dollar-a-month attendants. Another of the same sort, on one occasion, cursed me with a degree of brutality which I prefer not to recall, much less record. And a few days later the climax was appropriately capped when still another attendant perpetrated an outrage which a sane man would have resented to the point of homicide. He was a man of the coarsest type. His hands would have done credit to a longshoreman—

fingers knotted and nearly twice the normal size. Because I refused to obey a peremptory command, and this at a time when I habitually refused even on pain of imagined torture to obey or to speak, this brute not only cursed me with abandon, he deliberately spat upon me. I was a mental incompetent, but like many others in a similar position I was both by antecedents and by training a gentleman. Vitriol could not have seared my flesh more deeply than the venom of this human viper stung my soul! Yet, as I was rendered speechless by delusions, I could offer not so much as a word of protest. I trust that it is not now too late, however, to protest in behalf of the thousands of outraged patients in private and state hospitals whose mute submission to such indignities has never been recorded.

Of the readiness of an unscrupulous owner to employ inferior attendants, I shall offer a striking illustration. The capable attendant who acted as my protector at this sanatorium has given me an affidavit embodying certain facts which, of course, I could not have known at the time of their occurrence. The gist of this sworn statement is as follows: One day a man—seemingly a tramp—approached the main building of the sanatorium and inquired for the owner. He soon found him, talked with him a few minutes, and an hour or so later he was sitting at the bedside of an old and infirm man. This aged patient had recently been committed to the institution by relatives who had labored under the common delusion that the payment of a considerable sum of money each week would insure kindly treatment. When this tramp-attendant first appeared, all his visible worldly possessions were contained in a small bundle which he carried under his arm. So filthy were his person and his clothes that he received a compulsory bath and another suit before being assigned to duty. He then began to earn his four dollars and fifty cents a week by sitting several hours a day in the room with the aged man, sick unto death. My informant soon engaged him in conversation. What did he learn? First, that the uncouth stranger had never before so much as crossed the threshold of a hospital. His last job had been as a member of a section-gang on a railroad. From the roadbed of a railway to the bedside of a man about to die was indeed a change which might have taxed the adaptability of a more versatile being. But coarse as he was, this unkempt novice did not abuse his charge—except in so far as his inability to interpret or anticipate wants contributed to the sick man's distress. My own attendant, realizing that the patient was suffering for the want of skilled attention, spent a part of his time in this unhappy room, which was but across the hall from my own. The end soon came.

My attendant, who had had training as a nurse, detected the unmistakable signs of impending death. He forthwith informed the owner of the sanatorium that the patient was in a dying condition, and urged him (a doctor) to go at once to the bedside. The doctor refused to comply with the request on the plea that he was at the time "too busy." When at last he did visit the room, the patient was dead. Then came the supervisor, who took charge of the body. As it was being carried from the room the supervisor, the "handy man" of the owner, said: "There goes the best paying patient the institution had; the doctor" (meaning the owner) "was getting eighty-five dollars a week out of him." Of this sum not more than twenty dollars at most, at the time this happened, could be considered as "cost of maintenance." The remaining sixty-five dollars went into the pocket of the owner. Had the man lived for one year, the owner might have pocketed (so far as this one case was concerned) the neat but wicked profit of thirty-three hundred and eighty dollars. And what would the patient have received? The same privilege of living in neglect and dying neglected.

VIII

For the first few weeks after my arrival at the sanatorium, I was cared for by two attendants, one by day and one by night. I was still helpless, being unable to put my feet out of bed, much less upon the floor, and it was necessary that I be continually watched lest an impulse to walk should seize me. After a month or six weeks, however, I grew stronger, and from that time only one person was assigned to care for me. He was with me all day, and slept at night in the same room.

The earliest possible dismissal of one of my two attendants was expedient for the family purse; but such are the deficiencies in the prevailing treatment of the insane that relief in one direction often occasions evil in another. No sooner was the expense thus reduced than I was subjected to a detestable form of restraint which amounted to torture. To guard me at night while the remaining attendant slept, my hands were imprisoned in what is known as a "muff." A muff, innocent enough to the eyes of those who have never worn one, is in reality a relic of the Inquisition. It is an instrument of restraint which has been in use for centuries and even in many of our public and private institutions is still in use. The muff I wore was made of canvas, and differed in construction from a muff designed for the hands of fashion only in the inner partition, also of canvas, which separated my hands, but allowed them

46

to overlap. At either end was a strap which buckled tightly around the wrist and was locked.

The assistant physician, when he announced to me that I was to be subjected at night to this restraint, broke the news gently—so gently that I did not then know, nor did I guess for several months, why this thing was done to me. And thus it was that I drew deductions of my own which added not a little to my torture.

The gas jet in my room was situated at a distance, and stronger light was needed to find the keyholes and lock the muff when adjusted. Hence, an attendant was standing by with a lighted candle. Seating himself on the side of the bed, the physician said: "You won't try again to do what you did in New Haven, will you?" Now one may have done many things in a city where he has lived for a score of years, and it is not surprising that I failed to catch the meaning of the doctor's question. It was only after months of secret puzzling that I at last did discover his reference to my attempted suicide. But now the burning candle in the hands of the attendant, and a certain similarity between the doctor's name and the name of a man whose trial for arson I once attended out of idle curiosity, led me to imagine that in some way I had been connected with that crime. For months I firmly believed I stood charged as an accomplice.

The putting on of the muff was the most humiliating incident of my life. The shaving of my legs and the wearing of the court-plaster brand of infamy had been humiliating, but those experiences had not overwhelmed my very heart as did this bitter ordeal. I resisted weakly, and, after the muff was adjusted and locked, for the first time since my mental collapse I wept. And I remember distinctly why I wept. The key that locked the muff unlocked in imagination the door of the home in New Haven which I believed I had disgraced—and seemed for a time to unlock my heart. Anguish beat my mind into a momentary sanity, and with a wholly sane emotion I keenly felt my imagined disgrace. My thoughts centred on my mother. Her (and other members of the family) I could plainly see at home in a state of dejection and despair over her imprisoned and heartless son. I wore the muff each night for several weeks, and for the first few nights the unhappy glimpses of a ruined home recurred and increased my sufferings.

It was not always as an instrument of restraint that the muff was employed. Frequently it was used as a means of discipline on account of supposed stubborn disobedience. Many times was I roughly overpowered by two attendants who locked my hands and coerced me to do whatever I had refused to do. My arms and hands were my only weapons of defence. My feet were still in plaster casts, and my back had been so severely injured as to necessitate my lying flat upon it most of the time. It was thus that these unequal fights were fought. And I had not even the satisfaction of tongue-lashing my oppressors, for I was practically speechless.

My attendants. like most others in such institutions,

were incapable of understanding the operations of my mind, and what they could not understand they would seldom tolerate. Yet they were not entirely to blame. They were simply carrying out to the letter orders received from the doctors.

To ask a patient in my condition to take a little medicated sugar seemed reasonable. But from my point of view my refusal was justifiable. That innocuous sugar disc to me seemed saturated with the blood of loved ones; and so much as to touch it was to shed their blood—perhaps on the very scaffold on which I was destined to die. For myself I cared little. I was anxious to die, and eagerly would I have taken the sugar disc had I had any reason to believe that it was deadly poison. The sooner I could die and be forgotten, the better for all with whom I had ever come in contact. To continue to live was simply to be the treacherous tool of unscrupulous detectives, eager to exterminate my innocent relatives and friends, if so their fame could be made secure in the annals of their craft.

But the thoughts associated with the taking of the medicine were seldom twice alike. If before taking it something happened to remind me of mother, father, some other relative, or a friend, I imagined that compliance would compromise, if not eventually destroy, that particular person. Who would not resist when meek acceptance would be a confession which would doom his own mother or father to prison, or ignominy, or death? It was for this that I was reviled, for this, subjected to cruel restraint.

They thought I was stubborn. In the strict sense of the word there is no such thing as a stubborn insane person. The truly stubborn men and women in the world are sane; and the fortunate prevalence of sanity may be approximately estimated by the preponderance of stubbornness in society at large. When one possessed of the power of recognizing his own errors continues to hold an unreasonable belief—that is stubbornness. But for a man bereft of reason to adhere to an idea which to him seems absolutely correct and true because he has been deprived of the means of detecting his error— that is not stubbornness. It is a symptom of his disease, and merits the indulgence of forbearance, if not genuine sympathy. Certainly the afflicted one deserves no punishment. As well punish with a blow the cheek that is disfigured by the mumps.

The attendant who was with me most of the time while I remained at the sanatorium was the kindly one already mentioned. Him I regarded, however, as a detective, or, rather, as two detectives, one of whom watched me by day, and the other—a perfect double—by night. He was an enemy, and his professed sympathy—which I now know was genuine—only made me hate him the more. As he was ignorant of the methods of treatment in vogue in hospitals for the insane, it was several weeks before he dared put in jeopardy his position by presuming to shield me against unwise orders of the doctors. But when at last he awoke to the situation, he repeatedly intervened in my behalf. More than once the doctor who was both owner and superintend-

ent threatened to discharge him for alleged officiousness.
But better judgment usually held the doctor's wrath
in check, for he realized that not one attendant in a
hundred was so competent.

Not only did the friendly attendant frequently exhibit more wisdom than the superintendent, but he also
obeyed the dictates of a better conscience than that of
his nominal superior, the assistant physician.   On three
occasions this man treated me with a signal lack of
consideration, and in at least one instance he was vicious.   When this latter incident occurred, I was both
physically and mentally helpless.   My feet were swollen
and still in plaster bandages.   I was all but mute, uttering only an occasional expletive when forced to perform
acts against my will.

One morning Doctor No-name (he represents a type)
entered my room.

"Good morning! How are you feeling?" he asked.
No answer.

"Aren't you feeling well?"
No answer.

"Why don't you talk?" he asked with irritation.

Still no answer, except perhaps a contemptuous look
such as is so often the essence of eloquence. Suddenly,
and without the slightest warning, as a petulant child
locked in a room for disobedience might treat a pillow,
he seized me by an arm and jerked me from the bed.
It was fortunate that the bones of my ankles and feet,
not yet thoroughly knitted, were not again injured.
And this was the performance of the very man who had,

locked my hands in the muff, that I might not injure myself!

"Why don't you talk?" he again asked.

Though rather slow in replying, I will take pleasure in doing so by sending that doctor a copy of this book —my answer—if he will but send me his address.

It is not a pleasant duty to brand any physician for cruelty and incompetence, for the worst that ever lived has undoubtedly done many good deeds. But here is the type of man that has wrought havoc among the helpless insane. And the owner represented a type that has too long profited through the misfortunes of others. "Pay the price or put your relative in a public institution!" is the burden of his discordant song before commitment. "Pay or get out!" is his jarring refrain when satisfied that the family's resources are exhausted. I later learned that this grasping owner had bragged of making a profit of $98,000 in a single year. About twenty years later he left an estate of approximately $1,500,000. Some of the money, however, wrung from patients and their relatives in the past may yet benefit similar sufferers in the future, for, under the will of the owner, several hundred thousand dollars will eventually be available as an endowment for the institution.

IX

IT was at the sanatorium that my ankles were finally
restored to a semblance of their former utility. They
were there subjected to a course of heroic treatment;
but as to-day they permit me to walk, run, dance, and
play tennis and golf, as do those who have never
been crippled, my hours of torture endured under
my first attempts to walk are almost pleasant to recall.
About five months from the date of my injury I was
allowed, or rather compelled, to place my feet on the
floor and attempt to walk. My ankles were still swollen,
absolutely without action, and acutely sensitive to the
slightest pressure. From the time they were hurt
until I again began to talk—two years later—I asked
not one question as to the probability of my ever regaining the use of them. The fact was, I never expected to
walk naturally again. The desire of the doctors to have
me walk I believed to be inspired by the detectives, of
whom, indeed, I supposed the doctor himself to be
one. Had there been any confession to make, I am sure
it would have been yielded under the stress of this ultimate torture. The million needle points which, just
prior to my mental collapse, seemed to goad my brain,
now centred their unwelcome attention on the soles of
my feet. Had the floor been studded with minute
stilettos my sufferings could hardly have been more

intense. For several weeks assistance was necessary with each attempt to walk, and each attempt was an ordeal. Sweat stood in beads on either foot, wrung from my blood by agony. Believing that it would be only a question of time when I should be tried, condemned, and executed for some one of my countless felonies, I thought that the attempt to prevent my continuing a cripple for the brief remainder of my days was prompted by anything but benevolence.

The superintendent would have proved himself more humane had he not peremptorily ordered my attendant to discontinue the use of a support which, until the plaster bandages were removed, had enabled me to keep my legs in a horizontal position when I sat up. His order was that I should put my legs down and keep them down, whether it hurt or not. The pain was of course intense when the blood again began to circulate freely through tissues long unused to its full pressure, and so evident was my distress that the attendant ignored the doctor's command and secretly favored me. He would remove the forbidden support for only a few minutes at a time, gradually lengthening the intervals until at last I was able to do without the support entirely. Before long and each day for several weeks I was forced at first to stagger and finally to walk across the room and back to the bed. The distance was increased as the pain diminished, until I was able to walk without more discomfort than a comparatively pleasant sensation of lameness. For at least two months after my feet first touched the floor I had to be carried

up and downstairs, and for several months longer I went
flat-footed.

Delusions of persecution—which include "delusions
of self-reference"—though a source of annoyance while
I was in an inactive state, annoyed and distressed me
even more when I began to move about and was obliged
to associate with other patients. To my mind, not
only were the doctors and attendants detectives; each
patient was a detective and the whole institution was a
part of the Third Degree. Scarcely any remark was
made in my presence that I could not twist into a
cleverly veiled reference to myself. In each person
I could see a resemblance to persons I had known, or to
the principals or victims of the crimes with which I
imagined myself charged. I refused to read; for to
read veiled charges and fail to assert my innocence was
to incriminate both myself and others. But I looked
with longing glances upon all printed matter and, as
my curiosity was continually piqued, this enforced
abstinence grew to be well-nigh intolerable.

It became again necessary to the family purse that
every possible saving be made. Accordingly, I was transferred from the main building, where I had a private
room and a special attendant, to a ward where I was to
mingle, under an aggregate sort of supervision, with
fifteen or twenty other patients. Here I had no special
attendant by day, though one slept in my room at night.

Of this ward I had heard alarming reports—and these
from the lips of several attendants. I was, therefore,
greatly disturbed at the proposed change. But, the

transfer once accomplished, after a few days I really
liked my new quarters better than the old. During the
entire time I remained at the sanatorium I was more
alert mentally than I gave evidence of being. But not
until after my removal to this ward, where I was left
alone for hours every day, did I dare to show my alert-
ness. Here I even went so far on one occasion as to joke
with the attendant in charge. He had been trying to
persuade me to take a bath. I refused, mainly because
I did not like the looks of the bath room, which, with its
cement floor and central drain, resembled the room in
which vehicles are washed in a modern stable. After
all else had failed, the attendant tried the rôle of sym-
pathizer.

"Now I know just how you feel," he said, "I can put
myself in your place."

"Well, if you can, do it and take the bath yourself,"
was my retort.

The remark is brilliant by contrast with the dismal
source from which it escaped. "Escaped" is the word
for the fear that I should hasten my trial by exhibiting
too great a gain in health, mental or physical, was already
upon me; and it controlled much of my conduct during
the succeeding months of depression.

Having now no special attendant, I spent many hours
in my room, alone, but not absolutely alone, for somewhere the eye of a detective was evermore upon me.
Comparative solitude, however, gave me courage; and
soon I began to read, regardless of consequences.
During the entire period of my depression, every publi-

cation seemed to have been written and printed for me, and me alone. Books, magazines, and newspapers seemed to be special editions. The fact that I well knew how inordinate would be the cost of such a procedure in no way shook my belief in it. Indeed, that I was costing my persecutors fabulous amounts of money was a source of secret satisfaction. My belief in special editions of newspapers was strengthened by items which seemed too trivial to warrant publication in any except editions issued for a special purpose. I recall a seemingly absurd advertisement, in which the phrase, " Green Bluefish," appeared. At the time I did not know that " green " was a term used to denote " fresh " or " unsalted."

During the earliest stages of my illness I had lost count of time, and the calendar did not right itself until the day when I largely regained my reason. Meanwhile, the date on each newspaper was, according to my reckoning, two weeks out of the way. This confirmed my belief in the special editions as a part of the Third Degree.

Most sane people think that no insane person can reason logically. But this is not so. Upon unreasonable premises I made most reasonable deductions, and that at the time when my mind was in its most disturbed condition. Had the newspapers which I read on the day which I supposed to be February 1st borne a January date, I might not then, for so long a time, have believed in special editions. Probably I should have inferred that the regular editions had been held back. But the newspapers I had were dated about two weeks *ahead*. Now if a sane person on February 1st receives a newspaper dated February 14th, he will be fully justified in thinking something wrong, either with the publication or with himself. But the shifted calendar which had planted itself in my mind meant as much to me as the true calendar does to any sane business man.   During the seven hundred and ninety-eight days of depression I drew countless incorrect deductions.   But, such as they were, they were deductions, and essentially the mental process was not other than that which takes place in a well-ordered mind.

My gradually increasing vitality, although it increased my fear of trial, impelled me to take new risks.   I began to read not only newspapers, but also such books as were placed within my reach.   Yet had they not been placed there, I should have gone without them, for I would never ask even for what I greatly desired and knew I could have for the asking.

Whatever love of literature I now have dates from this time, when I was a mental incompetent and confined in an institution.   Lying on a shelf in my room was a book by George Eliot.   For several days I cast longing glances at it and finally plucked up the courage to take little nibbles now and then.   These were so good that I grew bold and at last began openly to read the book.   Its contents at the time made but little impression on my mind, but I enjoyed it.   I read also some of Addison's essays; and had I been fortunate enough to have made myself familiar with these earlier in life, I might have been spared the delusion that I could detect, in many passages, the altering hand of my persecutors.

The friendly attendant, from whom I was now separated, tried to send his favors after me into my new quarters. At first he came in person to see me, but the superintendent soon forbade that, and also ordered him not to communicate with me in any way. It was this disagreement, and others naturally arising between such a doctor and such an attendant, that soon brought about the discharge of the latter. But "discharge" is hardly the word, for he had become disgusted with the institution, and had remained so long only because of his interest in me. Upon leaving, he informed the owner that he would soon cause my removal from the institution. This he did. I left the sanatorium in March, 1901, and remained for three months in the home of this kindly fellow, who lived with a grandmother and an aunt in Wallingford, a town not far from New Haven.

It is not to be inferred that I entertained any affection for my friendly keeper. I continued to regard him as an enemy; and my life at his home became a monotonous round of displeasure. I took my three meals a day. I would sit listlessly for hours at a time in the house. Daily I went out—accompanied, of course—for short walks about the town. These were not enjoyable. I believed everybody was familiar with my black record and expected me to be put to death. Indeed, I wondered why passers-by did not revile or even stone me. Once I was sure I heard a little girl call me "Traitor!" That, I believe, was my last "false voice," but it made such an impression that I can even now recall vividly the appearance of that dreadful child. It was not surprising that a piece of rope, old and frayed, which someone had carelessly thrown on a hedge by a cemetery that I sometimes passed, had for me great significance.

During these three months I again refused to read books, though within my reach, but I sometimes read newspapers. Still I would not speak, except under some unusual stress of emotion. The only time I took the initiative in this regard while living in the home of my attendant was on a bitterly cold and snowy day when I had the temerity to tell him that the wind had blown the blanket from a horse that had been standing for a long time in front of the house. The owner had come inside to transact some business with my attendant's relatives. In appearance he reminded me of the uncle to whom this book is dedicated. I imagined the mysterious caller was impersonating him and, by one of my curious mental processes, I deduced that it was incumbent on me to do for the dumb beast outside what I knew my uncle would have done had he been aware of its plight. My reputation for decency of feeling I believed to be gone forever; but I could not bear, in this situation, to be unworthy of my uncle, who, among those who knew him, was famous for his kindliness and humanity.

My attendant and his relatives were very kind and very patient, for I was still intractable. But their efforts to make me comfortable, so far as they had any effect, made keener my desire to kill myself. I shrank from death; but I preferred to die by my own hand and take the blame for it, rather than to be executed and bring lasting disgrace on my family, friends, and, I may add with truth, on Yale. For I reasoned that parents throughout the country would withhold their sons from a university which numbered among its graduates such a despicable being. But from any tragic act I was providentially restrained by the very delusion which gave birth to the desire—in a way which signally appeared on a later and, to me, a memorable day.

X

I AM in a position not unlike that of a man whose obituary notice has appeared prematurely. Few have ever had a better opportunity than I to test the affection of their relatives and friends. That mine did their duty and did it willingly is naturally a constant source of satisfaction to me. Indeed, I believe that this unbroken record of devotion is one of the factors which eventually made it possible for me to take up again my duties in the social and business world, with a comfortable feeling of continuity. I can, indeed, now view my past in as matter-of-fact a way as do those whose lives have been uniformly uneventful.

As I have seen scores of patients neglected by their relatives—a neglect which they resent and often brood upon—my sense of gratitude is the livelier, and especially so because of the difficulty with which friendly intercourse with me was maintained during two of the three years I was ill. Relatives and friends frequently called to see me. True, these calls were trying for all concerned. I spoke to none, not even to my mother and father. For, though they all appeared about as they used to do, I was able to detect some slight difference in look or gesture or intonation of voice, and this was enough to confirm my belief that they were impersonators, engaged in a conspiracy, not merely to entrap me, but to incriminate those whom they impersonated. It is not strange, then, that I refused to say anything to them, or to permit them to come near me. To have kissed the woman who was my mother, but whom I believed to be a federal conspirator, would have been an act of betrayal. These interviews were much harder for my relatives and friends than for me. But even for me they were ordeals; and though I suffered less at these moments than my callers, my sum of suffering was greater, for I was constantly anticipating these unwelcome, but eventually beneficial, visitations.

Suppose my relatives and friends had held aloof during this apparently hopeless period, what to-day would be my feelings toward them? Let others answer. For over two years I considered all letters forgeries. Yet the day came when I convinced myself of their genuineness and the genuineness of the love of those who sent them. Perhaps persons who have relatives among the more than a quarter of a million patients in institutions in this country to-day will find some comfort in this fact. To be on the safe and humane side, let every relative and friend of persons so afflicted remember the Golden Rule, which has never been suspended with respect to the insane. Go to see them, treat them sanely, write to them, keep them informed about the home circle; let not your devotion flag, nor accept any repulse.

The consensus now was that my condition was unlikely ever to improve, and the question of my commitment to some institution where incurable cases could be cared for came up for decision. While it was being considered, my attendant kept assuring me that it would be unnecessary to commit me to an institution if I would but show some improvement. So he repeatedly suggested that I go to New Haven and spend a day at home. At this time, it will be recalled, I was all but mute, so, being unable to beguile me into speech, the attendant one morning laid out for my use a more fashionable shirt than I usually wore, telling me to put it on if I wished to make the visit. That day it took me an unusually long time to dress, but in the end I put on the designated garment. Thus did one part of my brain outwit another.

I simply chose the less of two evils. The greater was to find myself again committed to an institution. Nothing else would have induced me to go to New Haven. I did not wish to go. To my best knowledge and belief, I had no home there, nor did I have any relatives or friends who would greet me upon my return. How could they, if still free, even approach me while I was surrounded by detectives? Then, too, I had a lurking suspicion that my attendant's offer was made in the belief that I would not dare accept it. By taking him at his word, I knew that I should at least have an opportunity to test the truth of many of his statements regarding my old home. Life had become insupportable; and back of my consent to make this experimental visit was a willingness to beard the detectives in their own den, regardless of consequences. With these and many other reflections I started for the train. The events of the journey which followed are of no moment. We soon reached the New Haven station; and, as I had expected, no relative or friend was there to greet us. This apparent indifference seemed to support my suspicion that my attendant had not told me the truth; but I found little satisfaction in uncovering his deceit, for the more of a liar I proved him to be, the worse would be my plight. We walked to the front of the station and stood there for almost half an hour. The unfortunate, but perfectly natural, wording of a question caused the delay.

"Well, shall we go home?" my attendant said.

How could I say, "Yes"? I had no home. I feel sure I should finally have said, "No," had he continued to put the question in that form. Consciously or unconsciously, however, he altered it. "Shall we go to 30 Trumbull Street?" That was what I had been waiting for. Certainly I would go to the house designated by that number. I had come to New Haven to see that house; and I had just a faint hope that its appearance and the appearance of its occupants might prove convincing.

At home my visit came as a complete surprise. I could not believe that my relatives—if they were relatives—had not been informed of my presence in the city, and their words and actions upon my arrival confirmed my suspicion and extinguished the faint hope I had briefly cherished. My hosts were simply the same old persecutors with whom I had already had too much to do. Soon after my arrival, dinner was served. I sat at my old place at the table, and secretly admired the skill with which he who asked the blessing imitated the language and the well-remembered intonation of my father's voice. But alas for the family!—I imagined my relatives banished and languishing in prison, and the old home confiscated by the government!

XI

THOUGH my few hours at home failed to prove that I did not belong in an institution, it served one good purpose. Certain relatives who had objected to my commitment now agreed that there was no alternative, and, accordingly, my eldest brother caused himself to be appointed my conservator. He had long favored taking such action, but other relatives had counseled delay. They had been deterred by that inbred dread of seeing a member of the family branded by law as a mental incompetent, and, to a degree, stigmatized by the prevailing unwarranted attitude of the public toward mental illness and the institutions in which mental cases are treated. The very thought was repellent; and a mistaken sense of duty—and perhaps a suggestion of pride—led them to wish me out of such an institution as long as possible.

Though at the time I dreaded commitment, it was the best possible thing that could befall me. To be, as I was, in the world but not of it, was exasperating. The constant friction that is inevitable under such conditions —conditions such as existed for me in the home of my attendant—can only aggravate the mental disturbance. Especially is this true of those laboring under delusions of persecution. Such delusions multiply with the complexity of the life led. It is the even-going routine of

67

institutional life which affords the indispensable quieting effect—provided that routine is well ordered, and not defeated by annoyances imposed by ignorant or indifferent doctors and attendants.

My commitment occurred on June 11th, 1901. The institution to which I was committed was a chartered, private institution, but not run for personal profit. It was considered one of the best of its kind in the country and was pleasantly situated. Though the view was a restricted one, a vast expanse of lawn, surrounded by groups of trees, like patches of primeval forest, gave the place an atmosphere which was not without its remedial effect. My quarters were comfortable, and after a little time I adjusted myself to my new environment.

Breakfast was served about half-past seven, though the hour varied somewhat according to the season—earlier in summer and later in winter. In the spring, summer, and autumn, when the weather was favorable, those able to go out of doors were taken after breakfast for walks within the grounds, or were allowed to roam about the lawn and sit under the trees, where they remained for an hour or two at a time. Dinner was usually served shortly after noon, and then the active patients were again taken out of doors, where they remained an hour or two doing much as they pleased, but under watchful eyes. About half-past three they returned to their respective wards, there to remain until the next day—except those who cared to attend the religious service which was held almost every afternoon in an endowed chapel.

In all institutions those confined in different kinds of

wards go to bed at different hours. The patients in the best wards retire at nine or ten o'clock. Those in the wards where more troublesome cases are treated go to bed usually at seven or eight o'clock. I, while undergoing treatment, have retired at all hours, so that I am in the better position to describe the mysteries of what is, in a way, one of the greatest secret societies in the world. I soon became accustomed to the rather agreeable routine, and had I not been burdened with the delusions which held me a prisoner of the police, and kept me a stranger to my old world, I should have been able to enjoy a comparatively happy existence in spite of all.

This new feeling of comparative contentment had not been brought about by any marked improvement in health. It was due directly and entirely to an environment more nearly in tune with my ill-tuned mind. While surrounded by sane people my mental inferiority had been painfully apparent to me, as well as to others. Here a feeling of superiority easily asserted itself, for many of my associates were, to my mind, vastly inferior to myself. But this stimulus did not affect me at once. For several weeks I believed the institution to be peopled by detectives, feigning insanity. The government was still operating the Third Degree, only on a grander scale. Nevertheless, I did soon come to the conclusion that the institution was what it purported to be—still cherishing the idea, however, that certain patients and attachés were detectives.

For a while after my arrival I again abandoned my new-found reading habit. But as I became accustomed

to my surroundings I grew bolder and resumed the
reading of newspapers and such books as were at hand.
There was a bookcase in the ward, filled with old numbers
of standard English periodicals; among them: *West-
minster Review, Edinburgh Review, London Quarterly,*
and *Blackwood's.* There were also copies of *Harper's*
and *The Atlantic Monthly,* dated a generation or more
before my first reading days. Indeed, some of the reviews were over fifty years old. But I had to read
their heavy contents or go without reading, for I would
not yet ask even for a thing I ardently desired. In
the room of one of the patients were thirty or forty
books belonging to him. Time and again I walked by
his door and cast longing glances at those books,
which at first I had not the courage to ask for or to take.
But during the summer, about the time I was getting
desperate, I finally managed to summon enough courage
to take them surreptitiously. It was usually while the
owner of these books was attending the daily service in
the chapel that his library became a circulating one.

The contents of the books I read made perhaps a
deeper impression on my memory than most books make
on the minds of normal readers. To assure myself of
the fact, I have since reread "The Scarlet Letter," and
I recognize it as an old friend. The first part of the
story, however, wherein Hawthorne describes his work
as a Custom House official and portrays his literary
personality, seems to have made scarcely any impression. This I attribute to my utter lack of interest
at that time in writers and their methods. I then

had no desire to write a book, nor any thought of ever doing so.

Letters I looked upon with suspicion. I never read them at the time they were received. I would not even open them; but generally, after a week or sometimes a month, I would secretly open and read them—forgeries of the detectives.

I still refused to speak, and exhibited physical activity only when the patients were taken out of doors. For hours I would sit reading books or newspapers, or apparently doing nothing. But my mind was in an active state and very sensitive. As the event proved, almost everything done or said within the range of my senses was making indelible impressions, though these at the time were frequently of such a character that I experienced great difficulty in trying to recall incidents which I thought I might find useful at the time of my appearance in court.

My ankles had not regained anything like their former strength. It hurt to walk. For months I continued to go flat-footed. I could not sustain my weight with heels lifted from the floor. In going downstairs I had to place my insteps on the edge of each step, or go one step at a time, like a child. Believing that the detectives were pampering me into prime condition, as a butcher fattens a beast for slaughter, I deliberately made myself out much weaker than I really was; and not a little of my inactivity was due to a desire to prolong my fairly comfortable existence, by deferring as long as possible the day of trial and conspicuous disgrace.

But each day still had its distressing incidents. Whenever the attendants were wanted at the office, an electric bell was rung. During the fourteen months that I remained in this hospital in a depressed condition, the bell in my ward rang several hundred times. Never did it fail to send through me a mild shock of terror, for I imagined that at last the hour had struck for my transportation to the scene of trial. Relatives and friends would be brought to the ward— heralded, of course, by a warning bell—and short interviews would be held in my room, during which the visitors had to do all the talking. My eldest brother, whom I shall refer to hereafter as my conservator, called often. He seldom failed to use one phrase which worried me.

"You are looking better and getting stronger," he would say. "We shall straighten you out yet."

To be "straightened out " was an ambiguous phrase which might refer to the end of the hangman's rope or to a fatal electric shock.

I preferred to be let alone, and the assistant physician in charge of my case, after several ineffectual attempts to engage me in conversation, humored my persistent taciturnity. For more than a year his only remarks to me were occasional conventional salutations. Subsequent events have led me to doubt the wisdom of his policy.

For one year no further attention was paid to me than to see that I had three meals a day, the requisite number of baths, and a sufficient amount of exercise. I was, however, occasionally urged by an attendant to write a letter to some relative, but that, of course, I refused to do. As I shall have many hard things to say about attendants in general, I take pleasure in testifying that, so long as I remained in a passive condition, those at this institution were kind, and at times even thoughtful. But there came a time when diplomatic relations with doctors and attendants became so strained that war promptly ensued.

It was no doubt upon the gradual, but sure improvement in my physical condition that the doctors were relying for my eventual return to normality. They were not without some warrant for this. In a way I had become less suspicious, but my increased confidence was due as much to an increasing indifference to my fate as to an improvement in health And there were other signs of improved mental vigor. I was still watchful, however, for a chance to end my life, and, but for a series of fortunate circumstances, I do not doubt that my choice of evils would have found tragic expression in an overt act.

Having convinced myself that most of my associates were really insane, and therefore (as I believed) disqualified as competent witnesses in a court of law, I would occasionally engage in conversation with a few whose evident incompetency seemed to make them safe confidants. One, a man who during his life had more than once been committed to an institution, took a very evident interest in me and persisted in talking to me, often much against my will. His persistent inquisitiveness seemed to support his own statement that he had

formerly been a successful life-insurance agent. He
finally gained my confidence to such a degree that
months before I finally began to talk to others I permitted
myself to converse frequently with him—but only when
we were so situated as to escape observation. I would
talk to him on almost any subject, but would not speak
about myself. At length, however, his admirable persistence overcame my reticence. During a conversation
held in June, 1902, he abruptly said, "Why you are kept
here I cannot understand. Apparently you are as sane
as anyone. You have never made any but sensible
remarks to me." Now for weeks I had been waiting for
a chance to tell this man my very thoughts. I had come
to believe him a true friend who would not betray me.

"If I should tell you some things which you apparently
don't know, you would understand why I am held here,"
I said.

"Well, tell me," he urged.

"Will you promise not to repeat my statements to any
one else?"

"I promise not to say a word."

"Well," I remarked, "you have seen certain persons
who have come here, professing to be relatives of mine."

"Yes, and they are your relatives, aren't they?"

"They look like my relatives, but they're not," was
my reply.

My inquisitive friend burst into laughter and said,
"Well, if you mean *that*, I shall have to take back what
I just said. You are really the craziest person I have
ever met, and I have met several."

"You will think differently some day," I replied; for I believed that when my trial should occur, he would appreciate the significance of my remark. I did not tell him that I believed these callers to be detectives; nor did I hint that I thought myself in the hands of the police.

Meanwhile, during July and August, 1902, I redoubled my activity in devising suicidal schemes; for I now thought my physical condition satisfactory to my enemies, and was sure that my trial could not be postponed beyond the next opening of the courts in September. I even went so far as to talk to one of the attendants, a medical student, who during the summer worked as an attendant at the hospital. I approached him artfully. First I asked him to procure from the library for me "The Scarlet Letter," "The House of the Seven Gables," and other books; then I talked medicine and finally asked him to lend me a textbook on anatomy which I knew he had in his possession. This he did, cautioning me not to let anyone know that he had done so. The book once secured, I lost no time in examining that part which described the heart, its functions, and especially its exact position in the body. I had scarcely begun to read when the young man returned and took the book from me, giving as his reason that an attendant had no right to let a patient read a medical work. Maybe his change of heart was providential.

As is usual in these institutions, all knives, forks, and other articles that might be used by a patient for

a dangerous purpose were counted by the attendants
after each meal. This I knew, and the knowledge had a
deterrent effect. I dared not take one. Though I might
at any time during the night have hanged myself, that
method did not appeal to me, and I kept it in mind only
as a last resort. To get possession of some sharp dagger-
like instrument which I could plunge into my heart at a
moment's notice—this was my consuming desire. With
such a weapon I felt that I could, when the crisis came,
rob the detectives of their victory. During the summer
months an employé spent his entire time mowing the
lawn with a large horse-drawn machine. This, when
not in use, was often left outdoors. Upon it was a square
wooden box, containing certain necessary tools, among
them a sharp, spike-like instrument, used to clean the
oil-holes when they became clogged. This bit of
steel was five or six inches long, and was shaped like a
pencil. For at least three months, I seldom went out
of doors that I did not go with the intention of purloin-
ing that steel spike. I intended then to keep it in my
room against the day of my anticipated transfer to jail.

It was now that my delusions protected me from the
very fate they had induced me to court. For had I not
believed that the eye of a detective was on me every
moment, I could have taken that spike a score of times.
Often, when it was not in use, I walked to the lawn-
mower and even laid my hand upon the tool-box. But
I dared not open it. My feelings were much like those
of Pandora about a certain other box. In my case,
however, the box upon which I looked with longing

had Hope without, and not within. Instinctively, perhaps, I realized this, for I did not lift the lid.

One day, as the patients were returning to their wards, I saw, lying directly in my path (I could even now point out the spot), the coveted weapon. Never have I seen anything that I wanted more. To have stooped and picked it up without detection would have been easy; and had I known, as I know now, that it had been carelessly dropped there, nothing could have prevented me from doing so and perhaps using it with fatal effect. But I believed it had been placed there deliberately and as a test, by those who had divined my suicidal purpose. The eye of the imagined detective, which, I am inclined to believe, and like to believe, was the eye of the real God, was upon me; and though I stepped directly over it, I did not pick up that thing of death.

XII

WHEN I had decided that my chance for securing the little stiletto spike was very uncertain, I at once busied myself with plans which were designed to bring about my death by drowning. There was in the ward a large bath tub. Access to it could be had at any time, except from the hour of nine (when the patients were locked in their rooms for the night) until the following morning. How to reach it during the night was the problem which confronted me. The attendant in charge was supposed to see that each patient was in his room before his door was locked. As it rarely happened that the patients were not in their rooms at the appointed time, the attendants naturally grew careless, and often locked a door without looking in. "Good night"—a salutation usually devoid of sentiment—might, or might not, elicit a response, and the absence of a response would not tend to arouse suspicion—especially in a case like mine, for I would sometimes say "good night," but more often not.

My simple and easy plan was to hide behind a piece of furniture in the corridor and there remain until the attendant had locked the doors of the rooms and gone to bed. I had even advanced so far in my plan as to select a convenient nook within twenty feet of my own room. Should the attendant, when about to lock the door, discover my absence, I should, of course, immediately reveal my hiding-place by leaving it; and it would have been an easy matter to convince him that I had done the thing as a test of his own vigilance. On the other hand, if I escaped discovery, I should then have nine hours at my disposal with little fear of interruption. True, the night watch passed through the ward once every hour. But death by drowning requires a time no longer than that necessary to boil an egg. I had even calculated how long it would take to fill the tub with water. To make sure of a fatal result, I had secreted a piece of wire which I intended so to use that my head, once under water, could by no possibility be raised above the surface in the inevitable death struggle.

I have said that I did not desire death; nor did I. Had the supposed detectives been able to convince me that they would keep their word, I would willingly have signed an agreement stipulating on my side that I must live the rest of my life in confinement, and on theirs that I should never undergo a trial for crime.

Fortunately, during these dismal preparations, I had not lost interest in other schemes which probably saved my life. In these the fellow-patient who had won my confidence played the rôle of my own private detective. That he and I could defeat the combined forces arrayed against me hardly seemed probable, but the seeming impossibility of so doing only lent zest to the undertaking. My friend, who, of course, did not realize that he was engaged in combat with the Secret Service, was allowed to go where he pleased within the limits of the city where the hospital was situated. Accordingly I determined to enlist his services. It was during July that, at my suggestion, he tried to procure copies of certain New Haven newspapers, of the date of my attempted suicide and the several dates immediately following. My purpose was to learn what motive had been ascribed to my suicidal act. I felt sure that the papers would contain at least hints as to the nature of the criminal charges against me. But my purpose I did not disclose to my friend. In due time he reported that no copies for the given dates were to be had. So *that* quest proved fruitless, and I attributed the failure to the superior strategy of the enemy.

Meanwhile, my friend had not stopped trying to convince me that my apparent relatives were not spurious; so one day I said to him: "If my relatives still live in New Haven, their addresses must be in the latest New Haven Directory. Here is a list containing the names and former addresses of my father, brother, and uncle. These were their addresses in 1900. To-morrow, when you go out, please see whether they appear in the New Haven Directory for 1902. These persons who present themselves to me as relatives pretend to live at these addresses. If they speak the truth, the 1902 Directory will corroborate them. I shall then have hope that a letter sent to any one of these addresses will reach relatives—and surely some attention will be paid to it."

The next day, my own good detective went to a local

publishing house where directories of important cities
throughout the country could be consulted. Shortly
after he went upon this errand, my conservator
appeared. He found me walking about the lawn.
At his suggestion we sat down. Bold in the assurance
that I could kill myself before the crisis came, I talked
with him freely, replying to many of his questions
and asking several. My conservator, who did not know
that I doubted his identity, commented with manifest
pleasure on my new-found readiness to talk. He would
have been less pleased, however, had he been able to
read my mind

Shortly after my conservator's departure, my fellow-
patient returned and informed me that the latest New
Haven Directory contained the names and addresses I
had given him. This information, though it did not
prove that my morning caller was no detective, did
convince me that my real brother still lived where he did
when I left New Haven, two years earlier. Now that my
delusions were growing weaker, my returning reason
enabled me to construct the ingenious scheme which,
I believe, saved my life; for, had I not largely regained
my reason *when I did*, I am inclined to believe that
my distraught mind would have destroyed itself and me,
before it could have been restored by the slow process of
returning health.

A few hours after my own private detective had given
me the information I so much desired, I wrote the first
letter I had written in twenty-six months. As letters go,
it is in a class by itself. I dared not ask for ink, so I wrote

with a lead pencil. Another fellow-patient in whom I had confidence, at my request, addressed the envelope; but he was not in the secret of its contents. This was an added precaution, for I thought the Secret Service men might have found out that I had a detective of my own and would confiscate any letters addressed by him or me. The next morning, *my* "detective" mailed the letter. That letter I still have, and I treasure it as any innocent man condemned to death would treasure a pardon. It should convince the reader that sometimes a mentally disordered person, even one suffering from many delusions, can think and write clearly. An exact copy of this—the most important letter I ever expect to be called upon to write—is here presented:

AUGUST 29, 1902.

DEAR GEORGE:

On last Wednesday morning a person who claimed to be George M. Beers of New Haven, Ct., clerk in the Director's Office of the Sheffield Scientific School and a brother of mine, called to see me.

Perhaps what he said was true, but after the events of the last two years I find myself inclined to doubt the truth of everything that is told me. He said that he would come and see me again sometime next week, and I am sending you this letter in order that you may bring it with you as a passport, provided you *are* the one who was here on Wednesday.

If you did not call as stated please say nothing about this letter to anyone, and when your double arrives, I'll tell him what I think of him. Would send other messages, but while things seem as they do at present it is impossible. Have had someone else address envelope for fear letter might be held up on the way.

Yours,

CLIFFORD W. B.

Though I felt reasonably confident that this message would reach my brother, I was by no means certain. I was sure, however, that, should he receive it, under no circumstances would he turn it over to anyone hostile to myself. When I wrote the words: "Dear George," my feeling was much like that of a child who sends a letter to Santa Claus after his childish faith has been shaken. Like the skeptical child, I felt there was nothing to lose, but everything to gain. "Yours" fully expressed such affection for relatives as I was then capable of — for the belief that I had disgraced, perhaps destroyed, my family prompted me to forbear to use the family name in the signature.

The thought that I might soon get in touch with my old world did not excite me. I had not much faith anyway that I was to re-establish former relations with it, and what little faith I had was all but destroyed on the morning of August 30th, 1902, when a short message, written on a slip of paper, reached me by the hand of an attendant. It informed me that my conservator would call that afternoon. I thought it a lie. I felt that any brother of mine would have taken the pains to send a letter in reply to the first I had written him in over two years. The thought that there had not been time for him to do so and that this message must have arrived by telephone did not then occur to me. What I believed was that my own letter had been confiscated. I asked one of the doctors to swear on his honor that it really was my own brother who was coming to see me. This he did. But abnormal suspicion robbed all men in my sight of whatever honor they may have had, and I was not fully reassured.

In the afternoon, as usual, the patients were taken out of doors, I among them. I wandered about the lawn and cast frequent and expectant glances toward the gate, through which I believed my anticipated visitor would soon pass. In less than an hour he appeared. I first caught sight of him about three hundred feet away, and, impelled more by curiosity than hope, I advanced to meet him. "I wonder what the lie will be this time," was the gist of my thoughts.

The person approaching me was indeed the counterpart of my brother as I remembered him. Yet he was no more my brother than he had been at any time during the preceding two years. He was still a detective. Such he was when I shook his hand. As soon as that ceremony was over, he drew forth a leather pocketbook. I instantly recognized it as one I myself had carried for several years prior to the time I was taken ill in 1900. It was from this that he took my recent letter.

"Here's my passport," he said.

"It's a good thing you brought it," I replied, as I glanced at it and again shook his hand—this time the hand of my own brother.

"Don't you want to read it?" he asked.

"There is no need of that. I am convinced."

After my long journey of exploration in the jungle of a tangled imagination, a journey which finally ended in my finding the person for whom I had long searched, my behavior differed very little from that of a great explorer

who, full of doubt after a long and perilous trip through
real jungles, found the man he sought and, grasping his
hand, greeted him with the simple and historic words,
"Dr. Livingstone, I presume?"

The very instant I caught sight of my letter in the
hands of my brother, all was changed. The thousands of
false impressions recorded during the seven hundred and
ninety-eight days of my depression seemed at once to
correct themselves. Untruth became Truth. A large
part of what was once my old world was again mine.
To me, at least, my mind seemed to have found itself, for
the gigantic web of false beliefs in which it had been
all but hopelessly enmeshed I now immediately recognized as a snare of delusions. That the Gordian knot
of mental torture should be cut and swept away by the
mere glance of a willing eye is like a miracle. Not a
few patients, however, suffering from certain forms of
mental disorder, regain a high degree of insight into their
mental condition in what might be termed a flash of divine enlightenment. Though insight regained seemingly
in an instant is a most encouraging symptom, power to
reason normally on all subjects cannot, of course, be so
promptly recovered. My new power to reason correctly on some subjects simply marked the transition
from depression, one phase of my disorder, to elation,
another phase of it. Medically speaking, I was as
mentally disordered as before—yet I was happy!

My memory during depression may be likened to a
photographic film, seven hundred and ninety-eight days
long. Each impression seems to have been made in a

negative way and then, in a fraction of a second, miraculously developed and made positive. Of hundreds of impressions made during that depressed period I had not before been conscious, but from the moment my mind, if not my full reason, found itself, they stood out vividly. Not only so, but other impressions registered during earlier years became clearer. Since that August 30th, which I regard as my second birthday (my first was on the 30th of another month), my mind has exhibited qualities which, prior to that time, were so latent as to be scarcely distinguishable. As a result, I find myself able to do desirable things I never before dreamed of doing—the writing of this book is one of them.

Yet had I failed to convince myself on August 30th, when my brother came to see me, that he was no spy, I am almost sure that I should have compassed my own destruction within the following ten days, for the next month, I believed, was the fatal one of opening courts. You will recall that it was death by drowning that impended. I liken my salvation itself to a prolonged process of drowning. Thousands of minutes of the seven hundred and ninety-eight days—and there were over one million of them, during which I had been borne down by intolerably burdensome delusions—were, I imagine, much like the last minutes of consciousness experienced by persons who drown. Many who have narrowly escaped that fate can testify to the vividness with which good and bad impressions of their entire life rush through their confused minds, and hold them in a grip of terror until a kind unconsciousness envelops them. Such

had been many of my moments. But the only unconsciousness which had deadened my sensibilities during
these two despondent years was that of sleep itself.
Though I slept fairly well most of the time, mine
was seldom a dreamless sleep. Many of my dreams
were, if anything, harder to bear than my delusions of
the day, for what little reason I had was absolutely
suspended in sleep. Almost every night my brain was
at battledore and shuttlecock with weird thoughts.
And if not all my dreams were terrifying, this fact seemed
to be only because a perverted and perverse Reason, in
order that its possessor might not lose the capacity for
suffering, knew how to keep Hope alive with visions
which supplied the contrast necessary for keen appreciation.

No man can be born again, but I believe I came as
near it as ever a man did. To leave behind what was in
reality a hell, and immediately have this good green
earth revealed in more glory than most men ever see it,
was one of the compensating privileges which make
me feel that my suffering was worth while.

I have already described the peculiar sensation which
assailed me when, in June, 1900, I lost my reason.
At that time my brain felt as though pricked by a
million needles at white heat. On this August 30th,
1902, shortly after largely regaining my reason, I had
another most distinct sensation in the brain. It started
under my brow and gradually spread until the entire
surface was affected. The throes of a dying Reason had
been torture. The sensations felt as my dead Reason

Was reborn were delightful. It seemed as though the refreshing breath of some kind Goddess of Wisdom were being gently blown against the surface of my brain. It was a sensation not unlike that produced by a menthol pencil rubbed ever so gently over a fevered brow. So delicate, so crisp and exhilarating was it that words fail me in my attempt to describe it. Few, if any, experiences can be more delightful. If the exaltation produced by some drugs is anything like it, I can easily understand how and why certain pernicious habits enslave those who contract them. For me, however, this experience was liberation, not enslavement.

XIII

AFTER two years of silence I found it no easy matter to carry on with my brother a sustained conversation. So weak were my vocal cords from lack of use that every few minutes I must either rest or whisper. And upon pursing my lips I found myself unable to whistle, notwithstanding the popular belief, drawn from vague memories of small-boyhood, that this art is instinctive. Those who all their lives have talked at will cannot possibly appreciate the enjoyment I found in using my regained power of speech. Reluctantly I returned to the ward; but not until my brother had left for home, laden with so much of my conversation that it took most of his leisure for the next two days to tell the family what I had said in two hours.

During the first few hours I seemed virtually normal. I had none of the delusions which had previously oppressed me; nor had I yet developed any of the expansive ideas, or delusions of grandeur, which soon began to crowd in upon me. So normal did I appear while talking to my brother that he thought I should be able to return home in a few weeks; and, needless to say, I agreed with him. But the pendulum, as it were, had swung too far. The human brain is too complex a mechanism to admit of any such complete readjustment in an instant. It is said to be composed of several million cells; and, that fact granted, it seems safe to say that every day, perhaps every hour, hundreds of thousands of the cells of my brain were now being brought into a state of renewed activity. Comparatively sane and able to recognize the important truths of life, I was yet insane as to many of its practical details. Judgment being King of the Realm of Thought, it was not surprising that my judgment failed often to decide correctly the many questions presented to it by its abnormally communicative subjects. At first I seemed to live a second childhood. I did with delight many things which I had first learned to do as a child—the more so as it had been necessary for me to learn again to eat and walk, and now to talk. I had much lost time to make up; and for a while my sole ambition seemed to be to utter as many thousand words a day as possible. My fellow-patients who for fourteen months had seen me walk about in silence—a silence so profound and inexorable that I would seldom heed their friendly salutations—were naturally surprised to see me in my new mood of unrestrained loquacity and irrepressible good humor. In short, I had come into that abnormal condition which is known to psychiatrists as elation.

For several weeks I believe I did not sleep more than two or three hours a night. Such was my state of elation, however, that all signs of fatigue were entirely absent; and the sustained and abnormal mental and physical activity in which I then indulged has left on my memory no other than a series of very pleasant impressions. Though based on fancy, the delights of some forms of mental disorder are real. Few, if any, sane persons would care to test the matter at so great a price; but those familiar with the "Letters of Charles Lamb " must know that Lamb, himself, underwent treatment for mental disease. In a letter to Coleridge, dated June 10th, 1796, he says: "At some future time I will amuse you with an account, as full as my memory will permit, of the strange turns my frenzy took. I look back upon it at times with a gloomy kind of envy; for, while it lasted, I had many, many hours of pure happiness. Dream not, Coleridge, of having tasted all the grandeur and wildness of Fancy till you have gone mad! All now seems to me vapid, comparatively so!"

As for me, the very first night vast but vague human-itarian projects began joyously to shape themselves in my mind. My garden of thoughts seemed filled with flowers which might properly be likened to the quick-blowing night-blooming cereus—that Delusion of Grandeur of all flowering plants that thinks itself prodigal enough if it but unmask its beauty to the moon! Few of my bold fancies, however, were of so fugitive and chaste a splendor.

The religious instinct is found in primitive man. It is not strange, therefore, that at this time the religious side of my nature was the first to display compelling activity. Whether or not this was due to my rescue from a living death, and my immediate appreciation of God's good-ness, both to me and to those faithful relatives who had done all the praying during the preceding two years— this I cannot say. But the fact stands out, that, whereas I had, while depressed, attached a sinister significance

to everything done or said in my presence, I now interpreted the most trifling incidents as messages from
God. The day after this transition I attended church.
It was the first service in over two years which I had
not attended against my will. The reading of a psalm
—the 45th — made a lasting impression upon me, and
the interpretation which I placed upon it furnishes
the key to my attitude during the first weeks of elation.
It seemed to me a direct message from Heaven.

The minister began: "My heart is inditing a good matter: I speak of the things which I have made touching the
king: my tongue is the pen of a ready writer."—Whose
heart but mine? And the things indited—what were
they but the humanitarian projects which had blossomed
in my garden of thoughts over night? When, a few days
later, I found myself writing very long letters with unwonted facility, I became convinced that my tongue was
to prove itself "the pen of a ready writer." Indeed, to
these prophetic words I trace the inception of an irresistible desire, of which this book is the first fruit.

"Thou art fairer than the children of men; grace is
poured into thy lips:" was the verse next read (by
myself and the congregation), to which the minister
responded, "Therefore God hath blessed thee for ever."
—"Surely, I have been selected as the instrument wherewith great reforms shall be effected," was my thought.
(All is grist that comes to the mill of a mind in elation—
then even divine encomiums seem not undeserved.)

"Gird thy sword upon thy thigh, O most mighty, with
thy glory and thy majesty"—a command to fight.

"And in thy majesty ride prosperously because of truth and meekness and righteousness;" replied the minister. "And thy right hand shall teach thee terrible things," —was another response. That I could speak the truth, I knew. "Meekness" I could not associate with myself, except that during the preceding two years I had suffered many indignities without open resentment. That my right hand with a pen should teach me terrible things— how to fight for reform—I firmly believed.

"Thine arrows are sharp in the heart of the King's enemies, whereby the people fall under thee," quoth the minister. Yes, my tongue could be as sharp as an arrow, and I should be able to stand up against those who should stand in the way of reform. Again: "Thou lovest righteousness, and hatest wickedness. Therefore God, thy God, hath anointed thee with the oil of gladness above thy fellows." The first sentence I did not apply to myself; but being then, as I supposed, a man restored to himself, it was easy to feel that I had been anointed with the oil of gladness above my fellows. "Oil of gladness" is, in truth, an apt phrase wherewith to describe elation.

The last two verses of the psalm corroborated the messages found in the preceding verses: "I will make thy name to be remembered in all generations:"—thus the minister. "Therefore shall the people praise thee for ever and ever," was the response I read. That spelled immortal fame for me, but only on condition that I should carry to a successful conclusion the mission of reform—an obligation placed upon me by God when He restored my reason.

When I set out upon a career of reform, I was impelled to do so by motives in part like those which seem to have possessed Don Quixote when he set forth, as Cervantes says, with the intention "of righting every kind of wrong, and exposing himself to peril and danger, from which in the issue he would obtain eternal renown and fame." In likening myself to Cervantes' mad hero my purpose is quite other than to push myself within the charmed circle of the chivalrous. What I wish to do is to make plain that a man abnormally elated may be swayed irresistibly by his best instincts, and that while under the spell of an exaltation, idealistic in degree, he may not only be willing, but eager to assume risks and endure hardships which under normal conditions he would assume reluctantly, if at all. In justice to myself, however, I may remark that my plans for reform have never assumed quixotic, and, therefore, impracticable, proportions. At no time have I gone a-tilting at windmills. A pen rather than a lance has been my weapon of offence and defence; for with its point I have felt sure that I should one day prick the civic conscience into a compassionate activity, and thus bring into a neglected field earnest men and women who should act as champions for those afflicted thousands least able to fight for themselves.

XIV

AFTER being without relatives and friends for over two years I naturally lost no time in trying again to get in touch with them; though I did heed my conservator's request that I first give him two or three days in which to acquaint intimates with the new turn my affairs had taken.

During the latter part of that first week I wrote many letters, so many, indeed, that I soon exhausted a liberal supply of stationery. This had been placed at my disposal at the suggestion of my conservator, who had wisely arranged that I should have whatever I wanted, if expedient. It was now at my own suggestion that the supervisor gave me large sheets of manila wrapping paper. These I proceeded to cut into strips a foot wide. One such strip, four feet long, would suffice for a mere *billet-doux;* but a real letter usually required several such strips pasted together. More than once letters twenty or thirty feet long were written; and on one occasion the accumulation of two or three days of excessive productivity, when spread upon the floor, reached from one end of the corridor to the other—a distance of about one hundred feet. My hourly output was something like twelve feet, with an average of one hundred and fifty words to the foot. Under the pressure of elation one takes pride in doing everything

in record time. Despite my speed my letters were
not incoherent. They were simply digressive, which was
to be expected, as elation befogs one's "goal idea."
Though these epistolary monstrosities were launched,
few reached those to whom they were addressed; for
my conservator had wisely ordered that my literary
output be sent in bulk to him. His action was exasperating, but later I realized that he had done me a great
favor when he interposed his judgment between my
red-hot mentality and the cool minds of the workaday world. Yet this interference with what I deemed
my rights proved to be the first step in the general
overruling of them by tactless attendants and, in particular, by a certain assistant physician.

I had always shown a strong inclination to super-
intend. In consequence, in my elated condition it was
but natural that I should have an excess of executive
impulses. In order to decrease this executive pressure
I proceeded to assume entire charge of that portion
of the hospital in which I happened at the moment
to be confined. What I eventually issued as impera-
tive orders were often presented at first as polite suggestions. But, if my suggestions were not accorded a
respectful hearing, and my demands acted upon at once,
I invariably supplemented them with vituperative ulti-
matums. These were double-edged, and involved me in
trouble quite as often as they gained the ends I sought.

The assistant physician in charge of my case, realizing
that he could not grant all of my requests, unwisely
decided to deny most of them. Had he been tactful,

he could have taken the same stand without arousing
my animosity. As it was, he treated me with a contemptuous sort of indifference which finally developed
into spite, and led to much trouble for us both. During
the two wild months that followed, the superintendent
and the steward could induce me to do almost anything
by simply requesting it. If two men out of three could
control me easily during such a period of mental excitement, is it not reasonable to suppose that the third man,
the assistant physician, could likewise have controlled
me had he treated me with consideration? It was
his undisguised superciliousness that gave birth to my
contempt for him. In a letter written during my second
week of elation, I expressed the opinion that he and I
should get along well together. But that was before I
had become troublesome enough to try the man's
patience. Nevertheless, it indicates that he could have
saved himself hours of time and subsequent worry, had
he met my friendly advances in the proper spirit, for
it is the quality of heart quite as much as the quantity
of mind that cures or makes happy the insane.

The literary impulse took such a hold on me that, when
I first sat down to compose a letter, I bluntly refused to
stop writing and go to bed when the attendant ordered
me to do so. For over one year this man had seen me
mute and meek, and the sudden and startling change
from passive obedience to uncompromising independence
naturally puzzled him. He threatened to drag me to my
room, but strangely enough decided not to do so. After
half an hour's futile coaxing, during which time an un-

wonted supply of blood was drawn to his brain, that surprised organ proved its gratitude by giving birth to a timely and sensible idea. With an unaccustomed resourcefulness, by cutting off the supply of light at the electric switch, he put the entire ward in darkness. Secretly I admired the stratagem, but my words on that occasion probably conveyed no idea of the approbation that lurked within me.

I then went to bed, but not to sleep. The ecstasy of elation made each conscious hour one of rapturous happiness, and my memory knows no day of brighter sunlight than those nights. The floodgates of thought were wide open. So jealous of each other were the thoughts that they seemed to stumble over one another in their mad rush to present themselves to my re-enthroned ego.

I naturally craved companionship, but there were not many patients whom I cared to talk with. I did, however, greatly desire to engage the assistant physician in conversation, as he was a man of some education and familiar with the history of my case. But this man, who had tried to induce me to speak when delusions had tied my tongue, now, when I was at last willing to talk, would scarcely condescend to listen; and what seemed to me his studied and ill-disguised avoidance only served to whet my desire to detain him whenever possible.

It was about the second week that my reformative turn of mind became acute. The ward in which I was confined was well furnished and as homelike as such a place could be, though in justice to my own home I must observe that the resemblance was not great. About the so-called violent ward I had far less favorable ideas. Though I had not been subjected to physical abuse during the first fourteen months of my stay here, I had seen unnecessary and often brutal force used by the attendants in managing several so-called violent patients, who, upon their arrival, had been placed in the ward where I was. I had also heard convincing rumors of rough treatment of irresponsible patients in the violent ward.

At once I determined to conduct a thorough investigation of the institution. In order that I might have proof that my intended action was deliberate, my first move was to tell one or two fellow-patients that I should soon transgress some rule in such a way as to necessitate my removal to the violent ward. At first I thought of breaking a few panes of glass; but my purpose was accomplished in another way—and, indeed, sooner than I had anticipated. My conservator, in my presence, had told the assistant physician that the doctors could permit me to telephone him whenever they should see fit. It was rather with the wish to test the unfriendly physician than to satisfy any desire to speak with my conservator that one morning I asked permission to call up the latter. That very morning I had received a letter from him. This the doctor knew, for I showed him the letter—but not its contents. It was on the letter that I based my demand, though in it my brother did not even intimate that he wished to speak to me. The doctor, however, had no way of knowing that my statement was not true. To deny my request was simply one of his ill-advised whims, and his refusal was given with customary curtness and contempt. I met his refusal in kind, and presented him with a trenchant critique of his character.

He said, "Unless you stop talking in that way I shall have you transferred to the Fourth Ward." (This was the violent ward.)

"Put me where you please," was my reply. "I'll put you in the gutter before I get through with you."

With that the doctor made good his threat, and the attendant escorted me to the violent ward—a willing, in fact, eager prisoner.

The ward in which I was now placed (September 13th, 1902) was furnished in the plainest manner. The floors were of hard wood and the walls were bare. Except when at meals or out of doors taking their accustomed exercise, the patients usually lounged about in one large room, in which heavy benches were used, it being thought that in the hands of violent patients, chairs might become a menace to others. In the dining room, however, there were chairs of a substantial type, for patients seldom run amuck at meal time. Nevertheless, one of these dining-room chairs soon acquired a history.

As my banishment had come on short notice, I had failed to provide myself with many things I now desired. My first request was that I be supplied with stationery. The attendants, acting no doubt on the doctor's orders, refused to grant my request; nor would they give me a lead pencil—which, luckily, I did not need, for I happened to have one. Despite their refusal I managed to get some scraps of paper, on which I was soon busily engaged in writing notes to those in authority. Some of these (as I learned later) were delivered, but no attention was paid to them. No doctor came near me until evening, when the one who had banished me made his regular round of inspection. When he appeared, the interrupted conversation of the morning was resumed—that is, by me—and in a similar vein. I again asked leave to telephone my conservator. The doctor again refused, and, of course, again I told him what I thought of him.

My imprisonment pleased me. I was where I most wished to be, and I busied myself investigating conditions and making mental notes. As the assistant physician could grant favors to the attendants, and had authority to discharge them, they did his bidding and continued to refuse most of my requests. In spite of their unfriendly attitude, however, I did manage to persuade the supervisor, a kindly man, well along in years, to deliver a note to the steward. In it I asked him to come at once, as I wished to talk with him. The steward, whom I looked upon as a friend, returned no answer and made no visit. I supposed he, too, had purposely ignored me. As I learned afterwards, both he and the superintendent were absent, else perhaps I should have been treated in a less high-handed manner by the assistant physician, who was not absent.

The next morning, after a renewal of my request and a repeated refusal, I asked the doctor to send me the "Book of Psalms" which I had left in my former room. With this request he complied, believing, perhaps, that some religion would at least do me no harm. I probably read my favorite psalm, the 45th; but most of my time I spent writing, on the flyleaves, psalms of my own. And if the value of a psalm is to be measured by the intensity of feeling portrayed, my compositions of that day rightly belonged beside the writings of David. My psalms were indited to those in authority at the hospital, and later in the day the supervisor—who proved himself a friend on many occasions—took the book to headquarters.

The assistant physician, who had mistaken my malevolent tongue for a violent mind, had placed me in an exile which precluded my attending the service which was held in the chapel that Sunday afternoon. Time which might better have been spent in church I therefore spent in perfecting a somewhat ingenious scheme for getting in touch with the steward. That evening, when the doctor again appeared, I approached him in a friendly way and politely repeated my request. He again refused to grant it. With an air of resignation I said, "Well, as it seems useless to argue the point with you and as the notes sent to others have thus far been ignored, I should like, with your kind permission, to kick a hole in your damned old building and to-morrow present myself to the steward in his office."

"Kick away!" he said with a sneer. He then entered an adjoining ward, where he remained for about ten minutes.

If you will draw in your mind, or on paper, a letter "L," and let the vertical part represent a room forty feet in length, and the horizontal part one of twenty, and if you will then picture me as standing in a doorway at the intersection of these two lines—the door to the dining room—and the doctor behind another door at the top of the perpendicular, forty feet away, you will have represented graphically the opposing armies just prior to the first real assault in what proved to be a siege of seven weeks.

The moment the doctor re-entered the ward, as he had to do to return to the office, I disappeared through my door—into the dining room. I then walked the length of that room and picked up one of the heavy wooden chairs, selected for my purpose while the doctor and his tame charges were at church. Using the chair as a battering-ram, without malice—joy being in my heart—I deliberately thrust two of its legs through an upper and a lower pane of a four-paned plate glass window. The only miscalculation I made was in failing to place myself directly in front of that window, and at a proper distance, so that I might have broken every one of the four panes. This was a source of regret to me, for I was always loath to leave a well-thought-out piece of work unfinished.

The crash of shattered and falling glass startled every one but me. Especially did it frighten one patient who happened to be in the dining room at the time. He fled. The doctor and the attendant who were in the adjoining room could not see me, or know what the trouble was; but they lost no time in finding out. Like the proverbial cold-blooded murderer who stands over his victim, weapon in hand, calmly awaiting arrest, I stood my ground, and, with a fair degree of composure, awaited the onrush of doctor and attendant. They soon had me in hand. Each taking an arm, they marched me to my room. This took not more than half a minute, but the time was not so short as to prevent my delivering myself of one more thumb-nail characterization of the doctor. My inability to recall that delineation, verbatim, entails no loss on literature. But one remark made as the doctor seized hold of me was apt, though not impromptu. "Well, doctor," I said, "knowing you to be a truthful man, I just took you at your word."

Senseless as this act appears it was the result of logical thinking. The steward had entire charge of the building and ordered all necessary repairs. It was he whom I desired above all others to see, and I reasoned that the breaking of several dollars' worth of plate glass (for which later, to my surprise, I had to pay) would compel his attention on grounds of economy, if not those of the friendly interest which I now believed he had abandoned. Early the next morning, as I had hoped, the steward appeared. He approached me in a friendly way (as had been his wont) and I met him in a like manner. "I wish you would leave a little bit of the building," he said good-naturedly.

"I will leave it all, and gladly, if you will pay some attention to my messages," was my rejoinder.

"Had I not been out of town," he replied, "I would have come to see you sooner." And this honest explanation I accepted.

I made known to the steward the assistant physician's behavior in balking my desire to telephone my conservator. He agreed to place the matter before the superintendent, who had that morning returned. As proof of gratitude, I promised to suspend hostilities until I had had a talk with the superintendent. I made it quite plain, however, that should he fail to keep his word, I would further facilitate the ventilation of the violent ward. My faith in mankind was not yet wholly restored.

XV

A FEW hours later, without having witnessed anything of particular significance, except as it befell myself, I was transferred to my old ward. The superintendent, who had ordered this rehabilitation, soon appeared, and he and I had a satisfactory talk. He gave me to understand that he himself would in future look after my case, as he realized that his assistant lacked the requisite tact and judgment to cope with one of my temperament—and with that, my desire to telephone my conservator vanished.

Now no physician would like to have his wings clipped by a patient, even indirectly, and without doubt the man's pride was piqued as his incompetence was thus made plain. Thereafter, when he passed through the ward, he and I had frequent tilts. Not only did I lose no opportunity to belittle him in the presence of attendants and patients, but I even created such opportunities; so that before long he tried to avoid me whenever possible. But it seldom was possible. One of my chief amusements consisted in what were really one-sided interviews with him. Occasionally he was so unwise as to stand his ground for several minutes, and his arguments on such occasions served only to keep my temper at a vituperative heat. If there were any epithets which I failed to apply to him during the succeeding weeks

of my association with him, they must have been coined
since. The uncanny admixture of sanity displayed by
me, despite my insane condition, was something this
doctor could not comprehend. Remarks of mine, which
he should have discounted or ignored, rankled as the
insults of a sane and free man would have done. And
his blunt and indiscriminate refusal of most of my
requests prolonged my period of mental excitement.

After my return to my old ward I remained there for a
period of three weeks. At that time I was a very self-
centred individual. My large and varied assortment of
delusions of grandeur made everything seem possible.
There were few problems I hesitated to attack. With
sufficient provocation I even attacked attendants—problems in themselves; but such fights as I subsequently
engaged in were fights either for my own rights or the
rights of others. Though for a while I got along fairly
well with the attendants and as well as could be expected
with the assistant physician, it soon became evident that
these men felt that to know me more was to love me less.
Owing to their lack of capacity for the work required of
them, I was able to cause them endless annoyance.
Many times a day I would tell the attendants what
to do and what not to do, and tell them what I should do
if my requests, suggestions, or orders were not immediately complied with. For over one year they had
seen me in a passive, almost speechless condition, and
they were, therefore, unable to understand my unwonted aggressions. The threat that I would chastise
them for any disobedience of my orders they looked upon

as a huge joke.   So it was, until one day I incontinently
cracked that joke against the head of one of them.

It began in this wise: Early in October there was
placed in the ward a man whose abnormality for the
most part consisted of an inordinate thirst for liquor.
He was over fifty years of age, well educated, traveled,
refined and of an artistic temperament.   Congenial companions were scarce where I was, and he and I were soon
drawn together in friendship. This man had been trapped
into the institution by the subterfuge of relatives.   As is
common in such cases, many "white" lies had been resorted to in order to save trouble for all concerned—
that is, all except the patient.   To be taken without
notice from one's home and by a deceitful, though
under the circumstances perhaps justifiable strategy,
placed in a ward with fifteen other men, all exhibiting insanity in varying degrees, is as heartbreaking an ordeal
as one can well imagine.   Yet such was this man's experience.   A free man one day, he found himself deprived of
his liberty the next, and branded with what he considered an unbearable disgrace.

Mr. Blank (as I shall call him) was completely unnerved.   As he was a stranger in what I well knew
was a strange world, I took him under my protecting
and commodious wing. I did all I could to cheer him
up, and tried to secure for him that consideration which
to me seemed indispensable to his well-being. Patients in his condition had never been forced, when
taking their exercise, to walk about the grounds with the
other patients.   At no time during the preceding four-

teen months had I seen a newly committed patient
forced to exercise against his will. One who objected
was invariably left in the ward, or his refusal was
reported to the doctor before further action was taken.
No sane person need stretch his imagination in order to
realize how humiliating it would be for this man to walk
with a crowd which greatly resembled a " chain gang."
Two by two, under guard, these hostages of misfortune
get the only long walks their restricted liberty allows
them. After the one or two occasions when this man did
walk with the gang, I was impressed with the not wholly
unreasonable thought that the physical exercise in no
way compensated for the mental distress which the sense
of humiliation and disgrace caused him to suffer. It
was delightfully easy for me to interfere in his behalf;
and when he came to my room, wrought up over the
prospect of another such humiliation and weeping bitterly, I assured him that he should take his exercise that
day when I did. My first move to accomplish the desired result was to approach, in a friendly way, the attendant in charge, and ask him to permit my new friend
to walk about the grounds with me when next I went.
He said he would do nothing of the kind—that he intended to take this man when he took the others. I said,
"For over a year I have been in this ward and so have
you, and I have never yet seen a man in Mr. Blank's
condition forced to go out of doors."

"It makes no difference whether you have or not,"
said the attendant, "he's going."

"Will you ask the doctor whether Mr. Blank can or

cannot walk about the grounds with my special attendant when I go?"

"No, I won't. Furthermore, it's none of your business."

"If you resort to physical force and attempt to take Mr. Blank with the other patients, you'll wish you hadn't," I said, as I walked away.

At this threat the fellow scornfully laughed. To him it meant nothing. He believed I could fight only with my tongue, and I confess that I myself was in doubt as to my power of fighting otherwise.

Returning to my room, where Mr. Blank was in waiting, I supported his drooping courage and again assured him that he should be spared the dreaded ordeal. I ordered him to go to a certain room at the farther end of the hall and there await developments—so that, should there be a fight, the line of battle might be a long one. He obeyed. In a minute or two the attendant was headed for that room. I followed closely at his heels, still threatening to attack him if he dared so much as lay a finger on my friend. Though I was not then aware of it, I was followed by another patient, a man who, though a mental case, had his lucid intervals and always a loyal heart. He seemed to realize that trouble was brewing and that very likely I should need help. Once in the room, the war of words was renewed, my sensitive and unnerved friend standing by and anxiously looking on.

"I warn you once more," I said, "if you touch Mr. Blank, I'll punch you so hard you'll wish you hadn't."

The attendant's answer was an immediate attempt to eject Mr. Blank from the room by force. Nothing could be more automatic than my action at that time; indeed, to this day I do not remember performing the act itself. What I remember is the determination to perform it and the subsequent evidence of its having been performed. At all events I had already made up my mind to do a certain thing if the attendant did a certain thing. He did the one and I did the other. Almost before he had touched Mr. Blank's person, my right fist struck him with great force in, on, or about the left eye. It was then that I became the object of the attendant's attention—but not his undivided attention—for as he was choking me, my unsuspected ally stepped up and paid the attendant a sincere compliment by likewise choking him. In the scuffle I was forced to the floor. The attendant had a grip upon my throat. My ward-mate had a double grip upon the attendant's throat. Thus was formed a chain with a weak, if not a missing, link in the middle. Picture, if you will, an insane man being choked by a supposedly sane one, and he in turn being choked by a temporarily sane insane friend of the assaulted one, and you will have Nemesis as nearly in a nutshell as any mere rhetorician has yet been able to put her.

That I was well choked is proved by the fact that my throat bore the crescent-shaped mark of my assailant's thumb nail. And I am inclined to believe that my rescuer, who was a very powerful man, made a decided impression on my assailant's throat. Had not the superintendent opportunely appeared at that moment, the man might soon have lapsed into unconsciousness, for I am sure my ally would never have released him until he had released me. The moment the attendant with his one good eye caught sight of the superintendent the scrimmage ended. This was but natural, for it is against the code of honor generally obtaining among attendants, that one should so far forget himself as to abuse patients in the presence of sane and competent witnesses.

The choking which I had just received served only to limber my vocal cords. I told the doctor all about the preliminary verbal skirmish and the needlessness of the fight. The superintendent had graduated at Yale over fifty years prior to my own graduation, and because of this common interest and his consummate tact we got along well together. But his friendly interest did not keep him from speaking his mind upon occasion, as his words at this time proved. "You don't know," he said, "how it grieves me to see you—a Yale man—act so like a rowdy."

"If fighting for the rights of a much older man, unable to protect his own interests, is the act of a rowdy, I'm quite willing to be thought one," was my reply.

Need I add that the attendant did not take Mr. Blank for a walk that morning? Nor, so far as I know, was the latter ever forced again to take his exercise against his will.

XVI

THE superintendent now realized that I was altogether too energetic a humanitarian to remain in a ward with so many other patients. My actions had a demoralizing effect upon them; so I was forthwith transferred to a private room, one of two situated in a small one-story annex. These new quarters were rather attractive, not unlike a bachelor apartment.

As there was no one here with whom I could interfere I got along without making any disturbance—that is, so long as I had a certain special attendant, a man suited to my temperament. He who was now placed over me understood human nature. He never resorted to force if argument failed to move me; and trifling transgressions, which would have led to a fight had he behaved like a typical attendant, he either ignored or privately reported to the doctor. For the whole period of my intense excitement there were certain persons who could control me, and certain others whose presence threw me into a state bordering on rage, and frequently into passions which led to distressing results.

Unfortunately for me, my good attendant soon left the institution to accept a more attractive business offer. He left without even a good-bye to me. Nothing proves more conclusively how important to me would have been his retention than this abrupt leave-taking which the doctor had evidently ordered, thinking perhaps that the prospect of such a change would excite me. However, I caused no trouble when the substitution was made, though I did dislike having placed over me a man with whom I had previously had misunderstandings. He was about my own age and it was by no means so easy to take orders from him as it had been to obey his predecessor, who was considerably older than myself. Then, too, this younger attendant disliked me because of the many disagreeable things I had said to him while we were together in a general ward. He weighed about one hundred and ninety pounds to my one hundred and thirty, and had evidently been selected to attend me because of his great strength. A choice based on mental rather than physical considerations would have been wiser. The superintendent, because of his advanced age and ill health, had been obliged again to place my case in the hands of the assistant physician, and the latter gave this new attendant certain orders. What I was to be permitted to do, and what not, was carefully specified. These orders, many of them unreasonable, were carried out to the letter. For this I cannot justly blame the attendant. The doctor had deprived him of the right to exercise what judgment he had.

At this period I required but little sleep. I usually spent part of the night drawing; for it was in September, 1902, while I was at the height of my wave of self-centred confidence, that I decided that I was destined to become a writer of books—or at least of one book; and now I thought I might as well be an artist, too, and illustrate my own works. In school I had never cared for drawing; nor at college either. But now my awakened artistic impulse was irresistible. My first self-imposed lesson was a free-hand copy of an illustration on a cover of *Life*. Considering the circumstances, that first drawing was creditable, though I cannot now prove the assertion; for inconsiderate attendants destroyed it, with many more of my drawings and manuscripts. From the very moment I completed that first drawing, honors were divided between my literary and artistic impulses; and a letter which, in due time, I felt impelled to write to the Governor of the State, incorporated art with literature. I wrote and read several hours a day and I spent as many more in drawing. But the assistant physician, instead of making it easy for me to rid myself of an excess of energy along literary and artistic lines, balked me at every turn, and seemed to delight in displaying as little interest as possible in my newly awakened ambitions. When everything should have been done to calm my abnormally active mind, a studied indifference and failure to protect my interests kept me in a state of exasperation.

But circumstances now arose which brought about the untimely stifling—I might better say strangulation—of my artistic impulses. The doctors were led—unwisely, I believe—to decide that absolute seclusion was the only thing that would calm my over-active brain. In consequence, all writing and drawing materials and all books were taken from me. And from October 18th until the first of the following January, except for one fortnight, I was confined in one or another small, barred room, hardly better than a cell in a prison and in some instances far worse.

A corn cob was the determining factor at this crisis. Seeing in myself an embryonic Raphael, I had a habit of preserving all kinds of odds and ends as souvenirs of my development. These, I believed, sanctified by my Midas-like touch, would one day be of great value. If the public can tolerate, as it does, thousands of souvenir hunters, surely one with a sick mind should be indulged in the whim for collecting such souvenirs as come within his reach. Among the odds and ends that I had gathered were several corn cobs. These I intended to gild and some day make useful by attaching to them small thermometers. But on the morning of October 18th, the young man in charge of me, finding the corn cobs, forthwith informed me that he would throw them away. I as promptly informed him that any such action on his part would lead to a fight. And so it did.

When this fight began, there were two attendants at hand. I fought them both to a standstill, and told them I should continue to fight until the assistant physician came to the ward. Thereupon, my special attendant, realizing that I meant what I said, held me while the other went for assistance. He soon returned, not with the assistant physician, but with a third attendant, and the fight was renewed. The one who had acted as messenger, being of finer fibre than the other two, stood at a safe distance. It was, of course, against the rules of the institution for an attendant to strike a patient, and, as I was sane enough to report with a fair chance of belief any forbidden blows, each captor had to content himself with holding me by an arm and attempting to choke me into submission. However, I was able to prevent them from getting a good grip on my throat, and for almost ten minutes I continued to fight, telling them all the time that I would not stop until a doctor should come. An assistant physician, but not the one in charge of my case, finally appeared. He gave orders that I be placed in the violent ward, which adjoined the private apartment I was then occupying, and no time was lost in locking me in a small room in that ward.

Friends have said to me: "Well, what is to be done when a patient runs amuck?" The best answer I can make is: "Do nothing to make him run amuck." Psychiatrists have since told me that had I had an attendant with the wisdom and ability to humor me and permit me to keep my priceless corn cobs, the fight in question, and the worse events that followed, would probably not have occurred—not that day, nor ever, had I at all times been properly treated by those in charge of me.

So again I found myself in the violent ward—but this time not because of any desire to investigate it. Art and literature being now more engrossing than my plans for reform, I became, in truth, an unwilling occupant of a room and a ward devoid of even a suggestion of the æsthetic. The room itself was clean, and under other circumstances might have been cheerful. It was twelve feet long, seven feet wide, and twelve high. A cluster of incandescent lights, enclosed in a semi-spherical glass globe, was attached to the ceiling. The walls were bare and plainly wainscotted, and one large window, barred outside, gave light. At one side of the door was an opening a foot square with a door of its own which could be unlocked only from without, and through which food could be passed to a supposedly dangerous patient. Aside from a single bed, the legs of which were screwed to the floor, the room had no furniture.

The attendant, before locking me in, searched me and took from me several lead pencils; but the stub of one escaped his vigilance. Naturally, to be taken from a handsomely furnished apartment and thrust into such a bare and unattractive room as this caused my already heated blood to approach the boiling point. Consequently, my first act was to send a note to the physician who regularly had charge of my case, requesting him to visit me as soon as he should arrive, and I have every reason to believe that the note was delivered. Whether or not this was so, a report of the morning's fight and my transfer must have reached him by some one of several witnesses. While waiting for an answer, I busied myself writing, and as I had no stationery I wrote on the walls. Beginning as high as I could reach, I wrote in columns, each about three feet wide. Soon the pencil became dull. But dull pencils are easily sharpened on the whetstone of wit. Stifling acquired traits, I permitted myself to revert momentarily to a primitive expedient. I gnawed the wood quite from the pencil, leaving only the graphite core. With a bit of graphite

a hand guided by the unerring insolence of elation
may artistically damn all men and things. That I
am inclined to believe I did; and I question whether
Raphael or Michael Angelo—upon whom I then looked
as mere predecessors—ever put more feeling per square
foot into their mural masterpieces. Every little while,
as if to punctuate my composition, and in an endeavor to get attention, I viciously kicked the door.

This first fight of the day occurred about 8 A.M.
For the three hours following I was left to thrash
about the room and work myself into a frenzy. I made
up my mind to compel attention. A month earlier,
shattered glass had enabled me to accomplish a certain
sane purpose. Again this day it served me. The opal-
escent half-globe on the ceiling seemed to be the most
vulnerable point for attack. How to reach and smash it
was the next question—and soon answered. Taking off
my shoes, I threw one with great force at my glass target
and succeeded in striking it a destructive blow.

The attendants charged upon my room. Their entrance was momentarily delayed by the door which stuck
fast. I was standing near it, and when it gave way, its
edge struck me on the forehead with force enough to have
fractured my skull had it struck a weaker part. Once in
the room, the two attendants threw me on the bed and
one choked me so severely that I could feel my eyes starting from their sockets. The attendants then put the
room in order; removed the glass—that is, all except one
small and apparently innocent, but as the event proved
well-nigh fatal, piece—took my shoes and again locked

me in my room—not forgetting, however, to curse me well for making them work for their living.

When the assistant physician finally appeared, I met him with a blast of invective which, in view of the events which quickly followed, must have blown out whatever spark of kindly feeling toward me he may ever have had. I demanded that he permit me to send word to my conservator asking him to come at once and look after my interests, for I was being unfairly treated. I also demanded that he request the superintendent to visit me at once, as I intended to have nothing more to do with the assistant physicians or attendants who were neglecting and abusing me. He granted neither demand.

The bit of glass which the attendants had overlooked was about the size of my thumb nail. If I remember rightly, it was not a part of the broken globe. It was a piece that had probably been hidden by a former occupant, in a corner of the square opening at the side of the door. At all events, if the pen is the tongue of a ready writer, so may a piece of glass be, under given conditions. As the thought I had in mind seemed an immortal one I decided to etch, rather than write with fugitive graphite. On the topmost panel of the door, which a few minutes before had dealt me so vicious a blow, I scratched a seven-word sentiment—sincere, if not classic: "God bless our Home, which is Hell."

The violent exercise of the morning had given me a good appetite and I ate my dinner with relish, though with some difficulty, for the choking had lamed my throat. On serving this dinner, the attendants again left me to my own devices. The early part of the afternoon I spent in vain endeavors to summon them and induce them to take notes to the superintendent and his assistant. They continued to ignore me. By sundown the furious excitement of the morning had given place to what might be called a deliberative excitement, which, if anything, was more effective. It was but a few days earlier that I had discussed my case with the assistant physician and told him all about the suicidal impulse which had been so strong during my entire period of depression. I now reasoned that a seeming attempt at suicide, a "fake" suicide, would frighten the attendants into calling this doctor whose presence I now desired—and desired the more because of his studied indifference. No man that ever lived, loved life more than I did on that day, and the mock tragedy which I successfully staged about dusk was, I believe, as good a farce as was ever perpetrated. If I had any one ambition it was to live long enough to regain my freedom and put behind prison bars this doctor and his burly henchmen. To compel attention that was my object.

At that season the sun set by half-past five and supper was usually served about that time. So dark was my room then that objects in it could scarcely be discerned. About a quarter of an hour before the attendant was due to appear with my evening meal I made my preparations. That the stage setting might be in keeping with the plot, I tore up such papers as I had with me, and also destroyed other articles in the room—as one might in a frenzy; and to complete the illusion of desperation, deliberately broke my watch. I then took off my suspenders, and tying one end to the head of the bedstead, made a noose of the other. This I adjusted comfortably about my throat. At the crucial moment I placed my pillow on the floor beside the head of the bed and sat on it—for this was to be an easy death. I then bore just enough weight on the improvised noose to give all a plausible look. And a last lifelike (or rather deathlike) touch I added by gurgling as in infancy's happy days.

No schoolboy ever enjoyed a prank more than I enjoyed this one. Soon I heard the step of the attendant, bringing my supper. When he opened the door, he had no idea that anything unusual was happening within. Coming as he did from a well-lighted room into one that was dark, it took him several seconds to grasp the situation —and then he failed really to take it in, for he at once supposed me to be in a semi-unconscious condition from strangulation. In a state of great excitement this brute of the morning called to his brute partner and I was soon released from what was nothing more than an amusing position, though they believed it one of torture or death. The vile curses with which they had addressed me in the morning were now silenced. They spoke kindly and expressed regret that I should have seen fit to resort to such an act. Their sympathy was as genuine as such men can feel, but a poor kind at best, for it was undoubtedly excited by the thought of what might be the consequences to them of their own neglect. While this unwonted stress of emotion threatened their peace of mind, I continued to play my part, pretending to be all but unconscious.

Shortly after my rescue from a very living death, the attendants picked me up and carried my limp body and laughing soul to an adjoining room, where I was tenderly placed upon a bed. I seemed gradually to revive.

"What did you do it for?" asked one.

"What's the use of living in a place like this, to be abused as I've been to-day?" I asked. "You and the doctor ignore me and all my requests. Even a cup of water between meals is denied me, and other requests which you have no right to refuse. Had I killed myself, both of you would have been discharged. And if my relatives and friends had ever found out how you had abused and neglected me, it is likely you would have been arrested and prosecuted."

Word had already been sent to the physician. He hurried to the ward, his almost breathless condition showing how my farce had been mistaken for a real tragedy. The moment he entered I abandoned the part I had been playing.

"Now that I have you three brutes where I want you, I'll tell you a few things you don't know," I said. "You probably think I've just tried to kill myself. It was simply a ruse to make you give me some attention. When I make threats and tell you that my one object in life is to live long enough to regain my freedom and lay bare the abuses which abound in places like this, you simply laugh at me, don't you? But the fact is, that's my ambition, and if you knew anything at all, you'd know that abuse won't drive me to suicide. You can continue to abuse me and deprive me of my rights, and keep me in exile from relatives and friends, but the time will come when I'll make you sweat for all this. I'll put you in prison where you belong. Or if I fail to do that, I can at least bring about your discharge from this institution. What's more, I will."

The doctor and attendants took my threats with characteristic nonchalance. Such threats, often enough heard in such places, make little or no impression, for they are seldom made good. When I made these threats, I really wished to put these men in prison. To-day I have no such desire, for were they not victims of the same vicious system of treatment to which I was subjected? In every institution where the discredited principles of "Restraint" are used or tolerated, the very atmosphere is brutalizing. Place a bludgeon in the hand of any man, with instructions to use it when necessary, and the gentler and more humane methods of persuasion will naturally be forgotten or deliberately abandoned.

Throughout my period of elation, especially the first months of it when I was doing the work of several normal men, I required an increased amount of fuel to generate the abnormal energy my activity demanded. I had a voracious appetite, and I insisted that the attendant give me the supper he was about to serve when he discovered me in the simulated throes of death. At first he refused, but finally relented and brought me a cup of tea and some buttered bread. Because of the severe choking administered earlier in the day it was with difficulty that I swallowed any food. I *had* to eat

slowly. The attendant, however, ordered me to hurry,
and threatened otherwise to take what little supper I
had. I told him that I thought he would not—that I
was entitled to my supper and intended to eat it with as
much comfort as possible. This nettled him, and by a
sudden and unexpected move he managed to take from
me all but a crust of bread. Even that he tried to snatch.
I resisted and the third fight of the day was soon on—and
that within five minutes of the time the doctor had left
the ward. I was seated on the bed. The attendant,
true to his vicious instincts, grasped my throat and
choked me with the full power of a hand accustomed
to that unmanly work. His partner, in the meantime,
had rendered me helpless by holding me flat on my
back while the attacking party choked me into breathless
submission. The first fight of the day was caused by a
corn cob; this of the evening by a crust of bread.

Were I to close the record of events of that October
day with an account of the assault just described, few, if
any, would imagine that I had failed to mention all the
abuse to which I was that day subjected. The fact is
that not the half has been told. As the handling of me
within the twenty-four hours typifies the worst, but,
nevertheless, the not unusual treatment of many patients in a like condition, I feel constrained to describe
minutely the torture which was my portion that night.

There are several methods of restraint in use to
this day in various institutions, chief among them
"mechanical restraint" and so-called "chemical restraint." The former consists in the use of instruments

of restraint, namely, strait-jackets or camisoles, muffs, straps, mittens, restraint or strong sheets, etc.—all of them, except on the rarest of occasions, instruments of neglect and torture. Chemical restraint (sometimes called medical restraint) consists in the use of temporarily paralyzing drugs—hyoscine being the popular "dose." By the use of such drugs a troublesome patient may be rendered unconscious and kept so for hours at a time. Indeed, very troublesome patients (especially when attendants are scarce) are not infrequently kept in a stupefied condition for days, or even for weeks—but only in institutions where the welfare of the patients is lightly regarded.

After the supper fight I was left alone in my room for about an hour. Then the assistant physician entered with three attendants, including the two who had figured in my farce. One carried a canvas contrivance known as a camisole. A camisole is a type of strait-jacket; and a very convenient type it is for those who resort to such methods of restraint, for it enables them to deny the use of strait-jackets at all. A strait-jacket, indeed, is not a camisole, just as electrocution is not hanging.

A camisole, or, as I prefer to stigmatize it, a strait-jacket, is really a tight-fitting coat of heavy canvas, reaching from neck to waist, constructed, however, on no ordinary pattern. There is not a button on it. The sleeves are closed at the ends, and the jacket, having no opening in front, is adjusted and tightly laced behind. To the end of each blind sleeve is attached a strong cord

The cord on the right sleeve is carried to the left of the body, and the cord on the left sleeve is carried to the right of the body. Both are then drawn tightly behind, thus bringing the arms of the victim into a folded position across his chest. These cords are then securely tied.

When I planned my ruse of the afternoon, I knew perfectly that I should soon find myself in a strait-jacket. The thought rather took my fancy, for I was resolved to know the inner workings of the violent ward.

The piece of glass with which I had that morning written the motto already quoted, I had appropriated for a purpose. Knowing that I should soon be put in the uncomfortable, but not necessarily intolerable embrace of a strait-jacket, my thought was that I might during the night, in some way or other, use this piece of glass to advantage—perhaps cut my way to a limited freedom. To make sure that I should retain possession of it, I placed it in my mouth and held it snugly against my cheek. Its presence there did not interfere with my speech; nor did it invite visual detection. But had I known as much about strait-jackets and their adjustment as I learned later, I should have resorted to no such futile expedient.

After many nights of torture, this jacket, at my urgent and repeated request, was finally adjusted in such manner that, had it been so adjusted at first, I need not have suffered any *torture* at all. This I knew at the time, for I had not failed to discuss the matter with a patient who on several occasions had been restrained in this same jacket.

On this occasion the element of personal spite entered into the assistant physician's treatment of me. The man's personality was apparently dual. His "Jekyll" personality was the one most in evidence, but it was the "Hyde" personality that seemed to control his actions when a crisis arose. It was "Doctor Jekyll" who approached my room that night, accompanied by the attendants. The moment he entered my room he became "Mr. Hyde." He was, indeed, no longer a doctor, or the semblance of one. His first move was to take the straitjacket in his own hands and order me to stand. Knowing that those in authority really believed I had that day attempted to kill myself, I found no fault with their wish to put me in restraint; but I did object to having this done by Jekyll-Hyde. Though a straitjacket should always be adjusted by the physician in charge, I knew that as a matter of fact the disagreeable duty was invariably assigned to the attendants. Consequently Jekyll-Hyde's eagerness to assume an obligation he usually shirked gave me the feeling that his motives were spiteful. For that reason I preferred to entrust myself to the uncertain mercies of a regular attendant; and I said so, but in vain. "If you will keep your mouth shut, I'll be able to do this job quicker," said Jekyll-Hyde.

"I'll shut my mouth as soon as you get out of this room and not before," I remarked. Nor did I. My abusive language was, of course, interlarded with the inevitable epithets. The more I talked, the more vindictive he became. He said nothing, but, unhappily for me, he expressed his pent-up feelings in something more effectual than words. After he had laced the jacket, and drawn my arms across my chest so snugly that I could not move them a fraction of an inch, I asked him to loosen the strait-jacket enough to enable me at least to take a full breath. I also requested him to give me a chance to adjust my fingers, which had been caught in an unnatural and uncomfortable position.

"If you will keep still a minute, I will," said Jekyll–Hyde. I obeyed, and willingly too, for I did not care to suffer more than was necessary. Instead of loosening the appliance as agreed, this doctor, now livid with rage, drew the cords in such a way that I found myself more securely and cruelly held than before. This breach of faith threw me into a frenzy. Though it was because his continued presence served to increase my excitement that Jekyll-Hyde at last withdrew, it will be observed that he did not do so until he had satisfied an unmanly desire which an apparently lurking hatred had engendered. The attendants soon withdrew and locked me up for the night.

No incidents of my life have ever impressed themselves more indelibly on my memory than those of my first night in a strait-jacket. Within one hour of the time I was placed in it I was suffering pain as intense as any I ever endured, and before the night had passed it had become almost unbearable. My right hand was so held that the tip of one of my fingers was all but cut by the nail of another, and soon knifelike pains began to shoot through my right arm as far as the shoulder. After four or five hours the excess of pain rendered me partially insensible to it. But for fifteen consecutive hours I remained in that instrument of torture; and not until the twelfth hour, about breakfast time the next morning, did an attendant so much as loosen a cord.

During the first seven or eight hours, excruciating pains racked not only my arms, but half of my body. Though I cried and moaned, in fact, screamed so loudly that the attendants must have heard me, little attention was paid to me—possibly because of orders from Mr. Hyde after he had again assumed the rôle of Doctor Jekyll. I even begged the attendants to loosen the jacket enough to ease me a little. This they refused to do, and they even seemed to enjoy being in a position to add their considerable mite to my torture.

Before midnight I really believed that I should be unable to endure the torture and retain my reason. A peculiar pricking sensation which I now felt in my brain, a sensation exactly like that of June, 1900, led me to believe that I might again be thrown out of touch with the world I had so lately regained. Realizing the awfulness of that fate, I redoubled my efforts to effect my rescue. Shortly after midnight I did succeed in gaining the attention of the night watch. Upon entering my room he found me flat on the floor. I had fallen from the bed and perforce remained absolutely helpless where I lay. I could not so much as lift my head. This, however, was not the fault of the straitjacket. It was because I could not control the muscles of my neck which that day had been so mauled. I

could scarcely swallow the water the night watch was
good enough to give me. He was not a bad sort;
yet even he refused to let out the cords of the strait-
jacket. As he seemed sympathetic, I can attribute
his refusal to nothing but strict orders issued by the
doctor.

It will be recalled that I placed a piece of glass in my
mouth before the strait-jacket was adjusted. At midnight the glass was still there. After the refusal of the
night watch, I said to him: "Then I want you to go to
Doctor Jekyll" (I, of course, called him by his right
name; but to do so now would be to prove myself as
brutal as Mr. Hyde himself). "Tell him to come here
at once and loosen this jacket. I can't endure the torture much longer. After fighting two years to regain
my reason, I believe I'll lose it again. You have
always treated me kindly. For God's sake, get the
doctor!"

"I can't leave the main building at this time," the
night watch said. (Jekyll-Hyde lived in a house about
one-eighth of a mile distant, but within the hospital
grounds.)

"Then will you take a message to the assistant
physician who stays here?" (A colleague of Jekyll-
Hyde had apartments in the main building.)

"I'll do that," he replied.

"Tell him how I'm suffering. Ask him to please come
here at once and ease this strait-jacket. If he doesn't,
I'll be as crazy by morning as I ever was. Also tell him
I'll kill myself unless he comes, and I can do it, too. I

have a piece of glass in this room and I know just what I'll do with it."

The night watch was as good as his word. He afterwards told me that he had delivered my message. The doctor ignored it. He did not come near me that night, nor the next day, nor did Jekyll-Hyde appear until his usual round of inspection about eleven o'clock the next morning.

"I understand that you have a piece of glass which you threatened to use for a suicidal purpose last night," he said, when he appeared.

"Yes, I have, and it's not your fault or the other doctor's that I am not dead. Had I gone mad, in my frenzy I might have swallowed that glass."

"Where is it?" asked the doctor, incredulously.

As my strait-jacket rendered me armless, I presented the glass to Jekyll-Hyde on the tip of a tongue he had often heard, but never before seen.

XVII

AFTER fifteen interminable hours the strait-jacket was removed. Whereas just prior to its putting on I had been in a vigorous enough condition to offer stout resistance when wantonly assaulted, now, on coming out of it, I was helpless. When my arms were released from their constricted position, the pain was intense. Every joint had been racked. I had no control over the fingers of either hand, and could not have dressed myself had I been promised my freedom for doing so.

For more than the following week I suffered as already described, though of course with gradually decreasing intensity as my racked body became accustomed to the unnatural positions it was forced to take. This first experience occurred on the night of October 18th, 1902. I was subjected to the same unfair, unnecessary, and unscientific ordeal for twenty-one consecutive nights and parts of each of the corresponding twenty-one days. On more than one occasion, indeed, the attendant placed me in the strait-jacket during the day for refusing to obey some trivial command. This, too, without an explicit order from the doctor in charge, though perhaps he acted under a general order.

During most of this time I was held also in seclusion in a padded cell. A padded cell is a vile hole. The side walls are padded as high as a man can reach, as is also the inside of the door. One of the worst features of such cells is the lack of ventilation, which deficiency of course aggravates their general unsanitary condition. The cell which I was forced to occupy was practically without heat, and as winter was coming on, I suffered intensely from the cold. Frequently it was so cold I could see my breath. Though my canvas jacket served to protect part of that body which it was at the same time racking, I was seldom comfortably warm; for, once uncovered, my arms being pinioned, I had no way of rearranging the blankets. What little sleep I managed to get I took lying on a hard mattress placed on the bare floor. The condition of the mattress I found in the cell was such that I objected to its further use, and the fact that another was supplied, at a time when few of my requests were being granted, proves its disgusting condition.

For this period of three weeks—from October 18th until November 8th, 1902, when I left this institution and was transferred to a state hospital—I was continuously either under lock and key (in the padded cell or some other room) or under the eye of an attendant. Over half the time I was in the snug, but cruel embrace of a strait-jacket—about three hundred hours in all.

While being subjected to this terrific abuse I was held in exile. I was cut off from all direct and all *honest* indirect communication with my legally appointed conservator—my own brother—and also with all other relatives and friends. I was even cut off from satisfactory communication with the superintendent. I saw him but twice, and then for so short a time that I was unable to give him any convincing idea of my plight.   These interviews occurred on two Sundays that fell within my period of exile, for it was on Sunday that the superintendent usually made his weekly round of inspection.

What chance had I of successfully pleading my case, while my pulpit was a padded cell, and the congregation—with the exception of the superintendent —the very ones who had been abusing me?   At such times my pent-up indignation poured itself forth in such a disconnected way that my protests were robbed of their right ring of truth.   I was not incoherent in speech.   I was simply voluble and digressive— a natural incident of elation.   Such notes as I managed to write on scraps of paper were presumably confiscated by Jekyll-Hyde.   At all events, it was not until some months later that the superintendent was informed of my treatment, when, at my request (though I was then elsewhere), the Governor of the State discussed the subject with him.   How I brought about that discussion while still virtually a prisoner in another place will be narrated in due time.   And not until several days after I had left this institution and had been placed in another, when for the first time in six weeks I saw my conservator, did *he* learn of the treatment to which I had been subjected.   From his office in New Haven he had telephoned several times to the assistant physician and inquired about my condition. Though Jekyll-Hyde did tell him that I was highly excited and difficult to control, he did not even hint that I was being subjected to any unusual restraint. Doctor Jekyll deceived everyone, and — as things turned out — deceived himself; for had he realized then that I should one day be able to do what I have since done, his brutality would surely have been held in check by his discretion.

How helpless, how at the mercy of his keepers, a patient may be is further illustrated by the conduct of this same man. Once, during the third week of my nights in a strait-jacket, I refused to take certain medicine which an attendant offered me. For some time I had been regularly taking this innocuous concoction without protest; but I now decided that, as the attendant refused most of my requests, I should no longer comply with all of his. He did not argue the point with me. He simply reported my refusal to Doctor Jekyll. A few minutes later Doctor Jekyll—or rather Mr. Hyde— accompanied by three attendants, entered the padded cell. I was robed for the night—in a strait-jacket. Mr. Hyde held in his hand a rubber tube. An attendant stood near with the medicine. For over two years, the common threat had been made that the "tube" would be resorted to if I refused medicine or food. I had begun to look upon it as a myth; but its presence in the hands of an oppressor now convinced me of its reality. I saw that the doctor and his bravos meant business; and as I had already endured torture enough, I determined to make every concession this time and escape what seemed to be in store for me.

"What are you going to do with that?" I asked, eyeing the tube.

"The attendant says you refuse to take your medicine. We are going to make you take it."

"I'll take your old medicine," was my reply.

"You have had your chance."

"All right," I said. "Put that medicine into me any way you think best. But the time will come when you'll wish you hadn't. When that time does come it won't be easy to prove that you had the right to force a patient to take medicine he had offered to take. I know something about the ethics of your profession. You have no right to do anything to a patient except what's good for him. You know that. All you are trying to do is to punish me, and I give you fair warning I'm going to camp on your trail till you are not only discharged from this institution, but expelled from the State Medical Society as well. You are a disgrace to your profession, and that society will attend to your case fast enough when certain members of it, who are friends of mine, hear about this. Furthermore, I shall report your conduct to the Governor of the State. He can take some action even if this is *not* a state institution. Now, damn you, do your worst!"

Coming from one in my condition, this was rather straight talk. The doctor was visibly disconcerted. Had he not feared to lose caste with the attendants who stood by, I think he would have given me another chance. But he had too much pride and too little manhood to recede from a false position already taken. I no longer resisted,

even verbally, for I no longer wanted the doctor to desist. Though I did not anticipate the operation with pleasure, I was eager to take the man's measure. He and the attendants knew that I usually kept a trick or two even up the sleeve of a strait-jacket, so they took added precautions. I was flat on my back, with simply a mattress between me and the floor. One attendant held me. Another stood by with the medicine and with a funnel through which, as soon as Mr. Hyde should insert the tube in one of my nostrils, the dose was to be poured. The third attendant stood near as a reserve force. Though the insertion of the tube, when skilfully done, need not cause suffering, the operation as conducted by Mr. Hyde was painful. Try as he would, he was unable to insert the tube properly, though in no way did I attempt to balk him. His embarrassment seemed to rob his hand of whatever cunning it may have possessed. After what seemed ten minutes of bungling, though it was probably not half that, he gave up the attempt, but not until my nose had begun to bleed. He was plainly chagrined when he and his bravos retired. Intuitively I felt that they would soon return. That they did, armed with a new implement of war. This time the doctor inserted between my teeth a large wooden peg—to keep open a mouth which he usually wanted shut. He then forced down my throat a rubber tube, the attendant adjusted the funnel, and the medicine, or rather liquid—for its medicinal properties were without effect upon me—was poured in.

As the scant reports sent to my conservator during

these three weeks indicated that I was not improving as he had hoped, he made a special trip to the institution to investigate in person. On his arrival he was met by none other than Doctor Jekyll, who told him that I was in a highly excited condition, which, he intimated, would be aggravated by a personal interview. Now for a man to see his brother in such a plight as mine would be a distressing ordeal, and, though my conservator came within a few hundred feet of my prison cell, it naturally took but a suggestion to dissuade him from coming nearer. Doctor Jekyll did tell him that it had been found necessary to place me in "restraint" and "seclusion" (the professional euphemisms for "strait-jacket," "padded cell," etc.), but no hint was given that I had been roughly handled. Doctor Jekyll's politic dissuasion was no doubt inspired by the knowledge that if ever I got within speaking distance of my conservator, nothing could prevent my giving him a circumstantial account of my sufferings—which account would have been corroborated by the blackened eye I happened to have at the time. Indeed, in dealing with my conservator the assistant physician showed a degree of tact which, had it been directed toward myself, would have sufficed to keep me tolerably comfortable.

My conservator, though temporarily stayed, was not convinced. He felt that I was not improving where I was, and he wisely decided that the best course would be to have me transferred to a public institution—the State Hospital. A few days later the judge who had originally committed me ordered my transfer. Nothing was said to me about the proposed change until the moment of departure, and then I could scarcely believe my ears.   In fact I did not believe my informant; for three weeks of abuse, together with my continued inability to get in touch with my conservator, had so shaken my reason that there was a partial recurrence of old delusions.   I imagined myself on the way to the State Prison, a few miles distant; and not until the train had passed the prison station did I believe that I was really on my way to the State Hospital.

XVIII

THE State Hospital in which I now found myself, the third institution to which I had been committed, though in many respects above the average of such institutions, was typical. It commanded a wide view of a beautiful river and valley. This view I was permitted to enjoy—at first. Those in charge of the institution which I had just left did not give my new custodians any detailed account of my case. Their reticence was, I believe, occasioned by chagrin rather than charity. Tamers of wild men have as much pride as tamers of wild animals (but unfortunately less skill) and to admit defeat is a thing not to be thought of. Though private institutions are prone to shift their troublesome cases to state institutions, there is too often a deplorable lack of sympathy and co-operation between them, which, in this instance, however, proved fortunate for me.

From October 18th until the early afternoon of November 8th, at the private institution, I had been classed as a raving maniac. The *name* I had brought upon myself by experimental conduct; the *condition* had been aggravated and perpetuated by the stupidity of those in authority over me. And it was the same experimental conduct on my part, and stupidity on the part of my new custodians, which gave rise, two weeks later, to a similar situation. On Friday, November 7th, I was in a strait-jacket. On November 9th and 10th I was apparently as tractable as any of the twenty-three hundred patients in the State Hospital—conventionally clothed, mild mannered, and, seemingly, right minded. On the 9th, the day after my arrival, I attended a church service held at the hospital. My behavior was not other than that of the most pious worshipper in the land. The next evening, with most exemplary deportment, I attended one of the dances which are held every fortnight during the winter. Had I been a raving maniac, such activities would have led to a disturbance; for maniacs, of necessity, disregard the conventions of both pious and polite society. Yet, on either of these days, had I been in the private institution which I had recently left, I should have occupied a cell and worn a strait-jacket.

The assistant superintendent, who received me upon my arrival, judged me by my behavior. He assigned me to one of two connecting wards—the best in the hospital—where about seventy patients led a fairly agreeable life. Though no official account of my case had accompanied my transfer, the attendant who had acted as escort and guard had already given an attendant at the State Hospital a brief account of my recent experiences. Yet when this report finally reached the ears of those in authority, they wisely decided not to transfer me to another ward so long as I caused no trouble where I was. Finding myself at last among friends, I lost no time in asking for writing and drawing materials, which had so rudely been taken from me three weeks earlier. My request was promptly granted. The doctors and attendants treated me kindly and I again began to enjoy life. My desire to write and draw had not abated. However, I did not devote my entire time to those pursuits, for there were plenty of congenial companions about. I found pleasure in talking—more pleasure by far than others did in listening. In fact I talked incessantly, and soon made known, in a general way, my scheme for reforming institutions, not only in my native State, but, of course, throughout the world, for my grandiose perspective made the earth look small. The attendants had to bear the brunt of my loquacity, and they soon grew weary. One of them, wishing to induce silence, ventured to remark that I was so "crazy" I could not possibly keep my mouth shut for even one minute. It was a challenge which aroused my fighting spirit.

"I'll show you that I can stop talking for a whole day," I said. He laughed, knowing that of all difficult tasks this which I had imposed upon myself was, for one in my condition, least likely of accomplishment. But I was as good as my boast. Until the same hour the next day I refused to speak to anyone. I did not even reply to civil questions; and, though my silence was deliberate and good-natured, the assistant physician seemed to consider it of a contumacious variety, for he threatened to transfer me to a less desirable ward unless I should again begin to talk.

That day of self-imposed silence was about the longest I have ever lived, for I was under a word pressure sufficient to have filled a book. Any psychiatrist will admit that my performance was remarkable, and he will further agree that it was, at least, an indication of a high degree of self-control. Though I have no desire to prove that at this period I was not in an abnormal condition, I do wish to show that I had a degree of self-control that probably would have enabled me to remain in the best ward at this institution had I not been intent —abnormally intent, of course, and yet with a high degree of deliberation—upon a reformative investigation. The crest of my wave of elation had been reached early in October. It was now (November) that the curve representing my return to normality should have been continuous and diminishing. Instead, it was kept violently fluctuating—or at least its fluctuations were aggravated—by the impositions of those in charge of me, induced sometimes, I freely admit, by deliberate and purposeful transgressions of my own. My condition during my three weeks of exile just ended, had been, if anything, one of milder excitement than that which had obtained previously during the first seven weeks of my period of elation. And my condition during the two weeks I now remained in the best ward in the State Hospital was not different from my condition during the preceding three weeks of torture, or the succeeding three weeks of abuse and privation, except in so far as a difference was occasioned by the torture and privation themselves.

Though I had long intended to effect reforms in existing methods of treatment, my reckless desire to in-

vestigate violent wards did not possess me until I myself had experienced the torture of continued confinement
in one such ward before coming to this state institution.
It was simple to deduce that if one could suffer such
abuses as I had while a patient in a private institution—
nay, in two private institutions—brutality must exist in
a state hospital also. Thus it was that I entered the
State Hospital with a firm resolve to inspect personally every type of ward, good and bad.

But I was in no hurry to begin. My recent experience had exhausted me, and I wished to regain strength
before subjecting myself to another such ordeal. This
desire to recuperate controlled my conduct for a while,
but its influence gradually diminished as life became
more and more monotonous. I soon found the good
ward entirely too polite. I craved excitement—action.
And I determined to get it regardless of consequences;
though I am free to confess I should not have had the
courage to proceed with my plan had I known what was
in store for me.

About this time my conservator called to see me. Of
course, I told him all about my cruel experiences at the
private institution. My account surprised and distressed him. I also told him that I knew for a fact that
similar conditions existed at the State Hospital, as I had
heard convincing rumors to that effect. He urged me
to behave myself and remain in the ward where I was,
which ward, as I admitted, was all that one could desire
—provided one had schooled himself to desire that sort
of thing.

The fact that I was under lock and key and behind what were virtually prison bars in no way gave me a sense of helplessness. I firmly believed that I should find it easy to effect my escape and reach home for the Thanksgiving Day celebration. And, furthermore, I knew that, should I reach home, I should not be denied my portion of the good things to eat before being returned to the hospital. Being under the spell of an intense desire to investigate the violent ward, I concluded that the time for action had come. I reasoned, too, that it would be easier and safer to escape from that ward—which was on a level with the ground—than from a ward three stories above it. The next thing I did was to inform the attendants (not to mention several of the patients) that within a day or two I should do something to cause my removal to it. They of course did not believe that I had any idea of deliberately inviting such a transfer. My very frankness disarmed them.

On the evening of November 21st, I went from room to room collecting all sorts of odds and ends belonging to other patients. These I secreted in my room. I also collected a small library of books, magazines and newspapers. After securing all the booty I dared, I mingled with the other patients until the time came for going to bed. The attendants soon locked me in my junk shop and I spent the rest of the night setting it in disorder. My original plan had been to barricade the door during the night, and thus hold the doctors and attendants at bay until those in authority had accepted my ultimatum, which was to include a Thanksgiving visit at home. But before morning I had slightly altered my plan. My sleepless night of activity had made me ravenously hungry, and I decided that it would be wiser not only to fill my stomach, but to lay by other supplies of food before submitting to a siege. Accordingly I set things to rights and went about my business the next morning as usual. At breakfast I ate enough for two men, and put in my pockets bread enough to last for twenty-four hours at least. Then I returned to my room and at once barricaded the door. My barricade consisted of a wardrobe, several drawers which I had removed from the bureau, and a number of books— among them "Paradise Lost" and the Bible. These, with conscious satisfaction, I placed in position as a keystone. Thus the floor space between the door and the opposite wall of the room was completely filled. My roommate, a young fellow in the speechless condition in which I had been during my period of depression, was in the room with me. This was accidental. It was no part of my plan to hold him as a hostage, though I might finally have used him as a pawn in the negotiations, had my barricade resisted the impending attack longer than it did.

It was not long before the attendants realized that something was wrong. They came to my door and asked me to open it. I refused, and told them that to argue the point would be a waste of time. They tried to force an entrance. Failing in that, they reported to the assistant physician, who soon appeared. At first he parleyed with me. I good-naturedly, but emphatically, told him that I could not be talked out of the position I had taken; nor could I be taken out of it until I was ready to surrender, for my barricade was one that would surely hold. I also announced that I had carefully planned my line of action and knew what I was about. I complimented him on his hitherto tactful treatment of me, and grandiloquently—yet sincerely—thanked him for his many courtesies. I also expressed entire satisfaction with the past conduct of the attendants. In fact, on part of the institution I put the stamp of my approval. "But," I said, "I know there are wards in this hospital where helpless patients are brutally treated; and I intend to put a stop to these abuses at once. Not until the Governor of the State, the judge who committed me, and my conservator come to this door will I open it. When they arrive, we'll see whether or not patients are to be robbed of their rights and abused."

My speech was made through a screen transom over the door. For a few minutes the doctor continued his persuasive methods, but that he should even imagine that I would basely recede from my high and mighty position only irritated me the more.

"You can stand outside that door all day if you choose," I said. "I won't open it until the three men I have named appear. I have prepared for a siege; and I have enough food in this room to keep me going for a day anyway."

Realizing at last that no argument would move

me, he set about forcing an entrance. First he tried to remove the transom by striking it with a stout stick. I gave blow for blow and the transom remained in place. A carpenter was then sent for, but before he could go about his work one of the attendants managed to open the door enough to thrust in his arm and shove aside my barricade. I did not realize what was being done until it was too late to interfere. The door once open, in rushed the doctor and four attendants. Without ceremony I was thrown upon the bed, with two or three of the attacking force on top of me. Again I was choked, this time by the doctor. The operation was a matter of only a moment. But before it was over I had the good fortune to deal the doctor a stinging blow on the jaw, for which (as he was about my own age and the odds were five to one) I have never felt called upon to apologize.

Once I was subdued, each of the four attendants attached himself to a leg or an arm and, under the direction and leadership of the doctor, I was carried bodily through two corridors, down two flights of stairs, and to the violent ward. My dramatic exit startled my fellow-patients, for so much action in so short a time is seldom seen in a quiet ward. And few patients placed in the violent ward are introduced with so impressive an array of camp-followers as I had that day.

All this to me was a huge joke, with a good purpose behind it. Though excited I was good-natured and, on the way to my new quarters, I said to the doctor: "Whether you believe it or not, it's a fact that I'm going to reform these institutions before I'm done. I raised this rumpus to make you transfer me to the violent ward. What I want you to do now is to show me the worst you've got."

"You needn't worry," the doctor said. "You'll get it."

He spoke the truth.

XIX

EVEN for a violent ward my entrance was spectac-
ular—if not dramatic. The three attendants regularly
in charge naturally jumped to the conclusion that, in
me, a troublesome patient had been foisted upon them.
They noted my arrival with an unpleasant curiosity,
which in turn aroused *my* curiosity, for it took but a
glance to convince me that my burly keepers were typical
attendants of the brute-force type. Acting on the order
of the doctor in charge, one of them stripped me of my
outer garments; and, clad in nothing but underclothes,
I was thrust into a cell.

Few, if any, prisons in this country contain worse
holes than this cell proved to be. It was one of five,
situated in a short corridor adjoining the main ward.
It was about six feet wide by ten long and of a good
height. A heavily screened and barred window admitted
light and a negligible quantity of air, for the ventilation
scarcely deserved the name. The walls and floor were
bare, and there was no furniture. A patient confined here
must lie on the floor with no substitute for a bed but one
or two felt druggets. Sleeping under such conditions
becomes tolerable after a time, but not until one has
become accustomed to lying on a surface nearly as hard
as a stone. Here (as well, indeed, as in other parts of
the ward) for a period of three weeks I was again forced

to breathe and rebreathe air so vitiated that even when I occupied a larger room in the same ward, doctors and attendants seldom entered without remarking its quality.

My first meal increased my distaste for my semi-sociological experiment. For over a month I was kept in a half-starved condition. At each meal, to be sure, I was given as much food as was served to other patients, but an average portion was not adequate to the needs of a patient as active as I was at this time.

Worst of all, winter was approaching and these, my first quarters, were without heat. As my olfactory nerves soon became uncommunicative, the breathing of foul air was not a hardship. On the other hand, to be famished the greater part of the time was a very conscious hardship. But to be half-frozen, day in and day out for a long period, was exquisite torture. Of all the suffering I endured, that occasioned by confinement in cold cells seems to have made the most lasting impression. Hunger is a local disturbance, but when one is cold, every nerve in the body registers its call for help. Long before reading a certain passage of De Quincey's I had decided that cold could cause greater suffering than hunger; consequently, it was with great satisfaction that I read the following sentences from his "Confessions": "O ancient women, daughters of toil and suffering, among all the hardships and bitter inheritances of flesh that ye are called upon to face, not one—not even hunger—seems in my eyes comparable to that of nightly cold. . . . A more killing curse there does not exist for man or woman than the bitter combat between

the weariness that prompts sleep and the keen, searching cold that forces you from that first access of sleep
to start up horror-stricken, and to seek warmth vainly
in renewed exercise, though long since fainting under
fatigue."

The hardness of the bed and the coldness of the room
were not all that interfered with sleep.   The short
corridor in which I was placed was known as the "Bull
Pen"—a phrase eschewed by the doctors.   It was usually
in an uproar, especially during the dark hours of the
early morning.   Patients in a state of excitement may
sleep during the first hours of the night, but seldom all
night; and even should one have the capacity to do
so, his companions in durance would wake him with a
shout or a song or a curse or the kicking of a door.
A noisy and chaotic medley frequently continued without interruption for hours at a time.   Noise, unearthly
noise, was the poetic license allowed the occupants of
these cells.   I spent several days and nights in one or
another of them, and I question whether I averaged
more than two or three hours' sleep a night during that
time.   Seldom did the regular attendants pay any attention to the noise, though even they must at times have
been disturbed by it.   In fact the only person likely to
attempt to stop it was the night watch, who, when he
did enter a cell for that purpose, almost invariably
kicked or choked the noisy patient into a state of temporary quiet.   I noted this and scented trouble.

Drawing and writing materials having been again
taken from me, I cast about for some new occupation.

I found one in the problem of warmth. Though I gave repeated expression to the benumbed messages of my tortured nerves, the doctor refused to return my clothes. For a semblance of warmth I was forced to depend upon ordinary undergarments and an extraordinary imagination. The heavy felt druggets were about as plastic as blotting paper and I derived little comfort from them until I hit upon the idea of rending them into strips. These strips I would weave into a crude Rip Van Winkle kind of suit; and so intricate was the warp and woof that on several occasions an attendant had to cut me out of these sartorial improvisations. At first, until I acquired the destructive knack, the tearing of one drugget into strips was a task of four or five hours. But in time I became so proficient that I could completely destroy more than one of these six-by-eight-foot druggets in a single night. During the following weeks of my close confinement I destroyed at least twenty of them, each worth, as I found out later, about four dollars; and I confess I found a peculiar satisfaction in the destruction of property belonging to a State which had deprived me of all my effects except underclothes. But my destructiveness was due to a variety of causes. It was occasioned primarily by a "pressure of activity," for which the tearing of druggets served as a vent. I was in a state of mind aptly described in a letter written during my first month of elation, in which I said, "I'm as busy as a nest of ants."

Though the habit of tearing druggets was the outgrowth of an abnormal impulse, the habit itself lasted longer than it could have done had I not, for so long a time, been deprived of suitable clothes and been held a prisoner in cold cells. But another motive soon asserted itself. Being deprived of all the luxuries of life and most of the necessities, my mother wit, always conspiring with a wild imagination for something to occupy my time, led me at last to invade the field of invention. With appropriate contrariety, an unfamiliar and hitherto almost detested line of investigation now attracted me. Abstruse mathematical problems which had defied solution for centuries began to appear easy. To defy the State and its puny representatives had become mere child's play. So I forthwith decided to overcome no less a force than gravity itself.

My conquering imagination soon tricked me into believing that I could lift myself by my boot-straps— or rather that I could do so when my laboratory should contain footgear that lent itself to the experiment. But what of the strips of felt torn from the druggets? Why, these I used as the straps of my missing boots; and having no boots to stand in, I used my bed as boots. I reasoned that for my scientific purpose a man in bed was as favorably situated as a man in boots. Therefore, attaching a sufficient number of my felt strips to the head and foot of the bed (which happened not to be screwed to the floor), and, in turn, attaching the free ends to the transom and the window guard, I found the problem very simple. For I next joined these cloth cables in such manner that by pulling downward

I effected a readjustment of stress and strain, and my bed, *with me in it*, was soon dangling in space. My sensations at this momentous instant must have been much like those which thrilled Newton when he solved one of the riddles of the universe. Indeed, they must have been more intense, for Newton, knowing, had his doubts; I, not knowing, had no doubts at all. So epoch-making did this discovery appear to me that I noted the exact position of the bed so that a wondering posterity might ever afterward view and revere the exact spot on the earth's surface whence one of man's greatest thoughts had winged its way to immortality.

For weeks I believed I had uncovered a mechanical principle which would enable man to defy gravity. And I talked freely and confidently about it. That is, I proclaimed the impending results. The intermediate steps in the solution of my problem I ignored, for good reasons. A blind man may harness a horse. So long as the horse is harnessed, one need not know the office of each strap and buckle. Gravity was harnessed— that was all. Meanwhile I felt sure that another sublime moment of inspiration would intervene and clear the atmosphere, thus rendering flight of the body as easy as a flight of imagination.

XX

WHILE my inventive operations were in progress, I was chafing under the unjust and certainly unscientific treatment to which I was being subjected. In spite of my close confinement in vile cells, for a period of over three weeks I was denied a bath. I do not regret this deprivation, for the attendants, who at the beginning were unfriendly, might have forced me to bathe in water which had first served for several other patients. Though such an unsanitary and disgusting practice was contrary to rules, it was often indulged in by the lazy brutes who controlled the ward.

I continued to object to the inadequate portions of food served me. On Thanksgiving Day (for I had not succeeded in escaping and joining in the celebration at home) an attendant, in the unaccustomed rôle of a ministering angel, brought me the usual turkey and cranberry dinner which, on two days a year, is provided by an intermittently generous State. Turkey being the *rara avis* of the imprisoned, it was but natural that I should desire to gratify a palate long insulted. I wished not only to satisfy my appetite, but to impress indelibly a memory which for months had not responded to so agreeable a stimulus. While lingering over the delights of this experience I forgot all about the ministering angel. But not for long. He soon returned. Observing that I had scarcely touched my feast, he said, "If you don't eat that dinner in a hurry, I'll take it from you."

"I don't see what difference it makes to you whether I eat it in a hurry or take my time about it," I said. "It's the best I've had in many a day, and I have a right to get as much pleasure out of it as I can."

"We'll see about that," he replied, and, snatching it away, he stalked out of the room, leaving me to satisfy my hunger on the memory of vanished luxuries. Thus did a feast become a fast.

Under this treatment I soon learned to be more noisy than my neighbors. I was never without a certain humor in contemplating not only my surroundings, but myself; and the demonstrations in which I began to indulge were partly in fun and partly by way of protest. In these outbursts I was assisted, and at times inspired, by a young man in the room next mine. He was about my own age and was enjoying the same phase of exuberance as myself. We talked and sang at all hours of the night. At the time we believed that the other patients enjoyed the spice which we added to the restricted variety of their lives, but later I learned that a majority of them looked upon us as the worst of nuisances.

We gave the doctors and attendants no rest—at least not intentionally. Whenever the assistant physician appeared, we upbraided him for the neglect which was then our portion. At one time or another we were banished to the Bull Pen for these indiscretions. And had there been a viler place of confinement still, our performances in the Bull Pen undoubtedly would have brought us to it. At last the doctor hit upon the expedient of transferring me to a room more remote from my inspiring, and, I may say, conspiring, companion. Talking to each other ceased to be the easy pastime it had been; so we gradually lapsed into a comparative silence which must have proved a boon to our ward-mates. The megaphonic Bull Pen, however, continued with irregularity, but annoying certainty to furnish its quota of noise.

On several occasions I concocted plans to escape, and not only that, but also to liberate others. That I did not make the attempt was the fault—or merit, perhaps—of a certain night watch, whose timidity, rather than sagacity, impelled him to refuse to unlock my door early one morning, although I gave him a plausible reason for the request. This night watch, I learned later, admitted that he feared to encounter me single-handed. And on this particular occasion well might he, for, during the night, I had woven a spider-web net in which I intended to enmesh him. Had I succeeded, there would have been a lively hour for him in the violent ward—had I failed, there would have been a lively hour for me. There were several comparatively sane patients (especially my elated neighbor) whose willing assistance I could have secured. Then the regular attendants could have been held prisoners in their own room, if, indeed, we had not in turn overpowered them and transferred them to the Bull Pen, where the several victims of their abuse might have given them a deserved dose of their own medicine. This scheme of mine was a prank rather than a plot. I had an inordinate desire to prove that one *could* escape if he had a mind to do so. Later I boasted to the assistant physician of my unsuccessful attempt. This boast he evidently tucked away in his memory.

My punishment for harmless antics of this sort was prompt in coming. The attendants seemed to think their whole duty to their closely confined charges consisted in delivering three meals a day. Between meals he was a rash patient who interfered with their leisure. Now one of my greatest crosses was their continued refusal to give me a drink when I asked for it. Except at meal time, or on those rare occasions when I was permitted to go to the wash room, I had to get along as best I might with no water to drink, and that too at a time when I was in a fever of excitement. My polite requests were ignored; impolite demands were answered with threats and curses. And this war of requests, demands, threats, and curses continued until the night of the fourth day of my banishment. Then the attendants made good their threats of assault. That they had been trying to goad me into a fighting mood I well knew, and often accused them of their mean purpose. They brazenly admitted that they were simply waiting for a chance to "slug" me, and promised to punish me well as soon as I should give them a slight excuse for doing so.

On the night of November 25th, 1902, the head attendant and one of his assistants passed my door. They were returning from one of the dances which, at intervals during the winter, the management provides for the nurses and attendants. While they were within hearing, I asked for a drink of water. It was a carefully worded request. But they were in a hurry to get to bed, and refused me with curses. Then I replied in kind.

"If I come there I'll kill you," one of them said.

"Well, you won't get in if I can help it," I replied, as I braced my iron bedstead against the door.

My defiance and defences gave the attendants the excuse for which they had said they were waiting; and my success in keeping them out for two or three minutes only served to enrage them. By the time they had gained entrance they had become furies. One was a young man of twenty-seven. Physically he was a fine specimen of manhood; morally he was deficient— thanks to the dehumanizing effect of several years in the employ of different institutions whose officials countenanced improper methods of care and treatment. It was he who now attacked me in the dark of my prison room. The head attendant stood by, holding a lantern which shed a dim light.

The door once open, I offered no further resistance. First I was knocked down. Then for several minutes I was kicked about the room—struck, kneed and choked. My assailant even attempted to grind his heel into my cheek. In this he failed, for I was there protected by a heavy beard which I wore at that time. But my shins, elbows, and back were cut by his heavy shoes; and had I not instinctively drawn up my knees to my elbows for the protection of my body, I might have been seriously, perhaps fatally, injured. As it was, I was severely cut and bruised. When my strength was nearly gone, I feigned unconsciousness. This ruse alone saved me from further punishment, for usually a premeditated assault is not ended until the patient is mute and helpless. When they had accomplished their purpose, they left me huddled in a corner to wear out the night as best I might—to live or die for all they cared.

Strange as it may seem, I slept well. But not at once. Within five minutes I was busily engaged writing an account of the assault. A trained war correspondent could not have pulled himself together in less time. As usual I had recourse to my bit of contraband lead pencil, this time a pencil which had been smuggled to me the very first day of my confinement in the Bull Pen by a sympathetic fellow-patient. When he had pushed under my cell door that little implement of war, it had loomed as large in my mind as a battering-ram. Paper I had none; but I had previously found walls to be a fair substitute. I therefore now selected and wrote upon a rectangular spot—about three feet by two — which marked the reflection of a light in the corridor just outside my transom.

The next morning, when the assistant physician appeared, he was accompanied as usual by the guilty head attendant who, on the previous night, had held the lantern.

"Doctor," I said, "I have something to tell you,"— and I glanced significantly at the attendant. "Last night I had a most unusual experience. I have had many imaginary experiences during the past two years and a half, and it may be that last night's was not real. Perhaps the whole thing was phantasmagoric—like what I used to see during the first months of my illness. Whether it was so or not I shall leave you to judge. It just happens to be my impression that I was brutally assaulted last night. If it was a dream, it is the first thing of the kind that ever left visible evidence on my body."

With that I uncovered to the doctor a score of bruises and lacerations. I knew these would be more impressive than any words of mine. The doctor put on a knowing look, but said nothing and soon left the room. His guilty subordinate tried to appear unconcerned, and I really believe he thought me not absolutely sure of the events of the previous night, or at least unaware of his share in them.

XXI

NEITHER of the attendants involved in the assault upon me was discharged. This fact made me more eager to gain wider knowledge of conditions. The self-control which had enabled me to suspend speech for a whole day now stood me in good stead. It enabled me to avert much suffering that would have been my portion had I been like the majority of my ward-mates. Time and again I surrendered when an attendant was about to chastise me. But at least a score of patients in the ward were not so well equipped mentally, and these were viciously assaulted again and again by the very men who had so thoroughly initiated me into the mysteries of their black art.

I soon observed that the only patients who were not likely to be subjected to abuse were the very ones least in need of care and treatment. The violent, noisy, and troublesome patient was abused because he was violent, noisy, and troublesome. The patient too weak, physically or mentally, to attend to his own wants was frequently abused because of that very helplessness which made it necessary for the attendants to wait upon him.

Usually a restless or troublesome patient placed in the violent ward was assaulted the very first day. This procedure seemed to be a part of the established code of dishonor. The attendants imagined that the best way to gain control of a patient was to cow him from the first. In fact, these fellows — nearly all of them ignorant and untrained—seemed to believe that "violent cases" could not be handled in any other way. One attendant, on the very day he had been discharged for choking a patient into an insensibility so profound that it had been necessary to call a physician to restore him, said to me, " They are getting pretty damned strict these days, discharging a man simply for *choking* a patient." This illustrates the attitude of many attendants. On the other hand, that the discharged employé soon secured a position in a similar institution not twenty miles distant illustrates the attitude of some hospital managements.

I recall the advent of a new attendant—a young man studying to become a physician. At first he seemed inclined to treat patients kindly, but he soon fell into brutal ways. His change of heart was due partly to the brutalizing environment, but more directly to the attitude of the three hardened attendants who mistook his consideration for cowardice and taunted him for it. Just to prove his mettle he began to assault patients, and one day knocked me down simply for refusing to stop my prattle at his command. That the environment in some institutions is brutalizing, was strikingly shown in the testimony of an attendant at a public investigation in Kentucky, who said, " When I came here, if anyone had told me I would be guilty of striking patients I would have called him crazy himself, but now I take delight in punching hell out of them."

I found also that an unnecessary and continued lack of out-door exercise tended to multiply deeds of violence. Patients were supposed to be taken for a walk at least once a day, and twice, when the weather permitted. Yet those in the violent ward (and it is they who most need the exercise) usually got out of doors only when the attendants saw fit to take them. For weeks a ward-mate—a man sane enough to enjoy freedom, had he had a home to go to—kept a record of the number of our walks. It showed that we averaged not more than one or two a week for a period of two months. This, too, in the face of many pleasant days, which made the close confinement doubly irksome. The lazy fellows on whose leisure we waited preferred to remain in the ward, playing cards, smoking, and telling their kind of stories. The attendants needed regular exercise quite as much as the patients and when they failed to employ their energy in this healthful way, they were likely to use it at the expense of the bodily comfort of their helpless charges.

If lack of exercise produced a need of discipline, each disciplinary move, on the other hand, served only to inflame us the more. Some wild animals can be clubbed into a semblance of obedience, yet it is a treacherous obedience at best, and justly so. And that is the only kind of obedience into which a *man* can be clubbed. To imagine otherwise of a human being, sane or insane, is the very essence of insanity itself. A temporary leisure may be won for the aggressor, but in the long run he will be put to greater inconvenience than he would be by a more humane method. It was repression and wilful frustration of reasonable desires which kept me a seeming maniac and made seeming maniacs of others. Whenever I was released from lock and key and permitted to mingle with the so-called violent patients, I was surprised to find that comparatively few were by nature troublesome or noisy. A patient, calm in mind and passive in behavior three hundred and sixty days in the year, may, on one of the remaining days, commit some slight transgression, or, more likely, be goaded into one by an attendant or needlessly led into one by a tactless physician. His indiscretion may consist merely in an unmannerly announcement to the doctor of how lightly the latter is regarded by the patient. At once he is banished to the violent ward, there to remain for weeks, perhaps indefinitely.

XXII

LIKE fires and railroad disasters, assaults seemed to come in groups. Days would pass without a single outbreak. Then would come a veritable carnival of abuse —due almost invariably to the attendants' state of mind, not to an unwonted aggressiveness on the part of the patients. I can recall as especially noteworthy several instances of atrocious abuse. Five patients were chronic victims. Three of them, peculiarly irresponsible, suffered with especial regularity, scarcely a day passing without bringing to them its quota of punishment. One of these, almost an idiot, and quite too inarticulate to tell a convincing story even under the most favorable conditions, became so cowed that, whenever an attendant passed, he would circle his oppressor as a whipped cur circles a cruel master. If this avoidance became too marked, the attendant would then and there chastise him for the implied, but unconscious insult.

There was a young man, occupying a cell next to mine in the Bull Pen, who was so far out of his mind as to be absolutely irresponsible. His offence was that he could not comprehend and obey. Day after day I could hear the blows and kicks as they fell upon his body, and his incoherent cries for mercy were as painful to hear as they are impossible to forget. That he survived is surprising. What wonder that this man, who was "violent," or who was made violent, would not permit the attendants to dress him! But he had a half-witted friend, a ward-mate, who could coax him into his clothes when his oppressors found him most intractable.

Of all the patients known to me, the one who was assaulted with the greatest frequency was an incoherent and irresponsible man of sixty years. This patient was restless and forever talking or shouting, as any man might if oppressed by such delusions as his. He was profoundly convinced that one of the patients had stolen his stomach—an idea inspired perhaps by the remarkable corpulency of the person he accused. His loss he would wofully voice even while eating. Of course, argument to the contrary had no effect; and his monotonous recital of his imaginary troubles made him unpopular with those whose business it was to care for him. They showed him no mercy. Each day—including the hours of the night, when the night watch took a hand —he was belabored with fists, broom handles, and frequently with the heavy bunch of keys which attendants usually carry on a long chain. He was also kicked and choked, and his suffering was aggravated by his almost continuous confinement in the Bull Pen. An exception to the general rule (for such continued abuse often causes death), this man lived a long time—five years, as I learned later.

Another victim, forty-five years of age, was one who had formerly been a successful man of affairs. His was a forceful personality, and the traits of his sane days influenced his conduct when he broke down mentally. He was in the expansive phase of paresis, a phase distinguished by an exaggerated sense of well-being, and by delusions of grandeur which are symptoms of this form as well as of several other forms of mental disease. Paresis, as everyone knows, is considered incurable and victims of it seldom live more than three or four years. In this instance, instead of trying to make the patient's last days comfortable, the attendants subjected him to a course of treatment severe enough to have sent even a sound man to an early grave. I endured privations and severe abuse for one month at the State Hospital. This man suffered in all ways worse treatment for many months.

I became well acquainted with two jovial and witty Irishmen. They were common laborers. One was a hodcarrier, and a strapping fellow. When he arrived at the institution, he was at once placed in the violent ward, though his "violence" consisted of nothing more than an annoying sort of irresponsibility. He irritated the attendants by persistently doing certain trivial things after they had been forbidden. The attendants made no allowance for his condition of mind. His repetition of a forbidden act was interpreted as deliberate disobedience. He was physically powerful, and they determined to cow him. Of the master assault by which they attempted to do this I was not an eyewitness. But I was an ear witness. It was committed behind a closed door; and I heard the dull thuds of the blows, and I heard the cries for mercy until there was no breath left in the man with which he could beg even for his life. For days, that wrecked Hercules dragged himself about the ward moaning pitifully. He complained of pain in his side and had difficulty in breathing, which would seem to indicate that some of his ribs had been fractured. This man was often punished, frequently for complaining of the torture already inflicted. But later, when he began to return to the normal, his good-humor and native wit won for him an increasing degree of good treatment.

The other patient's arch offence—a symptom of his disease—was that he gabbled incessantly. He could no more stop talking than he could right his reason on command. Yet his failure to become silent at a word was the signal for punishment. On one occasion an attendant ordered him to stop talking and take a seat at the further end of the corridor, about forty feet distant. He was doing his best to obey, even running to keep ahead of the attendant at his heels. As they passed the spot where I was sitting, the attendant felled him with a blow behind the ear; and, in falling, the patient's head barely missed the wall.

Addressing me, the attendant said, "Did you see that?"

"Yes," I replied, "and I'll not forget it."

"Be sure to report it to the doctor," he said, which remark showed his contempt, not only for me, but for those in authority.

The man who had so terribly beaten me was particularly flagrant in ignoring the claims of age. On more than one occasion he viciously attacked a man of over fifty, who, however, seemed much older. He was a Yankee sailing-master, who in his prime could have thrashed his tormentor with ease. But now he was helpless and could only submit. However, he was not utterly abandoned by his old world. His wife called often to see him; and, because of his condition, she was permitted to visit him in his room. Once she arrived a few hours after he had been cruelly beaten. Naturally she asked the attendants how he had come by the hurts —the blackened eye and bruised head. True to the code, they lied. The good wife, perhaps herself a Yankee, was not thus to be fooled; and her growing belief that her husband had been assaulted was confirmed by a sight she saw before her visit was ended. Another patient, a foreigner who was a target for abuse, was knocked flat two or three times as he was roughly forced along the corridor. I saw this little affair and I saw that the good wife saw it. The next day she called again and took her husband home. The result was that after a few (probably sleepless) nights, she had to return him to the hospital and trust to God rather than the State to protect him.

Another victim was a man sixty years of age. He was quite inoffensive, and no patient in the ward seemed to attend more strictly to his own business. Shortly after my transfer from the violent ward this man was so viciously attacked that his arm was broken. The attendant (the man who had so viciously assaulted me) was summarily discharged. Unfortunately, however, the relief afforded the insane was slight and brief, for this same brute, like another whom I have mentioned, soon secured a position in another institution—this one, however, a thousand miles distant.

Death by violence in a violent ward is after all not an unnatural death—for a violent ward. The patient of whom I am about to speak was also an old man—over sixty. Both physically and mentally he was a wreck. On being brought to the institution he was at once placed in a cell in the Bull Pen, probably because of his previous history for violence while at his own home. But his violence (if it ever existed) had already spent itself, and had come to be nothing more than an utter incapacity to obey. His offence was that he was too weak to attend to his common wants. The day after his arrival, shortly before noon, he lay stark naked and helpless upon the bed in his cell. This I know, for I went to investigate immediately after a ward-mate had informed me of the vicious way in which the head attendant had assaulted the sick man. My informant was a man whose word regarding an incident of this character I would take as readily as that of any man I know. He came to me, knowing that I had taken upon myself the duty of reporting such abominations. My informant feared to take the initiative, for, like many other patients who believe themselves doomed to continued confinement, he feared to invite abuse at the hands of vengeful attendants. I therefore promised him that I would report the case as soon as I had an opportunity.

All day long this victim of an attendant's unmanly passion lay in his cell in what seemed to be a semi-conscious condition. I took particular pains to observe his condition, for I felt that the assault of the morning might result in death. That night, after the doctor's regular tour of inspection, the patient in question was transferred to a room next my own. The mode of transfer impressed itself upon my memory. Two attendants—one of them being he who had so brutally beaten the patient—placed the man in a sheet and, each taking an end, carried the hammocklike contrivance, with its inert contents, to what proved to be its last resting-place above ground. The bearers seemed as much concerned about their burden as one might be about a dead dog, weighted and ready for the river.

That night the patient died. Whether he was murdered none can ever know. But it is my honest opinion that he was. Though he might never have recovered, it is plain that he would have lived days, perhaps months. And had he been humanely, nay, scientifically, treated, who can say that he might not have been restored to health and home?

The young man who had been my companion in mischief in the violent ward was also terribly abused. I am sure I do not exaggerate when I say that on ten occasions, within a period of two months, this man was cruelly assaulted, and I do not know how many times he suffered assaults of less severity. After one of these chastisements, I asked him why he persisted in his petty transgressions when he knew that he thereby invited such body-racking abuse.

"Oh," he said, laconically, "I need the exercise."

To my mind, the man who, with such gracious humor, could refer to what was in reality torture deserved to live a century. But an unkind fate decreed that he should die young. Ten months after his commitment to the State Hospital he was discharged as improved—but not cured. This was not an unusual procedure; nor was it in his case apparently an unwise one, for he seemed fit for freedom. During the first month of regained liberty, he hanged himself. He left no message of excuse. In my opinion, none was necessary. For aught any man knows, the memories of the abuse, torture, and injustice which were so long his portion may have proved to be the last straw which overbalanced the desire to live.

Patients with less stamina than mine often submitted with meekness; and none so aroused my sympathy as those whose submission was due to the consciousness that they had no relatives or friends to support them in a fight for their rights. On behalf of these, with my usual piece of smuggled lead pencil, I soon began to indite and submit to the officers of the institution, letters in which I described the cruel practices which came under my notice. My reports were perfunctorily accepted and at once forgotten or ignored. Yet these letters, so far as they related to overt acts witnessed, were lucid and should have been convincing. Furthermore, my allegations were frequently corroborated by bruises on the bodies of the patients. My usual custom was to write an account of each assault and hand it to the doctor in authority.

Frequently I would submit these reports to the attendants with instructions first to read and then deliver them to the superintendent or the assistant physician. The men whose cruelty I thus laid bare read with evident but perverted pleasure my accounts of assaults, and laughed and joked about my ineffectual attempts to bring them to book.

XXIII

I REFUSED to be a martyr. Rebellion was my watch-word. The only difference between the doctor's opinion of me and mine of him was that he could refuse utter-ance to his thoughts. Yes—there was another differ-ence. Mine could be expressed only in words—his in grim acts.

I repeatedly made demands for those privileges to which I knew I was entitled. When he saw fit to grant them, I gave him perfunctory thanks. When he refused —as he usually did—I at once poured upon his head the vials of my wrath. One day I would be on the friend-liest terms with the doctor, the next I would upbraid him for some denial of my rights—or, as frequently happened, for not intervening in behalf of the rights of others.

It was after one of these wrangles that I was placed in a cold cell in the Bull Pen at eleven o'clock one morning. Still without shoes and with no more covering than under-clothes, I was forced to stand, sit, or lie upon a bare floor as hard and cold as the pavement outside. Not until sundown was I provided even with a drugget, and this did little good, for already I had become thoroughly chilled. In consequence I contracted a severe cold which added greatly to my discomfort and might have led to serious results had I been of less sturdy fibre.

This day was the thirteenth of December and the twenty-second of my exile in the violent ward. I remember it distinctly for it was the seventy-seventh birthday of my father, to whom I wished to write a congratulatory letter. This had been my custom for years when absent from home on that anniversary. And well do I remember when, and under what conditions, I asked the doctor for permission. It was night. I was flat on my drugget-bed. My cell was lighted only by the feeble rays of a lantern held by an attendant to the doctor on this his regular visit. At first I couched my request in polite language. The doctor merely refused to grant it. I then put forth my plea in a way calculated to arouse sympathy. He remained unmoved. I then pointed out that he was defying the law of the State which provided that a patient should have stationery—a statute, the spirit of which at least meant that he should be permitted to communicate with his conservator. It was now three weeks since I had been permitted to write or send a letter to anyone. Contrary to my custom, therefore, I made my final demand in the form of a concession. I promised that I would write only a conventional note of congratulation, making no mention whatever of my plight. It was a fair offer; but to accept it would have been an implied admission that there was something to conceal, and for this, if for no other reason, it was refused.

Thus, day after day, I was repressed in a manner which probably would have driven many a sane man to vio-

lence. Yet the doctor would frequently exhort me to play
the gentleman. Were good manners and sweet submission ever the product of such treatment? Deprived of my
clothes, of sufficient food, of warmth, of all sane companionship and of my liberty, I told those in authority
that so long as they should continue to treat me as the
vilest of criminals, I should do my best to complete the
illusion. The burden of proving my sanity was placed
upon me. I was told that so soon as I became polite and
meek and lowly I should find myself in possession of
my clothes and of certain privileges. In every instance
I must earn my reward before being entrusted with it.
If the doctor, instead of demanding of me all the negative
virtues in the catalogue of spineless saints, had given
me my clothes on the condition that they would be taken
from me again if I so much as removed a button, his
course would doubtless have been productive of good
results. Thus I might have had my clothes three weeks
earlier than I did, and so been spared much suffering
from the cold.

I clamored daily for a lead pencil. This little luxury
represents the margin of happiness for hundreds of the
patients, just as a plug or package of tobacco represents
the margin of happiness for thousands of others; but for
seven weeks no doctor or attendant gave me one. To be
sure, by reason of my somewhat exceptional persistence
and ingenuity, I managed to be always in possession of
some substitute for a pencil, surreptitiously obtained, a
fact which no doubt had something to do with the doctor's
indifference to my request. But my inability to secure

a pencil in a legitimate way was a needless source of annoyance to me, and many of my verbal indiscretions were directly inspired by the doctor's continued refusal.

It was an assistant physician, other than the one regularly in charge of my case, who at last relented and presented me with a good, whole lead pencil. By so doing he placed himself high on my list of benefactors; for that little shaftlike implement, magnified by my lively appreciation, became as the very axis of the earth.

XXIV

A FEW days before Christmas my most galling deprivation was at last removed. That is, my clothes were restored. These I treated with great respect. Not so much as a thread did I destroy. Clothes, as is known, have a sobering and civilizing effect, and from the very moment I was again provided with presentable outer garments my conduct rapidly improved. The assistant physician with whom I had been on such variable terms of friendship and enmity even took me for a sleigh-ride. With this improvement came other privileges or, rather, the granting of my rights. Late in December I was permitted to send letters to my conservator. Though some of my blood-curdling letters were confiscated, a few detailing my experiences were forwarded. The account of my sufferings naturally distressed my conservator, but, as he said when he next visited me: "What could I have done to help you? If the men in this State whose business it is to run these institutions cannot manage you, I am at a loss to know what to do." True, he could have done little or nothing, for he did not then know the ins and outs of the baffling situation into which the ties of blood had drawn him.

About the middle of January the doctor in charge of my case went for a two weeks' vacation. During his absence an older member of the staff took charge of

the violent ward.   A man of wider experience and more
liberal ideas than his predecessor, he at once granted me
several real privileges.   One day he permitted me to
pay a brief visit to the best ward—the one from which I
had been transferred two months earlier.   I thus was able
again to mingle with many seemingly normal men, and
though I enjoyed this privilege upon but one occasion,
and then only for a few hours, it gave me intense satisfaction.

Altogether the last six weeks of the fourteen during
which I was confined in the violent ward were comfortable and relatively happy.   I was no longer subjected
to physical abuse, though this exemption was largely
due to my own skill in avoiding trouble.   I was no longer
cold and hungry.   I was allowed a fair amount of out-
door exercise which, after my close confinement, proved
to be a delightful shock.   But, above all, I was again
given an adequate supply of stationery and drawing
materials, which became as tinder under the focussed
rays of my artistic eagerness.   My mechanical investigations were gradually set aside.   Art and literature
again held sway.   Except when out of doors taking
my allotted exercise, I remained in my room reading,
writing, or drawing.   This room of mine soon became
a Mecca for the most irrepressible and loquacious characters in the ward.   But I soon schooled myself to shut
my ears to the incoherent prattle of my unwelcome
visitors.   Occasionally, some of them would become ob-
streperous—perhaps because of my lordly order to leave
the room.   Often did they threaten to throttle me; but

I ignored the threats, and they were never carried out. Nor was I afraid that they would be. Invariably I induced them to obey.

The drawings I produced at this time were crude. For the most part they consisted of copies of illustrations which I had cut from magazines that had miraculously found their way into the violent ward. The heads of men and women interested me most, for I had decided to take up portraiture. At first I was content to draw in black and white, but I soon procured some colors and from that time on devoted my attention to mastering pastel.

In the world of letters I had made little progress. My compositions were for the most part epistles addressed to relatives and friends and to those in authority at the hospital. Frequently the letters addressed to the doctors were sent in sets of three—this to save time, for I was very busy. The first letter of such a series would contain my request, couched in friendly and polite terms. To this I would add a postscript, worded about as follows: "If, after reading this letter, you feel inclined to refuse my request, please read letter number two." Letter number two would be severely formal—a business-like repetition of the request made in letter number one. Again a postscript would advise the reader to consult letter number three, if the reading of number two had failed to move him. Letter number three was invariably a brief philippic in which I would consign the unaccommodating doctor to oblivion.

In this way I expended part of my prodigious supply

of feeling and energy.   But I had also another way of
reducing my creative pressure.   Occasionally, from
sheer excess of emotion, I would burst into verse, of a
quality not to be doubted.   Of that quality the reader
shall judge, for I am going to quote a "creation" written
under circumstances which, to say the least, were adverse.
Before writing these lines I had never attempted verse
in my life—barring intentionally inane doggerel.   And,
as I now judge these lines, it is probably true that even
yet I have never written a poem.   Nevertheless, my
involuntary, almost automatic outburst is at least suggestive of the fervor that was in me.   These fourteen
lines were written within thirty minutes of the time I
first conceived the idea; and I present them substantially
as they first took form.   From a psychological standpoint at least, I am told, they are not without interest.

LIGHT

Man's darkest hour is the hour before he's born,
Another is the hour just before the Dawn;
From Darkness unto Life and Light he leaps,
To Life but once,—to Light as oft as God wills he should.
'Tis God's own secret, why
Some live long, and others early die;
For Life depends on Light, and Light on God,
Who hath given to Man the perfect knowledge
That Grim Despair and Sorrow end in Light
And Life everlasting, in realms
Where darkest Darkness becomes Light;
But not the Light Man knows,
Which only is Light
Because God told Man so.

These verses, which breathe religion, were written in an environment which was anything but religious. With curses of ward-mates ringing in my ears, some subconscious part of me seemed to force me to write at its dictation. I was far from being in a pious frame of mind myself, and the quality of my thought surprised me then—as it does now.

XXV

THOUGH I continued to respect my clothes, I did not at once cease to tear such material as would serve me in my scientific investigations. Gravity being conquered, it was inevitable that I should devote some of my time to the invention of a flying-machine. This was soon perfected—in my mind; and all I needed, that I might test the device, was my liberty. As usual I was unable to explain how I should produce the result which I so confidently foretold. But I believed and proclaimed that I should, ere long, fly to St. Louis and claim and receive the one-hundred-thousand-dollar reward offered by the Commission of the Louisiana Purchase Exposition for the most efficient airship to be exhibited. The moment the thought winged its way through my mind, I had not only a flying-machine, but a fortune in the bank. Being where I could not dissipate my riches, I became a lavish verbal spender. I was in a mood to buy anything, and I whiled away many an hour planning what I should do with my fortune. The St. Louis prize was a paltry trifle. I reasoned that the man who could harness gravity had at his beck and call the world and all that therein is. This sudden accession of wealth made my vast humanitarian projects seem only the more feasible. What could be more delightful, I thought, than the furnishing and

financing of ideas of a magnitude to stagger humanity.
My condition was one of ecstatic suspense. Give me
my liberty and I would show a sleepy old world
what could be done to improve conditions, not only
among the insane, but along every line of beneficent
endeavor.

The city of my birth was to be made a garden-spot.
All defiling, smoke-begriming factories were to be banished to an innocuous distance. Churches were to give
way to cathedrals; the city itself was to become a paradise of mansions. Yale University was to be transformed into the most magnificent—yet efficient—seat of
learning in the world. For once, college professors were
to be paid adequate salaries, and alluring provision for
their declining years was to be made. New Haven
should become a very hotbed of culture. Art galleries,
libraries, museums and theatres of a dreamlike splendor
were to rise whenever and wherever I should will. Why
absurd? Was it not I who would defray the cost? The
famous buildings of the Old World were to be reproduced,
if, indeed, the originals could not be purchased, brought
to this country and reassembled. Not far from New
Haven there is a sandy plain, once the bed of the Connecticut River, but now a kind of miniature desert. I
often smile as I pass it on the train; for it was here, for
the edification of those who might never be able to visit
the Valley of the Nile, that I planned to erect a pyramid
that should out-Cheops the original. My harnessed
gravity, I believed, would not only enable me to overcome
existing mechanical difficulties, but it would make the

quarrying of immense monoliths as easy as the slicing
of bread, and the placing of them in position as easy as
the laying of bricks.

After all, delusions of grandeur are the most entertaining
of toys. The assortment which my imagination provided
was a comprehensive one. I had tossed aside the blocks
of childhood days. Instead of laboriously piling small
squares of wood one upon another in an endeavor to
build the tiny semblance of a house, I now, in this second
childhood of mine, projected against thin air phantom
edifices planned and completed in the twinkling of an
eye. To be sure, such houses of cards almost immediately superseded one another, but the vanishing of one
could not disturb a mind that had ever another interesting bauble to take its place. And therein lies part of the
secret of the happiness peculiar to that stage of elation
which is distinguished by delusions of grandeur—always
provided that he who is possessed by them be not subjected to privation and abuse. The sane man who can
prove that he is rich in material wealth is not nearly so
happy as the mentally disordered man whose delusions
trick him into believing himself a modern Crœsus. A
wealth of Midaslike delusions is no burden. Such a fortune, though a misfortune in itself, bathes the world in
a golden glow. No clouds obscure the vision. Optimism
reigns supreme. "Failure" and "impossible" are as
words from an unknown tongue. And the unique
satisfaction about a fortune of this fugitive type is that
its loss occasions no regret. One by one the phantom
ships of treasure sail away for parts unknown; until.

when the last ship has become but a speck on the mental horizon, the observer makes the happy discovery that his pirate fleet has left behind it a priceless wake of Reason!

XXVI

EARLY in March, 1902, having lived in a violent ward for nearly four months, I was transferred to another—a ward quite as orderly as the best in the institution, though less attractively furnished than the one in which I had first been placed. Here also I had a room to myself; in this instance, however, the room had not only a bed, but a chair and a wardrobe. With this elaborate equipment I was soon able to convert my room into a veritable studio. Whereas in the violent ward it had been necessary for me to hide my writing and drawing materials to keep other patients from taking them, in my new abode I was able to conduct my literary and artistic pursuits without the annoyances which had been inevitable during the preceding months.

Soon after my transfer to this ward I was permitted to go out of doors and walk to the business section of the city, two miles distant. But on these walks I was always accompanied. To one who has never surrendered any part of his liberty such surveillance would no doubt seem irksome; yet, to me, after being so closely confined, the ever-present attendant seemed a companion rather than a guard. These excursions into the sane and free world were not only a great pleasure, they were almost a tonic. To rub elbows with normal people tended to restore my mental poise. That

the casual passer-by had no way of knowing that I
was a patient, out for a walk about the city, helped
me gain that self-confidence so essential to the success
of one about to re-enter a world from which he had long
been cut off.

My first trips to the city were made primarily for the
purpose of supplying myself with writing and drawing
materials. While enjoying these welcome tastes of liberty, on more than one occasion I surreptitiously mailed
certain letters which I did not dare entrust to the doctor.
Under ordinary circumstances such an act on the part
of one enjoying a special privilege would be dishonor-
able. But the circumstances that then obtained were
not ordinary. I was simply protecting myself against
what I believed to be unjust and illegal confiscation of
letters.

I have already described how an assistant physician
arbitrarily denied my request that I be permitted to send
a birthday letter to my father, thereby not merely ex-
ceeding his authority and ignoring decency, but, consciously or unconsciously, stifling a sane impulse. That
this should occur while I was confined in the Bull Pen
was, perhaps, not so surprising. But about four months
later, while I was in one of the best wards, a similar,
though less open, interference occurred. At this time I
was so nearly normal that my discharge was a question
of but a very few months. Anticipating my return to
my old world, I decided to renew former relationships.
Accordingly, my brother, at my suggestion, informed
certain friends that I should be pleased to receive letters

from them. They soon wrote. In the meantime the
doctor had been instructed to deliver to me any and all
letters that might arrive. He did so for a time, and
that without censoring. As was to be expected, after
nearly three almost letterless years, I found rare
delight in replying to my reawakened correspondents.
Yet some of these letters, written for the deliberate
purpose of re-establishing myself in the sane world,
were destroyed by the doctor in authority. At the time,
not one word did he say to me about the matter. I had
handed him for mailing certain letters, unsealed. He
did not mail them, nor did he forward them to my conservator as he should have done, and had earlier agreed
to do with all letters which he could not see his way clear
to approve. It was fully a month before I learned that
my friends had not received my replies to their letters.
Then I accused the doctor of destroying them, and he,
with belated frankness, admitted that he had done so.
He offered no better excuse than the mere statement
that he did not approve of the sentiments I had expressed.
Another flagrant instance was that of a letter addressed
to me in reply to one of those which I had posted surreptitiously. The person to whom I wrote, a friend of
years' standing, later informed me that he had sent
the reply. I never received it. Neither did my conservator. Were it not that I feel absolutely sure that
the letter in question was received at the hospital
and destroyed, I should not now raise this point. But
such a point, if raised at all, must of course be made
without that direct proof which can come only from the

man guilty of an act which in the sane world is regarded as odious and criminal.

I therefore need not dilate on the reasons which made it necessary for me to smuggle, as it were, to the Governor of the State, a letter of complaint and instruction. This letter was written shortly after my transfer from the violent ward. The abuses of that ward were still fresh in my mind, and the memory of distressing scenes was kept vivid by reports reaching me from friends who were still confined there. These private sleuths of mine I talked with at the evening entertainments or at other gatherings. From them I learned that brutality had become more rife, if anything, since I had left the ward. Realizing that my crusade against the physical abuse of patients thus far had proved of no avail, I determined to go over the heads of the doctors and appeal to the ex-officio head of the institution, the Governor of the State.

On March 12th, 1903, I wrote a letter which so disturbed the Governor that he immediately set about an informal investigation of some of my charges. Despite its prolixity, its unconventional form and what, under other circumstances, would be characterized as almost diabolic impudence and familiarity, my letter, as he said months later when I talked with him, "rang true." The writing of it was an easy matter; in fact, so easy, because of the pressure of truth under which I was laboring at the time, that it embodied a compelling spontaneity.

The mailing of it was not so easy. I knew that the

only sure way of getting my thoughts before the Governor was to do my own mailing. Naturally no doctor could be trusted to send an indictment against himself and his colleagues to the one man in the State who had the power to institute such an investigation as might make it necessary for all to seek employment elsewhere. In my frame of mind, to wish to mail my letter was to know how to accomplish the wish. The letter was in reality a booklet. I had thoughtfully used waterproof India drawing ink in writing it, in order, perhaps, that a remote posterity might not be deprived of the document. The booklet consisted of thirty-two eight-by-ten-inch pages of heavy white drawing paper. These I sewed together. In planning the form of my letter I had forgotten to consider the slot of a letter-box of average size. Therefore I had to adopt an unusual method of getting the letter into the mails. My expedient was simple. There was in the town a certain shop where I traded. At my request the doctor gave me permission to go there for supplies. I was of course accompanied by an attendant, who little suspected what was under my vest. To conceal and carry my letter in that place had been easy; but to get rid of it after reaching my goal was another matter. Watching my opportunity, I slipped the missive between the leaves of a copy of the *Saturday Evening Post*. This I did, believing that some purchaser would soon discover the letter and mail it. Then I left the shop.

On the back of the wrapper I had endorsed the following words:

"Mr. Postmaster: This package is unsealed. Nevertheless it is first-class matter. Everything I write is necessarily first class. I have affixed two two-cent stamps. If extra postage is needed you will do the Governor a favor if you will put the extra postage on. Or affix 'due' stamps, and let the Governor pay his own bills, as he can well afford to. If you want to know who I am, just ask his Excellency, and oblige,

Yours truly,

?"

Flanking this notice, I had arrayed other forceful sentiments, as follows—taken from statutes which I had framed for the occasion:

"Any person finding letter or package—duly stamped and addressed—*must* mail same as said letter or package is really in hands of the Government the moment the stamp is affixed."

And again:

"Failure to comply with Federal Statute which forbids any one except addressee to open a letter renders one liable to imprisonment in State Prison."

My letter reached the Governor. One of the clerks at the shop in which I left the missive found and mailed it. From him I afterwards learned that my unique instructions had piqued his curiosity, as well as compelled my wished-for action. Assuming that the reader's curiosity may likewise have been piqued, I shall quote certain passages from this four-thousand-word epistle of protest. The opening sentence read as follows: "If you have had the courage to read the above " (referring to an unconventional heading) " I hope you will read on to the end of this epistle—thereby displaying real Christian fortitude and learning a few facts which I think should be brought to your attention."

I then introduced myself, mentioning a few common friends, by way of indicating that I was not without influential political connections, and proceeded as follows: "I take pleasure in informing you that I am in the Crazy Business and am holding my job down with ease and a fair degree of grace. Being in the Crazy Business, I understand certain phases of the business about which you know nothing. You as Governor are at present 'head devil' in this 'hell,' though I know you are unconsciously acting as 'His Majesty's' 1st Lieutenant."

I then launched into my arraignment of the treatment of the insane. The method, I declared, was "wrong from start to finish. The abuses existing here exist in every other institution of the kind in the country. They are all alike—though some of them are of course worse than others. Hell is hell the world over, and I might also add that hell is only a great big bunch of disagreeable details anyway. That's all an Insane Asylum is. If you don't believe it, just go crazy and take up your abode here. In writing this letter I am laboring under no mental excitement. I am no longer subjected to the abuses about which I complain. I am well and happy. In fact I never was so happy as I am now. Whether I am in perfect mental health or not, I shall leave for you to decide. If I am insane to-day I hope I may never recover my Reason."

First I assailed the management of the private institution where I had been strait-jacketed and referred to "Jekyll-Hyde" as "Dr. — —, M.D. (Mentally Deranged)." Then followed an account of the strait-jacket experience; then an account of abuses at the State Hospital. I described in detail the most brutal assault that fell to my lot. In summing up I said, "The attendants claimed next day that I had called them certain names. Maybe I did—though I don't believe I did at all. What of it? This is no young ladies' boarding school. Should a man be nearly killed because he swears at attendants who swear like pirates? I have seen at least fifteen men, many of them mental and physical wrecks, assaulted just as brutally as I was, and usually without a cause. I know that men's lives have been shortened by these brutal assaults. And that is only a polite way of saying that murder has been committed here." Turning next to the matter of the women's wards, I said: "A patient in this ward—a man in his right mind, who leaves here on Tuesday next—told me that a woman patient told him that she had seen many a helpless woman dragged along the floor by her hair, and had also seen them choked by attendants who used a wet towel as a sort of garrote. I have been through the mill and believe every word of the abuse. You will perhaps doubt it, as it seems impossible. Bear in mind, though, that everything bad and disagreeable is possible in an Insane Asylum."

It will be observed that I was shrewd enough to qualify a charge I could not prove.

When I came to the matter of the Bull Pen, I wasted

no words: "The Bull Pen," I wrote, "is a pocket edition of the New York Stock Exchange during a panic."

I next pointed out the difficulties a patient must overcome in mailing letters: "It is impossible for any one to send a letter to you *via* the office. The letter would be consigned to the waste-basket—unless it was a particularly crazy letter—in which case it might reach you, as you would then pay no attention to it. But a sane letter and a *true* letter, telling about the abuses which exist here would stand no show of being mailed. The way in which mail is tampered with by the medical staff is contemptible."

I then described my stratagem in mailing my letter to the Governor. Discovering that I had left a page of my epistolary booklet blank, I drew upon it a copy of Rembrandt's Anatomy Lesson, and under it wrote: "This page was skipped by mistake. Had to fight fifty-three days to get writing paper and I hate to waste any space—hence the masterpiece—drawn in five minutes. Never drew a line till September 26 (last) and never took lessons in my life. I think you will readily believe my statement." Continuing in the same half-bantering vein, I said: "I intend to immortalize all members of medical staff of State Hospital for Insane—when I illustrate my Inferno, which, when written, will make Dante's Divine Comedy look like a French Farce."

I then outlined my plans for reform: "Whether my suggestions meet with approval or not," I wrote, "will not affect the result—though opposition on your part would perhaps delay reforms. I have decided to devote the next few years of my life to correcting abuses now in existence in every asylum in this country.   I know how these abuses can be corrected and I intend—later on, when I understand the subject better—to draw up a Bill of Rights for the Insane.   Every State in the Union will pass it, because it will be founded on the Golden Rule.   I am desirous of having the co-operation of the Governor of Connecticut, but if my plans do not appeal to him I shall deal directly with his only superior, the President of the United States.   When Theodore Roosevelt hears my story his blood will boil.   I would write to him now, but I am afraid he would jump in and correct abuses too quickly.   And by doing it too quickly too little good would be accomplished."

Waxing crafty, yet, as I believed, writing truth, I continued: "I need money badly, and if I cared to, I could sell my information and services to the *New York World* or *New York Journal* for a large amount.   But I do not intend to advertise Connecticut as a Hell-hole of Iniquity, Insanity, and Injustice.   If the facts appeared in the public press at this time, Connecticut would lose caste with her sister States.   And they would profit by Connecticut's disgrace and correct the abuses before they could be put on the rack.   As these conditions prevail throughout the country, there is no reason why Connecticut should get all the abuse and criticism which would follow any such revelation of disgusting abuse; such inhuman treatment of human wrecks.   If publicity is necessary to force you to act—and I am sure it will not be necessary—I shall apply for a writ of habeas

corpus, and, in proving my sanity to a jury, I shall incidentally prove your own incompetence. Permitting such
a whirl-wind reformer to drag Connecticut's disgrace
into open court would prove your incompetence."

For several obvious reasons it is well that I did not at
that time attempt to convince a jury that I was mentally
sound. The mere outlining of my ambitious scheme for
reform would have caused my immediate return to the
hospital. That scheme, however, was a sound and
feasible one, as later events have proved. But, taking
hold of me, as it did, while my imagination was at white
heat, I was impelled to attack my problem with compromising energy and, for a time, in a manner so uncon-
vincing as to obscure the essential sanity of my cherished
purpose.

I closed my letter as follows: "No doubt you will consider certain parts of this letter rather 'fresh.' I apologize for any such passages now, but, as I have an Insane
License, I do not hesitate to say what I think. What's
the use when one is caged like a criminal?

"P. S. This letter is a confidential one—and is to be
returned to the writer upon demand."

The letter was eventually forwarded to my conservator and is now in my possession.

As a result of my protest the Governor immediately
interrogated the superintendent of the institution where
"Jekyll-Hyde" had tortured me. Until he laid before the
superintendent my charges against his assistant, the
doctor in authority had not even suspected that I had
been tortured. This superintendent took pride in his

institution. He was sensitive to criticism and it was natural that he should strive to palliate the offence of his subordinate. He said that I was a most troublesome patient, which was, indeed, the truth; for I had always a way of my own for doing the things that worried those in charge of me. In a word, I brought to bear upon the situation what I have previously referred to as "an uncanny admixture of sanity."

The Governor did not meet the assistant physician who had maltreated me. The reprimand, if there was to be any, was left to the superintendent to administer.

In my letter to the Governor I had laid more stress upon the abuses to which I had been subjected at this private institution than I had upon conditions at the State Hospital where I was when I wrote to him. This may have had some effect on the action he took, or rather failed to take. At any rate, as to the State Hospital, no action was taken. Not even a word of warning was sent to the officials, as I later learned; for before leaving the institution I asked them.

Though my letter did not bring about an investigation, it was not altogether without results. Naturally, it was with considerable satisfaction that I informed the doctors that I had outwitted them, and it was with even greater satisfaction that I now saw those in authority make a determined, if temporary, effort to protect helpless patients against the cruelties of attendants. The moment the doctors were convinced that I had gone over their heads and had sent a characteristic letter of protest to the Governor of the State, that moment they began to protect themselves with an energy born of a realization of their former shortcomings. Whether or not the management in question ever admitted that their unwonted activity was due to my successful stratagem, the fact remains that the summary discharge of several attendants accused and proved guilty of brutality immediately followed and for a while put a stop to wanton assaults against which for a period of four months I had protested in vain. Patients who still lived in the violent ward told me that comparative peace reigned about this time.

XXVII

My failure to force the Governor to investigate conditions at the State Hospital convinced me that I could not hope to prosecute my reforms until I should regain my liberty and re-establish myself in my old world. I therefore quitted the rôle of reformer-militant; and, but for an occasional outburst of righteous indignation at some flagrant abuse which obtruded itself upon my notice, my demeanor was that of one quite content with his lot in life.

I was indeed content—I was happy. Knowing that I should soon regain my freedom, I found it easy to forgive—taking great pains not to forget—any injustice which had been done me. Liberty is sweet, even to one whose appreciation of it has never been augmented by its temporary loss. The pleasurable emotions which my impending liberation aroused within me served to soften my speech and render me more tractable. This change the assistant physician was not slow to note, though he was rather slow in placing in me the degree of confidence which I felt I deserved. So justifiable, however, was his suspicion that even at the time I forgave him for it. I had on so many prior occasions "played possum" that the doctor naturally attributed complex and unfathomable motives to my most innocent acts. For a long time he seemed to think that I was trying to capture his confidence, win the privilege of an unlimited parole, and so effect my escape. Doubtless he had not forgotten the several plans for escape which I had dallied with and bragged about while in the violent ward.

Though I was granted considerable liberty during the months of April, May, and June, 1903, not until July did I enjoy a so-called unlimited parole which enabled me to walk about the neighboring city unattended. My privileges were granted so gradually that these first tastes of regained freedom, though delightful, were not so thrilling as one might imagine. I took everything as a matter of course, and, except when I deliberately analyzed my feelings, was scarcely conscious of my former deprivations.

This power to forget the past—or recall it only at will —has contributed much to my happiness. Some of those who have suffered experiences such as mine are prone to brood upon them, and I cannot but attribute my happy immunity from unpleasant memories to the fact that I have viewed my own case much as a physician might view that of a patient. My past is a thing apart. I can examine this or that phase of it in the clarifying and comforting light of reason, under a memory rendered somewhat microscopic. And I am further compensated by the belief that I have a distinct mission in life—a chance for usefulness that might never have been mine had I enjoyed unbroken health and uninterrupted liberty.

The last few months of my life in the hospital were much alike, save that each succeeding one brought with it an increased amount of liberty. My hours now passed pleasantly. Time did not drag, for I was engaged upon some enterprise every minute. I would draw, read, write, or talk. If any feeling was dominant, it was my feeling for art; and I read with avidity books on the technique of that subject. Strange as it may seem, however, the moment I again found myself in the world of business my desire to become an artist died almost as suddenly as it had been born. Though my artistic ambition was clearly an outgrowth of my abnormal condition, and languished when normality asserted itself, I am inclined to believe I should even now take a lively interest in the study of art if I were so situated as to be deprived of a free choice of my activities. The use of words later enthralled me because so eminently suited to my purposes.

During the summer of 1903, friends and relatives often called to see me. The talks we had were of great and lasting benefit to me. Though I had rid myself of my more extravagant and impossible delusions of grandeur—flying-machines and the like—I still discussed with intense earnestness other schemes, which, though allied to delusions of grandeur, were, in truth, still more closely allied to sanity itself. My talk was of that high, but perhaps suspicious type in which Imagination over-rules Common Sense. Lingering delusions, as it were, made great projects seem easy. That they were at least feasible under certain conditions, my mentors admitted. Only I was in an abnormal hurry to pro-duce results. Work that I later realized could not be accomplished in less than five or ten years, if, indeed, in a lifetime, I then believed could be accomplished in a year or two, and by me single-handed. Had I had none but mentally unbalanced people to talk with, I might have continued to cherish a distorted perspective. It was the unanimity of sane opinions that helped me to correct my own views; and I am confident that each talk with relatives and friends hastened my return to normality.

Though I was not discharged from the State Hospital until September 10th, 1903, during the preceding month I visited my home several times, once for three days. These trips were not only interesting, but steadying in effect. I willingly returned to the hospital when my parole expired. Though several friends expressed surprise at this willingness to enter again an institution where I had experienced so many hardships, to me my temporary return was not in the least irksome. As I had penetrated and conquered the mysteries of that dark side of life, it no longer held any terrors for me. Nor does it to this day. I can contemplate the future with a greater degree of complacency than can some of those whose lot in life has been uniformly fortunate. In fact, I said at that time that, should my condition ever demand it, I would again enter a hospital for the insane, quite as willingly as the average person now enters a hospital for the treatment of bodily ailments.

It was in this complacent and confident mood, and without any sharp line of transition, that I again began life in my old world of companionship and of business.

XXVIII

For the first month of regained freedom I remained at home. These weeks were interesting. Scarcely a day passed that I did not meet several former friends and acquaintances who greeted me as one risen from the dead. And well they might, for my three-year trip among the worlds—rather than around the world—was suggestive of complete separation from the everyday life of the multitude. One profound impression which I received at this time was of the uniform delicacy of feeling exhibited by my well-wishers. In no instance that I can recall was a direct reference made to the nature of my recent illness, until I had first made some remark indicating that I was not averse to discussing it. There was an evident effort on the part of friends and acquaintances to avoid a subject which they naturally supposed I wished to forget. Knowing that their studied avoidance of a delicate subject was inspired by a thoughtful consideration, rather than a lack of interest, I invariably forced the conversation along a line calculated to satisfy a suppressed, but perfectly proper, curiosity which I seldom failed to detect. My decision to stand on my past and look the future in the face has, I believe, contributed much to my own happiness, and, more than anything else, enabled my friends to view my past as I myself do.   By frankly referring to my illness, I put my friends and acquaintances at ease, and at a stroke rid them of that constraint which one must feel in the presence of a person constantly in danger of being hurt by a chance allusion to an unhappy occurrence.

I have said much about the obligation of the sane in reference to easing the burdens of those committed to institutions.   I might say almost as much about the attitude of the public toward those who survive such a period of exile, restored, but branded with a suspicion which only time can efface.   Though a former patient receives personal consideration, he finds it difficult to obtain employment.   No fair-minded man can find fault with this condition of affairs, for an inherent dread of insanity leads to distrust of one who has had a mental breakdown.   Nevertheless, the attitude is mistaken. Perhaps one reason for this lack of confidence is to be found in the lack of confidence which a former patient often feels in himself.   Confidence begets confidence, and those men and women who survive mental illness should attack their problem as though their absence had been occasioned by any one of the many circumstances which may interrupt the career of a person whose mind has never been other than sound. I can testify to the efficacy of this course, for it is the one I pursued.   And I think that I have thus far met with as great a degree of success as I might have reasonably expected had my career never been all but fatally interrupted.

Discharged from the State Hospital in September, 1903, late in October of that same year I went to New York. Primarily my purpose was to study art. I even went so far as to gather information regarding the several schools; and had not my artistic ambition taken wing, I might have worked for recognition in a field where so many strive in vain. But my business instinct, revivified by the commercially surcharged atmosphere of New York, soon gained sway, and within three months I had secured a position with the same firm for which I had worked when I first went to New York six years earlier. It was by the merest chance that I made this most fortunate business connection. By no stretch of my rather elastic imagination can I even now picture a situation that would, at one and the same time, have so perfectly afforded a means of livelihood, leisure in which to indulge my longing to write the story of my experiences, and an opportunity to further my humanitarian project.

Though persons discharged from mental hospitals are usually able to secure, without much difficulty, work as unskilled laborers, or positions where the responsibility is slight, it is often next to impossible for them to secure positions of trust. During the negotiations which led to my employment, I was in no suppliant mood. If anything, I was quite the reverse; and as I have since learned, I imposed terms with an assurance so sublime that any less degree of audacity might have put an end to the negotiations then and there. But the man with whom I was dealing was not only broad-minded, he was sagacious. He recognized immediately such an ability to take care of my own interests as argued an ability to protect those of his firm. But this alone would not have induced the average business man to employ me under the circumstances. It was the common-sense and rational attitude of my employer toward mental illness which determined the issue. This view, which is, indeed, exceptional to-day, will one day (within a few generations, I believe) be too commonplace to deserve special mention. As this man tersely expressed it: "When an employé is ill, he's ill, and it makes no difference to me whether he goes to a general hospital or a hospital for the insane. Should you ever find yourself in need of treatment or rest, I want you to feel that you can take it when and where you please, and work for us again when you are able."

Dealing almost exclusively with bankers, for that was the nature of my work, I enjoyed almost as much leisure for reading and trying to learn how to write as I should have enjoyed had I had an assured income that would have enabled me to devote my entire time to these pursuits. And so congenial did my work prove, and so many places of interest did I visit, that I might rather have been classed as a "commercial tourist" than as a commercial traveler. To view almost all of the natural wonders and places of historic interest east of the Mississippi, and many west of it; to meet and know representative men and women; to enjoy an almost uninterrupted leisure, and at the same time earn a livelihood—these advantages bear me out in the feeling that in securing the position I did, at the time I did, I enjoyed one of those rare compensations which Fate sometimes bestows upon those who survive unusual adversity.

XXIX

AFTER again becoming a free man, my mind would not abandon the miserable ones whom I had left behind. I thought with horror that my reason had been threatened and baffled at every turn. Without malice toward those who had had me in charge, I yet looked with abhorrence upon the system by which I had been treated. But I realized that I could not successfully advocate reforms in hospital management until I had first proved to relatives and friends my ability to earn a living. And I knew that, after securing a position in the business world, I must first satisfy my employers before I could hope to persuade others to join me in prosecuting the reforms I had at heart. Consequently, during the first year of my renewed business activity (the year 1904), I held my humanitarian project in abeyance and gave all my executive energy to my business duties. During the first half of that year I gave but little time to reading and writing, and none at all to drawing. In a tentative way, however, I did occasionally discuss my project with intimate friends; but I spoke of its consummation as a thing of the uncertain future. At that time, though confident of accomplishing my set purpose, I believed I should be fortunate if my projected book were published before my fortieth year. That I was able to publish it eight years earlier was due to one of those

unlooked for combinations of circumstances which sometimes cause a hurried change of plans.

Late in the autumn of 1904, a slight illness detained
me for two weeks in a city several hundred miles from
home. The illness itself amounted to little, and, so far
as I know, had no direct bearing on later results, except
that, in giving me an enforced vacation, it afforded me
an opportunity to read several of the world's great books.
One of these was "Les Misérables." It made a deep
impression on me, and I am inclined to believe it started
a train of thought which gradually grew into a purpose
so all-absorbing that I might have been overwhelmed
by it, had not my over-active imagination been brought
to bay by another's common sense. Hugo's plea for
suffering Humanity—for the world's miserable—struck
a responsive chord within me. Not only did it revive
my latent desire to help the afflicted; it did more. It
aroused a consuming desire to emulate Hugo himself,
by writing a book which should arouse sympathy for
and interest in that class of unfortunates in whose
behalf I felt it my peculiar right and duty to speak. I
question whether any one ever read "Les Misérables"
with keener feeling. By day I read the story until my
head ached; by night I dreamed of it.

To resolve to write a book is one thing; to write it—
fortunately for the public—is quite another. Though I
wrote letters with ease, I soon discovered that I knew
nothing of the vigils or methods of writing a book. Even
then I did not attempt to predict just when I should
begin to commit my story to paper. But, a month later,

a member of the firm in whose employ I was made a remark which acted as a sudden spur. One day, while discussing the business situation with me, he informed me that my work had convinced him that he had made no mistake in re-employing me when he did. Naturally I was pleased. I had vindicated his judgment sooner than I had hoped. Aside from appreciating and remembering his compliment, at the time I paid no more attention to it. Not until a fortnight later did the force of his remark exert any peculiar influence on my plans. During that time it apparently penetrated to some subconscious part of me—a part which, on prior occasions, had assumed such authority as to dominate my whole being. But, in this instance, the part that became dominant did not exert an unruly or even unwelcome influence. Full of interest in my business affairs one week, the next I not only had no interest in them, but I had begun even to dislike them. From a matter-of-fact man of business I was transformed into a man whose all-absorbing thought was the amelioration of suffering among the afflicted insane. Travelling on this high plane of ideal humanitarianism, I could get none but a distorted and dissatisfying view of the life I must lead if I should continue to devote my time to the comparatively deadening routine of commercial affairs.

Thus it was inevitable that I should focus my attention on my humanitarian project. During the last week of December I sought ammunition by making a visit to two of the institutions where I had once been a patient. I went there to discuss certain phases of the subject of reform with the doctors in authority. I was politely received and listened to with a degree of deference which was, indeed, gratifying. Though I realized that I was rather intense on the subject of reform, I did not have that clear insight into my state of mind which the doctors had. Indeed, I believe that only those expert in the detection of symptoms of a slightly disturbed mental condition could possibly have observed anything abnormal about me at that time. Only when I discussed my fond project of reform did I betray an abnormal stress of feeling. I could talk as convincingly about business as I had at any time in my life; for even at the height of this wave of enthusiasm I dealt at length with a certain banker who finally placed with my employers a large contract.

After conferring with the doctors, or rather—as it proved—exhibiting myself to them, I returned to New Haven and discussed my project with the President of Yale University. He listened patiently—he could scarcely do otherwise—and did me the great favor of interposing his judgment at a time when I might have made a false move. I told him that I intended to visit Washington at once, to enlist the aid of President Roosevelt; also that of Mr. Hay, Secretary of State. Mr. Hadley tactfully advised me not to approach them until I had more thoroughly crystallized my ideas. His wise suggestion I had the wisdom to adopt.

The next day I went to New York, and on January 1st, 1905, I began to write. Within two days I had written about fifteen thousand words—for the most part on the subject of reforms and how to effect them. One of the documents prepared at that time contained grandiloquent passages that were a portent of coming events—though I was ignorant of the fact. In writing about my project I said, "Whether I am a tool of God or a toy of the devil, time alone will tell; but there will be no misunderstanding Time's answer if I succeed in doing one-tenth of the good things I hope to accomplish. . . . Anything which is feasible in this philanthropic age can easily be put into practice. . . . A listener gets the impression that I hope to do a hundred years' work in a day. They are wrong there, for I'm not so in love with work—as such. I would like though to interest so many people in the accomplishment of my purpose that one hundred years' work might be done in a fraction of that time. Hearty co-operation brings quick results, and once you start a wave of enthusiasm in a sea of humanity, and have for the base of that wave a humanitarian project of great breadth, it will travel with irresistible and ever-increasing impulse to the ends of the earth—which is far enough. According to Dr. ——, many of my ideas regarding the solution of the problem under consideration are years and years in advance of the times. I agree with him, but that is no reason why we should not put 'the times' on board the express train of progress and give civilization a boost to a higher level, until it finally lands on a plateau where performance and perfection will be synonymous terms."

Referring to the betterment of conditions, I said,

"And this improvement can never be brought about without some central organization by means of which the best ideas in the world may be crystallized and passed along to those in charge of this army of afflicted ones. The methods to be used to bring about these results must be placed on the same high level as the idea itself. No yellow journalism or other sensational means should be resorted to. Let the thing be worked up secretly and confidentially by a small number of men who know their business. Then when the very best plan has been formulated for the accomplishment of the desired results, and men of money have been found to support the movement until it can take care of itself, announce to the world in a dignified and effective manner the organization and aims of the society, the name of which shall be —, decided later. . . . To start the movement will not require a whole lot of money. It will be started modestly and as financial resources of the society increase, the field will be broadened." . . . "The abuses and correction of same is a mere detail in the general scheme." . . . "It is too early to try to interest anyone in this scheme of preventing breakdowns, as there are other things of more importance to be brought about first—but it will surely come in time."

"'Uncle Tom's Cabin,'" I continued, "had a very decided effect on the question of slavery of the negro race. Why cannot a book be written which will free the helpless slaves of all creeds and colors confined to-day in the asylums and sanitariums throughout the world? That is, free them from unnecessary abuses to which

they are now subjected.   Such a book, I believe, can be
written and I trust that I may be permitted to live till
I am wise enough to write it.   Such a book might
change the attitude of the public towards those who
are unfortunate enough to have the stigma of mental
incompetency put upon them.   Of course, an insane
man is an insane man and while insane should be placed
in an institution for treatment, but when that man
comes out he should be as free from all taint as the man
is who recovers from a contagious disease and again
takes his place in society."   In conclusion, I said,
" From a scientific point of view there is a great field for
research. . . . Cannot some of the causes be discovered
and perhaps done away with, thereby saving the lives
of many—and millions in money?   It may come about
that some day something will be found which will prevent a complete and incurable mental breakdown. . . ."

Thus did I, as revealed by these rather crude, unre-
vised quotations, somewhat prophetically, if extrav-
agantly, box the compass that later guided the ship of
my hopes (not one of my phantom ships) into a safe
channel, and later into a safe harbor.

By way of mental diversion during these creative
days at the Yale Club, I wrote personal letters to
intimate friends.   One of these produced a result unlooked for.   There were about it compromising ear-
marks which the friend to whom it was sent recognized.
In it I said that I intended to approach a certain
man of wealth and influence who lived in New York,
with a view to securing some action that would lead to

reform. That was enough. My friend showed the letter to my brother—the one who had acted as my conservator. He knew at once that I was in an excited mental condition. But he could not very well judge the degree of the excitement; for when I had last talked with him a week earlier, I had not discussed my larger plans. Business affairs and my hope for business advancement had then alone interested me.

I talked with President Hadley on Friday; Saturday I went to New York; Sunday and Monday I spent at the Yale Club, writing; Tuesday, this telltale letter fell under the prescient eye of my brother. On that day he at once got in touch with me by telephone. We briefly discussed the situation. He did not intimate that he believed me to be in elation. He simply urged me not to attempt to interest anyone in my project until I had first returned to New Haven and talked with him. Now I had already gone so far as to invite my employers to dine with me that very night at the Yale Club for the purpose of informing them of my plans. This I did, believing it to be only fair that they should know what I intended to do, so that they might dispense with my services should they feel that my plans would in any way impair my usefulness as an employé. Of this dinner engagement, therefore, I told my brother. But so insistently did he urge me to defer any such conference as I proposed until I had talked with him that, although it was too late to break the dinner engagement, I agreed to avoid, if possible, any reference to my project. I also agreed to return home the next day.

That night my guests honored me as agreed. For an
hour or two we discussed business conditions and affairs
in general. Then, one of them referred pointedly to my
implied promise to unburden myself on a certain subject, the nature of which he did not at the time know.
I immediately decided that it would be best to "take
the bull by the horns," submit my plans, and, if necessary, sever my connection with the firm, should its members force me to choose (as I put it) between themselves
and Humanity. I then proceeded to unfold my scheme;
and, though I may have exhibited a decided intensity of
feeling during my discourse, at no time, I believe, did I
overstep the bounds of what appeared to be sane enthusiasm. My employers agreed that my purpose was commendable—that no doubt I could and would eventually
be able to do much for those I had left behind in a durance I so well knew to be vile. Their one warning was
that I seemed in too great a hurry. They expressed the
opinion that I had not been long enough re-established
in business to be able to persuade people of wealth and
influence to take hold of my project. And one of my
guests very aptly observed that I could not afford to be a
philanthropist, which objection I met by saying that all I
intended to do was to supply ideas for those who could
afford to apply them. The conference ended satisfac-
torily. My employers disclaimed any personal objection
to my proceeding with my project, if I would, and yet
remaining in their employ. They simply urged me to
"go slow." "Wait until you're forty," one of them said.
I then thought that I might do so. And perhaps I should

have waited so long, had not the events of the next two days put me on the right road to an earlier execution of my cherished plans.

The next day, January 4th, true to my word, I went home. That night I had a long talk with my brother. I did not suspect that a man like myself, capable of dealing with bankers and talking for several consecutive hours with his employers without arousing their suspicion as to his mental condition, was to be suspected by his own relatives. Nor, indeed, with the exception of my brother, who had read my suspiciously excellent letter, were any of my relatives disturbed; and he did nothing to disabuse my assurance. After our night conference he left for his own home, casually mentioning that he would see me again the next morning. That pleased me, for I was in a talkative mood and craved an interested listener.

When my brother returned the next morning, I willingly accepted his invitation to go with him to his office, where we could talk without fear of interruption. Arrived there, I calmly sat down and prepared to prove my whole case. I had scarcely "opened fire" when in walked a stranger—a strapping fellow, to whom my brother immediately introduced me. I instinctively felt that it was by no mere chance that this third party had so suddenly appeared. My eyes at once took in the dark blue trousers worn by the otherwise conventionally dressed stranger. That was enough. The situation became so clear that the explanations which followed were superfluous. In a word, I was under arrest, or in imminent danger of being arrested. To say that I was not in the least disconcerted would scarcely be true, for I had not divined my brother's clever purpose in luring me to his office. But I can say, with truth, that I was the coolest person in the room. I knew what I should do next, but my brother and the officer of the law could only guess. The fact is I did nothing. I calmly remained seated, awaiting the verdict which I well knew my brother, with characteristic decision, had already prepared. With considerable effort—for the situation, he has since told me, was the most trying one of his life—he informed me that on the preceding day he had talked with the doctors to whom I had so opportunely exhibited myself a week earlier. All agreed that I was in a state of elation which might or might not become more pronounced. They had advised that I be persuaded to submit voluntarily to treatment in a hospital, or that I be, if necessary, forcibly committed. On this advice my brother had proceeded to act. And it was well so; for, though I appreciated the fact that I was by no means in a normal state of mind, I had not a clear enough insight into my condition to realize that treatment and a restricted degree of liberty were what I needed, since continued freedom might further inflame an imagination already overwrought.

A few simple statements by my brother convinced me that it was for my own good and the peace of mind of my relatives that I should temporarily surrender my freedom. This I agreed to do. Perhaps the presence of two hundred pounds of brawn and muscle, representing the law, lent persuasiveness to my brother's words. In fact, I did assent the more readily because I admired the thorough, sane, fair, almost artistic manner in which my brother had brought me to bay. I am inclined to believe that, had I suspected that a recommitment was imminent, I should have fled to a neighboring State during the preceding night. Fortunately, however, the right thing was done in the right way at the right time. Though I had been the victim of a clever stratagem, not for one moment thereafter, in any particular, was I deceived. I was frankly told that several doctors had pronounced me elated, and that for my own good I *must* submit to treatment. I was allowed to choose between a probate court commitment which would have "admitted me" to the State Hospital, or a "voluntary commitment" which would enable me to enter the large private hospital where I had previously passed from depression to elation, and had later suffered tortures. I naturally chose the more desirable of the two disguised blessings, and agreed to start at once for the private hospital, the one in which I had been when depression gave way to elation. It was not that I feared again to enter the State Hospital. I simply wished to avoid the publicity which necessarily would have followed, for at that time the statutes of Connecticut did not provide for voluntary commitment to the state hospitals. Then, too, there were certain privileges which I knew I could not enjoy in a public institution. Having re-established myself in society and business I did not wish to forfeit that gain; and as the doctors believed that my period of elation would be short, it would have been sheer folly to advertise the fact that my mental health had again fallen under suspicion.

But before starting for the hospital I imposed certain conditions. One was that the man with the authoritative trousers should walk behind at such a distance that no friend or acquaintance who might see my brother and myself would suspect that I was under guard; the other was that the doctors at the institution should agree to grant my every request, no matter how trivial, so long as doing so could in no way work to my own injury. My privileges were to include that of reading and writing to my heart's content, and the procuring of such books and supplies as my fancy might dictate. All this was agreed to. In return I agreed to submit to the surveillance of an attendant when I went outside the hospital grounds. This I knew would contribute to the peace of mind of my relatives, who naturally could not rid themselves of the fear that one so nearly normal as myself might take it into his head to leave the State and resist further attempts at control. As I felt that I could easily elude my keeper, should I care to escape, his presence also contributed to *my* peace of mind, for I argued that the ability to outwit my guard would atone for the offence itself.

I then started for the hospital; and I went with a willingness surprising even to myself. A cheerful philosophy enabled me to turn an apparently disagreeable situation into one that was positively pleasing to me. I convinced myself that I could extract more real enjoyment from life during the ensuing weeks within the walls of a "retreat" than I could in the world outside. My one desire was to write, write, write. My fingers itched for a pen. My desire to write was, I imagine, as irresistible as is the desire of a drunkard for his dram. And the act of writing resulted in an intoxicating pleasure composed of a mingling of emotions that defies analysis.

That I should so calmly, almost eagerly, enter where devils might fear to tread may surprise the reader who already has been informed of the cruel treatment I had formerly received there. I feared nothing, for I knew all. Having seen the worst, I knew how to avoid the pitfalls into which, during my first experience at that hospital, I had fallen or deliberately walked. I was confident that I should suffer no abuse or injustice so long as the doctors in charge should live up to their agreement and treat me with unvarying fairness. This they did, and my quick recovery and subsequent discharge may be attributed partly to this cause. The assistant physicians who had come in contact with me during my first experience in this hospital were no longer there. They had resigned some months earlier, shortly after the death of the former superintendent. Thus it was that I started with a clean record, free from those prejudices which so often affect the judgment of a hospital physician who has treated a mental patient at his worst.

XXX

ON more than one occasion my chameleonlike temperament has enabled me to adjust myself to new conditions, but never has it served me better than it did at the time of which I write. A free man on New Year's Day, enjoying the pleasures of a congenial club life, four days later I found myself again under the lock and key of an institution for the insane. Never had I enjoyed. life in New York more than during those first days of that new year. To suffer so rude a change was, indeed, enough to arouse a feeling of discontent, if not despair; yet, aside from the momentary initial shock, my contentment was in no degree diminished. I can say with truth that I was as complacent the very moment I recrossed the threshold of that "retreat" as I had been when crossing and recrossing at will the threshold of my club.

Of everything I thought and did during the interesting weeks which followed, I have a complete record. The moment I accepted the inevitable, I determined to spend my time to good advantage. Knowing from experience that I must observe my own case, if I was to have any detailed record of it, I provided myself in advance with notebooks. In these I recorded, I might almost say, my every thought and action. The sane part of me, which fortunately was dominant, subjected its temporarily unruly part to a sort of scientific scrutiny and surveillance. From morning till night I dogged the steps of my restless body and my more restless imagination. I observed the physical and mental symptoms which I knew were characteristic of elation. An exquisite light-heartedness, an exalted sense of well-being, my pulse, my weight, my appetite—all these I observed and recorded with a care that would have put to the blush a majority of the doctors in charge of mental cases in institutions.

But this record of symptoms, though minute, was vague compared to my reckless analysis of my emotions. With a lack of reserve characteristic of my mood, I described the joy of living, which, for the most part, then consisted in the joy of writing. And even now, when I reread my record, I feel that I cannot overstate the pleasure I found in surrendering myself completely to that controlling impulse. The excellence of my composition seemed to me beyond criticism. And, as to one in a state of elation, things are pretty much as they seem, I was able to experience the subtle delights which, I fancy, thrill the soul of a master. During this month of elation I wrote words enough to fill a book nearly as large as this one. Having found that each filling of my fountain pen was sufficient for the writing of about twenty-eight hundred words, I kept a record of the number of times I filled it. This minute calculation I carried to an extreme. If I wrote for fifty-nine minutes, and then read for seventeen, those facts I recorded. Thus, in my diary and out of it, I wrote and wrote until the tips of my thumb and forefinger grew numb. As this numbness increased and general weariness of the hand set in, there came a gradual flagging of my creative impulse until a very normal unproductivity supervened.

The reader may well wonder in what my so-called insanity at this time consisted. Had I any of those impracticable delusions which had characterized my former period of elation? No, not one—unless an unreasonable haste to achieve my ambitions may be counted a delusion. My attention simply focussed itself on my project. All other considerations seemed of little moment. My interest in business waned to the vanishing point. Yet one thing should be noted: I did deliberately devote many hours to the consideration of business affairs. Realizing that one way to overcome an absorbing impulse is to divide the attention, I wrote a brief of the arguments I had often used when talking with bankers. In this way I was able to convince the doctors that my intense interest in literature and reform would soon spend itself.

A consuming desire to effect reforms had been the determining factor when I calmly weighed the situation with a view to making the best possible use of my impulse to write. The events of the immediate past had convinced me that I could not hope to interest people of wealth and influence in my humanitarian project until I had some definite plan to submit for their leisurely consideration. Further, I had discovered that an attempt to approach them directly disturbed my relatives and friends, who had not yet learned to dissociate

present intentions from past performances. I had,
therefore, determined to drill myself in the art of composition to the end that I might write a story of my life
which would merit publication.   I felt that such a book,
once written, wo uld do its own work, regardless of my
subsequent fortunes.   Other books had spoken ever.
from the grave; why should not my book so speak—if
necessary?

With this thought in mind I began not only to read
and write, but to test my impulse in order that I might
discover if it were a part of my very being, an abnormal
impulse, or a mere whim.   I reasoned that to compare
my own feelings toward literature, and my emotions
experienced in the heat of composition, with the
recorded feelings of successful men of letters, would give
me a clue to the truth on this question.   At this
time I read several books that could have served as a
basis for my deductions, but only one of them did I
have time to analyze and note in my diary.   That one
was, "Wit and Wisdom of the Earl of Beaconsfield."
The following passages from the pen of Disraeli I trans-
cribed in my diary with occasional comment.

"Remember who you are, and also that it is your duty
to excel.   Providence has given you a great lot.   Think
ever that you are born to perform great duties."   This
I interpreted in much the same spirit that I had interpreted the 45th Psalm on an earlier occasion.

"It was that noble ambition, the highest and best,
that must be born in the heart, and organized in the
brain, which will not let a man be content unless his

intellectual power is recognized by his race, and desires that it should contribute to their welfare."

"Authors—the creators of opinion."

"What appear to be calamities are often the sources of fortune."

"Change is inevitable in a progressive country. Change is constant." ("Then why," was my recorded comment, "cannot the changes I propose to bring about, be brought about?")

"The author is, as we must ever remember, of peculiar organization. He is a being born with a predisposition which with him is irresistible, the bent of which he cannot in any way avoid, whether it directs him to the abstruse researches of erudition or induces him to mount into the fervid and turbulent atmosphere of imagination."

"This," I wrote (the day after arriving at the hospital) "is a fair diagnosis of my case as it stands to-day, assuming, of course, that an author is one who loves to write, and can write with ease, even though what he says may have no literary value. My past proves that my organization is a peculiar one. I have for years (two and a half) had a desire to achieve success along literary lines. I believe that, feeling as I do to-day, nothing can prevent my writing. If I had to make a choice at once between a sure success in the business career ahead of me and doubtful success in the field of literature, I would willingly, yes confidently, choose the latter. I have read many a time about successful writers who learned how to write, and by dint of hard work ground out their ideas. If these men could succeed, why should not a man who is in danger of being ground up by an excess of ideas and imagination succeed, when he seems able to put those ideas into fairly intelligible English? He should and will succeed."

Therefore, without delay, I began the course of experiment and practice which culminated within a few months in the first draft of my story. Wise enough to realize the advantages of a situation free from the annoying interruptions of the workaday world, I enjoyed a degree of liberty seldom experienced by those in possession of complete legal liberty and its attendant obligations. When I wished to read, write, talk, walk, sleep, or eat, I did the thing I wished. I went to the theatre when the spirit moved me to do so, accompanied, of course, by an attendant, who on such occasions played the rôle of chum.

Friends called to see me and, at their suggestion or mine, invited me to dinner outside the walls of my "cloister." At one of these dinners an incident occurred which throws a clear light on my condition at the time. The friend, whose willing prisoner I was, had invited a common friend to join the party. The latter had not heard of my recent commitment. At my suggestion, he who shared my secret had agreed not to refer to it unless I first broached the subject. There was nothing strange in the fact that we three should meet. Just such impromptu celebrations had before occurred among us. We dined, and, as friends will, indulged in that exchange of thoughts which bespeaks intimacy. During our talk, I so shaped the conversation that the possibility of a recurrence of my mental illness was discussed. The uninformed friend derided the idea.

"Then, if I were to tell you," I remarked, "that I am at this moment supposedly insane—at least not normal—and that when I leave you to-night I shall go direct to the very hospital where I was formerly confined, there to remain until the doctors pronounce me fit for freedom, what would you say?"

"I should say that you are a choice sort of liar," he retorted.

This genial insult I swallowed with gratification. It was, in truth, a timely and encouraging compliment, the force of which its author failed to appreciate until my host had corroborated my statements.

If I could so favorably impress an intimate friend at a time when I was elated, it is not surprising that I should subsequently hold an interview with a comparative stranger—the cashier of a local bank—without betraying my state of mind. As business interviews go, this was in a class by itself. While my attendant stood guard at the door, I, an enrolled inmate of a hospital for the insane, entered the banking room and talked with a level-headed banker. And that interview was not without effect in subsequent negotiations which led to the closing of a contract amounting to one hundred and fifty thousand dollars.

The very day I re-entered the hospital I stopped on the way at a local hotel and procured some of the hostelry's stationery. By using this in the writing of personal and business letters I managed to conceal my condition and my whereabouts from all except near relatives and a few intimate friends who shared the secret. I quite enjoyed leading this legitimate double life. The situation appealed (not in vain) to my sense of humor. Many a smile did I indulge in when I closed a letter with such ambiguous phrases as the following: "Matters of importance necessitate my remaining where I am for an indefinite period." . . . "A situation has recently arisen which will delay my intended trip South. As soon as I have closed a certain contract (having in mind my contract to re-establish my sanity) I shall again take to the road." To this day few friends or acquaintances know that I was in semi-exile during the month of January, 1905. My desire to suppress the fact was not due, as already intimated, to any sensitiveness regarding the subject of insanity. What afterwards justified my course was that on regaining my freedom I was able, without embarrassment, again to take up my work. Within a month of my voluntary commitment, that is, in February, I started on a business trip through the Central West and South, where I remained until the following July. During those months I felt perfectly well, and have remained in excellent health ever since.

This second interruption of my career came at a time and in a manner to furnish me with strong arguments wherewith to support my contention that so-called madmen are too often man-made, and that he who is potentially mad may keep a saving grip on his own reason if he be fortunate enough to receive that kindly and intelligent treatment to which one on the brink of mental chaos is entitled. Though during this second period of elation I was never in a mood so reckless as that which obtained immediately after my recovery from depression in August, 1902, I was at least so excitable that, had those in authority attempted to impose upon me, I should have thrown discretion to the winds. To them, indeed, I frankly reiterated a terse dictum which I had coined during my first period of elation. "Just press the button of Injustice," I said, "and I'll do the rest!" This I meant, for fear of punishment does not restrain a man in the dare-devil grip of elation.

What fostered my self-control was a sense of gratitude. The doctors and attendants treated me as a gentleman. Therefore it was not difficult to prove myself one. My every whim was at least considered with a politeness which enabled me to accept a denial with a highly sane equanimity. Aside from mild tonics I took no other medicine than that most beneficial sort which inheres in kindness. The feeling that, though a prisoner, I could still command obligations from others led me to recognize my own reciprocal obligations, and was a constant source of delight. The doctors, by proving their title to that confidence which I tentatively gave them upon re-entering the institution, had no difficulty in convincing me that a temporary curtailment of some privileges was for my own good. They all evinced a consistent desire to trust me. In return I trusted them.

XXXI

ON leaving the hospital and resuming my travels, I felt sure that any one of several magazines or newspapers would willingly have had me conduct my campaign under its nervously commercial auspices; but a flash-in-the-pan method did not appeal to me. Those noxious growths, Incompetence, Abuse, and Injustice, had not only to be cut down, but rooted out. Therefore, I clung to my determination to write a book—an instrument of attack which, if it cuts and sears at all, does so as long as the need exists. Inasmuch as I knew that I still had to learn how to write, I approached my task with deliberation. I planned to do two things: first, to crystallize my thoughts by discussion—telling the story of my life whenever in my travels I should meet any person who inspired my confidence; second, while the subject matter of my book was shaping itself in my mind, to drill myself by carrying on a letter-writing campaign. Both these things I did—as certain indulgent friends who bore the brunt of my spoken and written discourse can certify. I feared the less to be dubbed a bore, and I hesitated the less, perhaps, to impose upon good-nature, because of my firm conviction that one in a position to help the many was himself entitled to the help of the few.

I wrote scores of letters of great length. I cared little

if some of my friends should conclude that I had been born a century too late; for, without them as confidants, I must write with no more inspiring object in view than the wastebasket. Indeed, I found it difficult to compose without keeping before me the image of a friend. Having stipulated that every letter should be returned upon demand, I wrote without reserve—my imagination had free rein. I wrote as I thought, and I thought as I pleased. The result was that within six months I found myself writing with a facility which hitherto had obtained only during elation. At first I was suspicious of this new-found and apparently permanent ease of expression—so suspicious that I set about diagnosing my symptoms. My self-examination convinced me that I was, in fact, quite normal. I had no irresistible desire to write, nor was there any suggestion of that exalted, or (technically speaking) euphoric, light-heartedness which characterizes elation. Further, after a prolonged period of composition, I experienced a comforting sense of exhaustion which I had not known while elated. I therefore concluded—and rightly—that my unwonted facility was the product of practice. At last I found myself able to conceive an idea and immediately transfer it to paper effectively.

In July, 1905, I came to the conclusion that the time for beginning my book was at hand. Nevertheless, I found it difficult to set a definite date. About this time I so arranged my itinerary that I was able to enjoy two summer—though stormy—nights and a day at the Summit House on Mount Washington. What better, thought I, than to begin my book on a plane so high as to be appropriate to this noble summit? I therefore began to compose a dedication. "To Humanity" was as far as I got. There the Muse forsook me.

But, returning to earth and going about my business, I soon again found myself in the midst of inspiring natural surroundings—the Berkshire Hills. At this juncture Man came to the assistance of Nature, and perhaps with an unconsciousness equal to her own. It was a chance remark made by an eminent man that aroused my subconscious literary personality to irresistible action. I had long wished to discuss my project with a man of great reputation, and if the reputation were international, so much the better. I desired the unbiased opinion of a judicial mind. Opportunely, I learned that the Hon. Joseph H. Choate was then at his summer residence at Stockbridge, Massachusetts. Mr. Choate had never heard of me and I had no letter of introduction. The exigencies of the occasion, however, demanded that I conjure one up, so I wrote my own letter of introduction and sent it:

RED LION INN,
STOCKBRIDGE, MASS.
August 18, 1905.

HON. JOSEPH H. CHOATE,
    Stockbridge, Massachusetts.

DEAR SIR:
    Though I might present myself at your door, armed with one of society's unfair skeleton-keys—a letter of introduction—I prefer to approach you as I now do: simply as a young man who honestly feels entitled to at least five minutes of your time, and as many

minutes more as you care to grant because of your interest in the subject to be discussed.

I look to you at this time for your opinion as to the value of some ideas of mine, and the feasibility of certain schemes based on them.

A few months ago I talked with President Hadley of Yale, and briefly outlined my plans. He admitted that many of them seemed feasible and would, if carried out, add much to the sum-total of human happiness. His only criticism was that they were "too comprehensive."

Not until I have staggered an imagination of the highest type will I admit that I am trying to do too much. Should you refuse to see me, believe me when I tell you that you will still be, as you are at this moment, the unconscious possessor of my sincere respect.

Business engagements necessitate my leaving here early on Monday next. Should you care to communicate with me, word sent in care of this hotel will reach me promptly.

Yours very truly,
CLIFFORD W. BEERS.

Within an hour I had received a reply, in which Mr. Choate said that he would see me at his home at ten o'clock the next morning.

At the appointed time, the door, whose lock I had picked with a pen, opened before me and I was ushered into the presence of Mr. Choate. He was graciousness itself—but pointed significantly at a heap of unanswered letters lying before him. I took the hint and within ten minutes briefly outlined my plans. After pronouncing my project a "commendable one," Mr. Choate offered the suggestion that produced results. "If you will submit your ideas in writing," he said, "I shall be glad to read your manuscript and assist you in any way I can. To consider fully your scheme would require several hours, and busy men cannot very well give you so much time. What they can do is to read your manuscript during their leisure moments."

Thus it was that Mr. Choate, by granting the interview, contributed to an earlier realization of my purposes. One week later I began the composition of this book. My action was unpremeditated, as my quitting Boston for less attractive Worcester proves. That very day, finding myself with a day and a half of leisure before me, I decided to tempt the Muse and compel myself to prove that my pen was, in truth, "the tongue of a ready writer." A stranger in the city, I went to a school of stenography and there secured the services of a young man who, though inexperienced in his art, was more skilled in catching thoughts as they took wing than I was at that time in the art of setting them free. Except in the writing of one or two conventional business letters, never before had I dictated to a stenographer. After I had startled him into an attentive mood by briefly outlining my past career and present purpose, I worked without any definite plan or brief, or reference to data. My narrative was therefore digressive and only roughly chronological. But it served to get my material in front of me for future shaping. At this task I hammered away three or four hours a day for a period of five weeks.

It so happened that Mr. Choate arrived at the same hotel on the day I took up my abode there, so that some of the toil he had inspired went on in his proximity, if not in his presence. I carefully kept out of his sight, however, lest he should think me a "crank" on the subject of reform, bent on persecuting his leisure.

As the work progressed my facility increased. In fact, I soon called in an additional stenographer to help in the snaring of my thoughts. This excessive productivity caused me to pause and again diagnose my condition. I could not fail now to recognize in myself symptoms hardly distinguishable from those which had obtained eight months earlier when it had been deemed expedient temporarily to restrict my freedom. But I had grown wise in adversity. Rather than interrupt my manuscript short of completion I decided to avail myself of a vacation that was due, and remain outside my native State—this, so that well-meaning but perhaps overzealous relatives might be spared unnecessary anxiety, and I myself be spared possible unwarranted restrictions. I was by no means certain as to the degree of mental excitement that would result from such continuous mental application; nor did I much care, so long as I accomplished my task. However, as I knew that "possession is nine points of the law," I decided to maintain my advantage by remaining in my literary fortress. And my resolve was further strengthened by certain cherished sentiments expressed by John Stuart Mill in his essay "On Liberty," which I had read and reread with an interest born of experience.

At last the first draft of the greater part of my story was completed. After a timely remittance (for, in strict accordance with the traditions of the craft, I had exhausted my financial resources) I started for home with a sigh of relief. For months I had been under the burden of a conscious obligation. My memory, stored with information which, if rightly used, could, I believed, brighten and even save unhappy lives, was to me as a basket of eggs which it was my duty to balance on a head whose poise was supposed to be none too certain. One by one, during the preceding five weeks, I had gently lifted my thoughts from their resting-place, until a large part of my burden had been so shifted as to admit of its being imposed upon the public conscience.

After I had lived over again the trials and the tortures of my unhappiest years—which was of course necessary in ploughing and harrowing a memory happily retentive— the completion of this first draft left me exhausted. But after a trip to New York, whither I went to convince my employers that I should be granted a further leave-of-absence, I resumed work. The ground for this added favor was that my manuscript was too crude to submit to any but intimate acquaintances. Knowing, perhaps, that a business man with a literary bee buzzing in his ear is, for the time, no business man at all, my employers readily agreed that I should do as I pleased during the month of October. They also believed me entitled to the favor, recognizing the force of my belief that I had a high obligation to discharge.

It was under the family rooftree that I now set up my literary shop. Nine months earlier an unwonted interest in literature and reform had sent me to an institution. That I should now in my own home be able to work out my destiny without unduly disturbing the peace of mind of relatives was a considerable satisfaction. In the very room where, during June, 1900, my reason had set out for an unknown goal, I redictated my account of that reason's experiences.

My leave-of-absence ended, I resumed my travels eagerly; for I wished to cool my brain by daily contact with the more prosaic minds of men of business. I went South. For a time I banished all thoughts of my book and project. But after some months of this change of occupation, which I thoroughly enjoyed, I found leisure in the course of wide travels to take up the work of elaboration and revision. A presentable draft of my story being finally prepared, I began to submit it to all sorts and conditions of minds (in accordance with Mill's dictum that only in that way can the truth be obtained). In my quest for criticism and advice, I fortunately decided to submit my manuscript to Professor William James of Harvard University, the most eminent of American psychologists and a masterful writer, who was then living. He expressed interest in my project; put my manuscript with others on his desk — but was somewhat reserved when it came to promising to read my story. He said it might be months before he could find time to do so. Within a fortnight, however, I received from him a characteristic letter. To me it came as a rescuing sun, after a period of groping about for an authoritative opinion that should put scoffers to flight. The letter read as follows:

95 Irving St., Cambridge, Mass.
July 1, 1906.

Dear Mr. Beers:

Having at last "got round" to your MS., I have read it with very great interest and admiration for both its style and its temper. I hope you will finish it and publish it.   It is the best written out "case" that I have seen; and you no doubt have put your finger on the weak spots of our treatment of the insane, and suggested the right line of remedy.   I have long thought that if I were a millionaire, with money to leave for public purposes, I should endow "Insanity" exclusively.

You were doubtless a pretty intolerable character when the maniacal condition came on and you were bossing the universe.   Not only ordinary "tact," but a genius for diplomacy must have been needed for avoiding rows with you; but you certainly were wrongly treated nevertheless; and the spiteful Assistant M.D. at —————— deserves to have his name published.   Your report is full of instructiveness for doctors and attendants alike.

The most striking thing in it to my mind is the sudden conversion of you from a delusional subject to a maniacal one—how the whole delusional system disintegrated the moment one pin was drawn out by your proving your brother to be genuine.   I never heard of so rapid a change in a mental system.

You speak of rewriting. Don't you do it.   You can hardly improve your book.   I shall keep the MS. a week longer as I wish to impart it to a friend.

Sincerely yours,

Wm. James.

Though Mr. James paid me the compliment of advising me not to rewrite my original manuscript, I did revise it quite thoroughly before publication. When my book was about to go to press for the first time and since its reception by the public was problematical,

I asked permission to publish the letter already quoted. In reply, Mr. James sent the following letter, also for publication.

95 IRVING ST., CAMBRIDGE, MASS.
November 10, 1907.

DEAR MR. BEERS:

You are welcome to use the letter I wrote to you (on July 1, 1906) after reading the first part of your MS. in any way your judgment prompts, whether as preface, advertisement, or anything else. Reading the rest of it only heightens its importance in my eyes. In style, in temper, in good taste, it is irreproachable. As for contents, it is fit to remain in literature as a classic account "from within" of an insane person's psychology.

The book ought to go far toward helping along that terribly needed reform, the amelioration of the lot of the insane of our country, for the Auxiliary Society which you propose is feasible (as numerous examples in other fields show), and ought to work important effects on the whole situation.

You have handled a difficult theme with great skill, and produced a narrative of absorbing interest to scientist as well as layman. It reads like fiction, but it is not fiction; and this I state emphatically, knowing how prone the uninitiated are to doubt the truthfulness of descriptions of abnormal mental processes.

With best wishes for the success of the book and the plan, both of which, I hope, will prove epoch-making, I remain,

Sincerely yours,
WM. JAMES.

Several times in my narrative, I have said that the seemingly unkind fate that robbed me of several probably happy and healthful years had hidden within it compensations which have offset the sufferings and the loss of those years. Not the least of the compensations has been the many letters sent to me by eminent men and women, who, having achieved results in their own work, are ever responsive to the efforts of anyone trying to reach a difficult objective. Of all the encouraging opinions I have ever received, one has its own niche in my memory. It came from William James a few months before his death, and will ever be an inspiration to me. Let my excuse for revealing so complimentary a letter be that it justifies the hopes and aspirations expressed in the course of my narrative, and shows them to be well on the way to accomplishment.

95 IRVING STREET, CAMBRIDGE,
January 17, 1910.

DEAR BEERS:

Your exegesis of my farewell in my last note to you was erroneous, but I am glad it occurred, because it brought me the extreme gratification of your letter of yesterday.

You are the most responsive and recognizant of human beings, my dear Beers, and it " sets me up immensely " to be treated by a practical man on practical grounds as you treat me. I inhabit such a realm of abstractions that I only get credit for what I do in that spectral empire; but you are not only a moral idealist and philanthropic enthusiast (and good fellow!), but a tip-top man of business in addition; and to have actually done anything that the like of you can regard as having helped him is an unwonted ground with me for self-gratulation. I think that your tenacity of purpose, foresight, tact, temper, discretion and patience, are beyond all praise, and I esteem it an honor to have been in any degree associated with you. Your name will loom big hereafter, for your movement must prosper, but mine will not survive unless some other kind of effort of mine saves it.

I am exceedingly glad of what you say of the Connecticut Society. May it prosper abundantly!

I thank you for your affectionate words which I return with
interest and remain, for I trust many years of this life,

Yours faithfully,
Wm. James.

At this point, rather than in the dusty corners of the
usual preface, I wish to express my obligation to Herbert
Wescott Fisher, whom I knew at school.   It was he who
led me to see my need of technical training, neglected in
earlier years.   To be exact, however, I must confess
that I read rather than studied rhetoric.   Close application to its rules served only to discourage me, so I
but lazily skimmed the pages of the works which he
recommended.   But my friend did more than direct
me to sources.   He proved to be the kindly mean
between the two extremes of stranger and intimate.
I was a prophet not without honor in his eyes.   Upon
an embarrassing wealth of material he brought to bear
his practical knowledge of the workmanship of writing;
and my drafting of the later parts and subsequent
revisions has been so improved by the practice received
under his scrupulous direction that he has had little
fault to find with them.   My debt to him is almost
beyond repayment.

Nothing would please me more than to express specifically my indebtedness to many others who have assisted
me in the preparation of my work.   But, aside from calling attention to the fact that physicians connected with
the State Hospital and with the private institution
referred to—the one not run for profit—exhibited rare
magnanimity (even going so far as to write letters which

helped me in my work), and, further, acknowledging anonymously (the list is too long for explicit mention) the invaluable advice given me by psychiatrists who have enabled me to make my work authoritative, I must be content to indite an all-embracing acknowledgment. Therefore, and with distinct pleasure, I wish to say that the active encouragement of casual, but trusted acquaintances, the inspiring indifference of unconvinced intimates, and the kindly scepticism of indulgent relatives, who, perforce, could do naught but obey an immutable law of blood-related minds—all these influences have conspired to render more sure the accomplishment of my heart's desire.

XXXII

"My heart's desire" is a true phrase. Since 1900, when my own breakdown occurred, not fewer than one million men and women in the United States alone have for like causes had to seek treatment in institutions, thousands of others have been treated outside of institutions, while other thousands have received no treatment at all. Yet, to use the words of one of our most conservative and best informed psychiatrists, "No less than half of the enormous toll which mental disease takes from the youth of this country can be prevented by the application, largely in childhood, of information and practical resources now available."

Elsewhere is an account of how my plan broadened from reform to cure, from cure to prevention, —how far, with the co-operation of some of this country's ablest specialists and most generous philanthropists, it has been realized, nationally and internationally, through the new form of social mechanism known as societies, committees, leagues or associations for mental hygiene.

More fundamental, however, than any technical reform, cure, or prevention—indeed, a condition precedent to all these—is a changed spiritual attitude toward the insane. They are still human: they love and hate, and have a sense of humor. The worst are usually responsive to kindness. In not a few cases their gratitude is livelier than that of normal men and women. Any person who has worked among the insane, and done his duty by them, can testify to cases in point; and even casual observers have noted the fact that the insane are oftentimes appreciative. Consider the experience of Thackeray, as related by himself in "Vanity Fair" (Chapter LVII). "I recollect," he writes, "seeing, years ago, at the prison for idiots and madmen, at Bicêtre, near Paris, a poor wretch bent down under the bondage of his imprisonment and his personal infirmity, to whom one of our party gave a halfpennyworth of snuff in a cornet or 'screw' of paper. The kindness was too much . . . He cried in an anguish of delight and gratitude; if anybody gave you and me a thousand a year, or saved our lives, we could not be so affected."

A striking exhibition of fine feeling on the part of a patient was brought to my attention by an assistant physician whom I met while visiting a State Hospital in Massachusetts. It seems that the woman in question had, at her worst, caused an endless amount of annoyance by indulging in mischievous acts which seemed to verge on malice. At that time, therefore, no observer would have credited her with the exquisite sensibility she so signally displayed when she had become convalescent and was granted a parole which permitted her to walk at will about the hospital grounds. After one of these walks, taken in the early spring, she rushed up to my informant and, with childlike simplicity, told him of the thrill of delight she had experienced in discovering the first flower of the year in full bloom—a dandelion, which, with characteristic audacity, had risked its life by braving the elements of an uncertain season.

"Did you pick it?" asked the doctor.

"I stooped to do so," said the patient; "then I thought of the pleasure the sight of it had given me—so I left it, hoping that someone else would discover it and enjoy its beauty as I did."

Thus it was that a woman, while still insane, unconsciously exhibited perhaps finer feeling than did Ruskin, Tennyson, and Patmore on an occasion the occurrence of which is vouched for by Mr. Julian Hawthorne. These three masters, out for a walk one chilly afternoon in late autumn, discovered a belated violet bravely putting forth from the shelter of a mossy stone. Not until these worthies had got down on all fours and done ceremonious homage to the flower did they resume their walk. Suddenly Ruskin halted and, planting his cane in the ground, exclaimed, "I don't believe, Alfred—Coventry, I don't believe that there are in all England three men besides ourselves who, after finding a violet at this time of year, would have had forbearance and fine feeling enough to refrain from plucking it."

The reader may judge whether the unconscious display of feeling by the obscure inmate of a hospital for the insane was not finer than the self-conscious raptures of these three men of world-wide reputation.

Is it not, then, an atrocious anomaly that the treatment often meted out to insane persons is the very treatment which would deprive some sane persons of their reason? Miners and shepherds who penetrate the mountain fastnesses sometimes become mentally unbalanced as a result of prolonged loneliness. But they usually know enough to return to civilization when they find themselves beginning to be affected with hallucinations. Delay means death. Contact with sane people, if not too long postponed, means an almost immediate restoration to normality. This is an illuminating fact. Inasmuch as patients cannot usually be set free to absorb, as it were, sanity in the community, it is the duty of those entrusted with their care to treat them with the utmost tenderness and consideration.

"After all," said a psychiatrist who had devoted a long life to work among the insane, both as an assistant physician and later as superintendent at various private and public hospitals, "what the insane most need is a *friend!*"

These words, spoken to me, came with a certain startling freshness. And yet it was the sublime and healing power of this same love which received its most signal demonstration two thousand years ago at the hands of one who restored to reason and his home that man of Scripture "who had his dwelling among the tombs; and no man could bind him, no, not with chains: Because that he had been often bound with fetters and chains, and the chains had been plucked asunder by him, and the fetters broken in pieces; neither could any man tame him. And always, night and day, he was in the

mountains, and in the tombs, crying, and cutting himself with stones. But when he saw Jesus afar off, he ran
and worshipped him, And cried with a loud voice, and
said, What have I to do with Thee, Jesus, Thou Son
of the Most High God? I adjure Thee by God, that
Thou torment me not."

EPILOGUE

And then what happened?—a question that may come to the mind of the reader. Having told the story of my least happy years and laid bare experiences which perhaps give a strange picture, I present supplementary material which tells, in part in autobiographic form, of happier years and of what has been accomplished by forces that evidently awaited the impulse of a story like mine to set them in motion. It has also been my privilege to help keep them in motion by founding The National and International Committees for Mental Hygiene, and The American Foundation for Mental Hygiene, and serving them continuously as an active officer ever since they came into existence.

EPILOGUE

THE MENTAL HYGIENE MOVEMENT

As I have noted in the preceding pages, this book was neither conceived nor written merely as an entertaining story; it was intended to serve as the opening gun in a permanent campaign for improvement in the care and treatment of mental sufferers, and the prevention, whenever possible, of mental illness itself. It was not conceived as an end in itself, but rather as the beginning —the first step—of a movement calculated to organize public opinion, scientific knowledge, and a humane application of that knowledge, into a unified force directed toward the attainment of the goal in view. I had abounding faith in the possibilities of such a movement. That faith has been justified by the origin and growth of the Mental Hygiene Movement since the first publication of this book a quarter-century ago. From its modest beginnings—a book, an ideal, and the determination to realize that ideal—the movement has spread not only across the continent, but around the world.

To-day The National Committee for Mental Hygiene, which I founded twenty-five years ago, is an ever-growing organism, firmly grounded on a sound basis of research and concrete achievements. To the Connecticut Society for Mental Hygiene, organized by me as a sort of demonstration project, there have been added nearly thirty more State Societies.   There are national societies in more than thirty countries, representing all the continents.   In 1930, the First International Congress on Mental Hygiene was held in Washington, at which time an International Committee was founded to coördinate the work of the national organizations and to help plan for future International Congresses, at intervals of about five years.   As an aid in financing the movement in this country, The American Foundation for Mental Hygiene was established in 1928, under virtually the same management as that of our National Committee.

The story of the building of this movement might well be entitled "The Romance of the Work."   For to me, at least, my "difficult enterprise"—as Charles W. Eliot termed it—has been a veritable romance, not lacking in thrills and dramatic moments, as one obstacle after another has been met and surmounted.

When the dream of an organized movement for mental health set forth in the pages of "A Mind That Found Itself" had become a living, active reality, I was repeatedly asked to add to my autobiography a personal account of the movement's origin and growth.   It may be interesting to furnish this sequel mainly in the form of letters which throw some sidelights on the movement and which afford, cumulatively, a more or less coherent picture of its growth.

The story of the work was an integral part of the narrative in earlier editions of my autobiography. Reasons for now making virtually two books of what was formerly one are reflected in the following letter from

Dr. Wilbur L. Cross, formerly Sterling Professor of English Literature and Dean of the Graduate School at Yale University:

New Haven, Connecticut.

September 12, 1921.

DEAR MR. BEERS:

Your extraordinary book I have followed with profound interest through its various editions since you showed me a typewritten copy of a preliminary draft more than fifteen years ago. I was absorbed in the story you then told. You may remember that I thought you had the material, which was at that time not wholly in literary form, for an autobiography comparable to De Quincey's "Confessions." Through your efforts has since been organized The National Committee for Mental Hygiene, with affiliated State Societies; and agencies similar to the National Committee have been established in foreign countries, and an "International Committee" is in process of formation.

After these accomplishments, it seems most fitting that you should now rearrange the contents of your book by giving the story of your experiences as one continuous narrative while reserving for an appendix all other matters. In the proofs of the revised 5th Edition of your autobiography, I read without a break the wonderful tale you told me many years ago. You have now produced a strange and thrilling account of your experiences, in such form that the gain for literature is immense.

In short, your book is destined to become a classic. Believe me,

> Yours most sincerely,
> WILBUR L. CROSS.

A leader in the field of psychiatry and mental hygiene, Dr. C. Macfie Campbell, Professor of Psychiatry at Harvard University, who did me the favor of examining the proofs of my revised edition, sent me the following letter:

> Cambridge, Massachusetts.
> September 20, 1921.

DEAR MR. BEERS:

I have just read the page proofs of the fifth edition of "A Mind That Found Itself," with the same fascination with which I read the book on its first appearance. Every reader, lay or medical, cannot but be carried away by the rush of the narrative. The psychopathologist may here and there modify the values given by the author and have personal interpretations to suggest, but he finds in the book both a story of absorbing interest and an important clinical document. I admire your courage and talent in having, like Mr. A. C. Benson in "Thy Rod and Thy Staff," transmuted a distressing personal experience into a valuable literary product. What I admire still more is that, while Mr. Benson has produced an essay of great beauty, you have furnished us not only with a literary ornament but with a powerful weapon and instrument of social progress.

It is a sharp weapon with which to smite the hydra-headed abuses connected with the treatment of insanity, abuses dependent on mediæval thought, medical ignorance, social indifference, personal greed and insensitiveness, political depravity, financial restrictions. Even more than as a weapon of offence is your book valuable as a peaceful instrument of social improvement. I do not suppose that, when you were so cheerfully forging this trenchant weapon and thinking of reform, you foresaw how rapid would be the development of the movement represented by The National Committee for Mental Hygiene, of which you were the inspiration. This movement, which had its origin in a desire to correct abuses, has developed into a broad health movement, dealing with those complex functions which mean most to human life.

The National Committee for Mental Hygiene has helped much in relation to the immediate practical problems of mental disorder and mental defect; it has emphasized the important bearing of these topics on such great social problems as delinquency and dependency of all types; it has consistently aimed at bringing into education principles of prophylactic value, which promise to develop a more robust personality than the traditional education; it would introduce into the management of industrial and economic problems the consideration of factors involving the personality of the individual worker, which in the past have been strangely neglected.

The field of mental hygiene is coextensive with the field of human endeavor; progress cannot be left altogether to the unorganized good-will of the well-meaning, but requires organization of forces and the clear formulation of problems and policies.

I, therefore, consider that in following up the publication of your book by the organization of The National Committee for Mental Hygiene, you have made a social contribution of very great value. Those who have vague ideas on the exact nature and scope of this important movement will find in "A Mind That Found Itself" a tale of intense human interest, and an admirable introduction to some of the practical problems of mental hygiene.

Cordially yours,
C. MACFIE CAMPBELL.

From William James came the following comments:

Cambridge, Massachusetts.

April 21, 1907.

DEAR MR. BEERS:

You ask for my opinion as to the advisability and feasibility of a National Society, such as you propose, for the improvement of conditions among the insane.

I have never ceased to believe that such improvement is one of the most "crying needs" of civilization; and the functions of such a society seem to me to be well drawn up by you. Your plea for its being founded before your book appears is well grounded, you being an author who naturally would like to cast seed upon ground already prepared for it to germinate practically without delay.

I have to confess to being myself a very impractical man, with no experience whatever in the details, difficulties, etc., of philanthropic or charity organization, so my opinion as to the *feasibility* of your plan is worth nothing, and is undecided. Of course the first consideration is to get your money, the second your Secretary and Trustees. All that *I* wish to bear witness to is the great need of a National Society such as you describe, or, failing that, of a society somewhere that might serve as a model in other States.

Nowhere is there massed together as much suffering as in the asylums. Nowhere is there so much sodden routine and fatalistic insensibility in those who have to treat it. Nowhere is an ideal treatment more costly. The officials in charge grow resigned to the conditions under which they have to labor. They cannot plead their cause as an auxiliary organization can plead it for them. Public opinion is too glad to remain ignorant. As mediator between officials, patients and the public conscience, a society such as you sketch is absolutely required and the sooner it gets under way the better.

Sincerely yours,
WILLIAM JAMES.

Incidentally, this letter, which appears in the second volume of "The Letters of William James," edited by his son, Henry James, is prefixed by this interesting note:

"[It] is addressed to an active promoter of reform in the treatment of the insane, the author of 'A Mind That Found Itself.' The Connecticut Society for Mental Hygiene and The National Committee for Mental Hygiene have already performed so great a public service that anyone may now see that in 1907 the time had come to employ such instrumentalities in improving the care of the insane. But when Mr. Beers, just out of an 'asylum' himself, appeared with the manuscript of his own story in his hands, it was not so clear that these agencies were needed, nor yet evident to anyone that he was a person who could bring about their organization.

"James's own opinion of the treatment of the insane is not in the least overstated in [this] letter. He recognized the genuineness of Mr. Beers's personal experience and its value for propaganda, and he immediately helped to get it published. From his first acquaintance with Mr. Beers, he gave time, counsel, and money to further the organization of The National Committee for Mental Hygiene; and he even departed, in its interest, from his fixed policy of 'keeping out of committees and societies.' He lived long enough to know that the movement had begun to gather momentum; and he drew great satisfaction from the knowledge."

In addition to receiving the endorsement of outstanding men like Professor James, it was most important to the success of my plan that I secure the approval of some medical men who had made a special study of mental diseases and had first-hand knowledge of the problem of State care of the insane. I took an important step in this direction by enlisting the interest of Dr. Adolf Meyer, who was then Director of the New York State Psychiatric Institute at Ward's Island, and who later became Director of the Phipps Psychiatric Clinic at The Johns Hopkins Hospital in Baltimore. I had been told that he was the one man of all others in his special field whose support should be secured, if possible. Through the courtesy of Dr. Stewart Paton, I was able to submit to Dr. Meyer the page proof of my book and outline my plans. This proved to be a most fortunate occurrence, as Dr. Meyer for a long time had wished that some auxiliary movement such as my plan called for might be inaugurated in this country. He and I, therefore, at once began to collaborate.

To Dr. Meyer belongs the credit for selecting the term "mental hygiene" to characterize the movement, an apt selection expressing not only the idea of the amelioration of conditions among the insane, but also that of prevention of mental disorders. And it was he, who, because of his profound knowledge of the scientific, medical, and social problems involved, did more than anyone else to place the initial work on a sound basis. After my manuscript and plans had been carefully examined by him, he sent me the following letter, which helped secure the coöperation of other psychiatrists and hospital officials whose support at that time was so essential to success:

Ward's Island
New York City.

October 27, 1907.

To Whom It May Concern:

Since about a month ago, when Mr. Clifford W. Beers was introduced to me by Dr. Stewart Paton, I have had an unusual experience in finding in him a man not only without a chip on his shoulder, but one with a sound and worthy conviction that something must be done to meet one of the most difficult, but also lamentably neglected problems of sociological improvement. Unlike so many ex-patients to whose efforts we owe in many ways the preposterous forms of legislation concerning the insane and many prejudices about the hospitals, Mr. Beers has given us a description of his personal experiences, has pointed out his own impressions and suggestions for remedy and has asked for advice with an open mind, with such willingness to accept and use new conceptions of matters not broadly enough viewed by him before that it looks as if we had at last what we need: a man for a cause. The difficulties to be met are such as to be unsurmountable to anyone who has not the personal experience and instinctive foundation for what must equal a religious vow of devotion of his life to a task before which others have become opportunistic, if not indifferent.

Mr. Beers plans to subordinate his activity to a body of men and women who shall be chosen by a temporary Board of Trustees of the cause. It will be a difficult task to find the not very common level-headed and well-informed persons in various parts of the country capable of organizing the public conscience of the people. Neglected by physicians and dreaded by the fiscal authorities, the facts are not available to-day, except in fragments] mixed up with innumerable extraneous considerations; the hospitals are closed corporations, the press injudicious in inquiry and reform, and those capable of judgment unable to get the facts. The crying needs persist in the meantime. Instead of a Federal land fund (the 12,225,000 acres bill and ideal of Dorothea Dix, which failed of adoption by Congress) we must have a permanent survey of the facts and efficient handling of what is not prevented. Information must be put into practical form for communication and teaching, and brought home where it will tell; in opportunities of work and education for physicians and coöperation between our educational forces and those who labor for physical hygiene and prophylaxis.

Most of us are already under too many definite obligations to meet the call for devoted work for the maintenance of an organization as well as can Mr. Beers. In my judgment, he deserves the assistance which will make it possible for others to join in the work which will be one of the greatest achievements of this country and of this century—less sensational than the breaking of chains, but more far-reaching and also more exacting in labor.

A Society for Mental Hygiene, with a capable and devoted and judicious agent of organization, will put an

end to the work of makeshift and short-sighted opportunism, and initiate work of prevention and of helping
the existing hospitals to attain what they should attain,
and further of adding those links which are needed to put
an end to conditions almost unfit for publication. What
officialism will never do alone must be helped along by
an organized body of persons who have set their hearts
on serious devotion to the cause.

If Mr. Beers gets the means to pursue his aim, he will
secure the body which will guarantee proper judgment in
a cause which has been a mere foster-child in the field of
charitable donations merely because it seemed too difficult. Here is a man who is not afraid of the task. May
he get the help to enable him to surround himself with
the best wisdom of our Nation!

ADOLF MEYER.

As was to be expected, the first person I invited to
become a member of the National Committee was
William James. His acceptance follows:

Cambridge, Massachusetts.

November 23, 1907.

DEAR MR. BEERS:

I gladly consent to serve as an honorary trustee of your
Society for Mental Hygiene.

I understand that our duties are primarily to let our
names serve as evidence for our belief in the utility of
such an auxiliary organization as your book proposes;
secondarily to appoint the working committee, secretary,

etc., when the thing reaches its working stage; and, finally, to act as general court of appeal in questions of policy about which the eventual active trustees might be in doubt.

I hope that most of the gentlemen whom you have thought of as possible trustees will feel as I do, that it is not only a duty, but a privilege to promote so humane a cause.

Sincerely yours,
WM. JAMES.

My early work received gratifying support in the form of acceptances of membership in The National Committee for Mental Hygiene by more than thirty outstanding leaders in various fields, among them Dr. Jacob Gould Schurman, Professor Russell H. Chittenden, Miss Jane Addams, Miss Julia C. Lathrop, Major Henry L. Higginson, Hon. George Wharton Pepper, Dr. Henry van Dyke, Dr. William L. Russell, Canon Anson Phelps Stokes, Dr. Frederick Peterson, and Dr. August Hoch.

Having secured the necessary support, I now felt secure in placing my book before the public. It was published in March, 1908, and immediately attracted wide and favorable attention in this country and abroad.

When "A Mind That Found Itself" was published, the projected National Committee for Mental Hygiene could have been founded at once. This, however, did not occur until February 19th, 1909, as it was thought best that a State Society should first be established by way of experiment on a smaller scale. Therefore the

Connecticut Society for Mental Hygiene, which began its work on May 6th, 1908, was founded. While serving as its Executive Secretary and developing its work and financial resources, I continued to enlist support for the National Committee. With bound copies of my book now available and a collection of favorable opinions in my possession, my task became easier. That is, it was easy to gain moral support. Securing funds for the work, however, was difficult. I therefore continued my efforts to secure not only acceptances of membership, but opinions likely to influence potential donors.

In acknowledging the receipt of a complimentary copy of my book, sent apparently at the psychological moment, the late Mr. Jacob A. Riis, under date of April 3rd, 1908, wrote:

"A woman, to whom a year or two ago I gave a lift that helped open the bars of the worse than prison in which she was confined without just cause, came into my office, the other day, with tears in her eyes and asked me to read your book, which she hailed as the promise of freedom for, she said, 'countless hundreds' of men and women as unfortunate as she was. And now to-day I found it upon my desk. I shall read it—I know already from the reviews what to expect—and I hope my poor friend is right. Meanwhile let me thank you very heartily for your gift. The world is so busy that it passes such suffering by unheeding because it 'has not time' to heed. If your book shall make it stop and pause, you have certainly rendered a service to your day that ought to be a monument indeed. *We will all help.*"

On April 10th, 1908, Mr. Riis wrote again, as follows:

"I have nearly finished your book and I am quite ready to help, for I see it is needed. My friend was right, and in losing your reason you found, I hope, ours for us in this pitiful matter."

In seeking advice as to the best way to organize The National Committee for Mental Hygiene, I naturally consulted those in charge of the work of similar organizations. Dr. Livingston Farrand, then the Executive Secretary of the National Tuberculosis Association, now President of Cornell University, wrote as follows, under date of April 25th, 1908:

"I read your book last night. The best proof of my interest is that I finished it before going to bed. It is one of the most striking and convincing documents that I have ever seen.

"I have long felt that one of the most important phases of the present great movement in the direction of preventive medicine, and at the same time one of the most neglected, is that of mental hygiene. There is no doubt at all that very great good could be accomplished by an educational campaign dealing with the causes, prevention and adequate treatment of abnormal mental conditions. I do not believe that there could be a better means of engaging public interest than by making an attack upon the present shocking abuses in the treatment of the insane the peg upon which to hang the broad educational movement, which, after all, is the object of chief importance.

After thinking over your propositions with some care, I see no reason why a national movement such as that you plan should not be entirely successful, and I am writing not only to thank you for the stimulus which your book has given me personally, but to assure you of hearty coöperation wherever possible in assisting such a movement. You have my very best wishes and renewed assurances of my coöperation."

On many occasions Dr. William H. Welch, the acknowledged leader of the medical profession in this country, then Dean of the School of Hygiene at The Johns Hopkins University, rendered great assistance. Under date of May 24th, 1908, he wrote:

"I am glad to see that your efforts are beginning to be fruitful and that State and National Societies are to be formed to carry on the work.

"Your book, which you kindly sent me, I read with great interest, and do not see how it can fail to be of great service. So far as I have observed, its reception both in the medical profession and by the general public has been sympathetic and encouraging. My copy has been loaned to several friends upon whom it has made a strong impression.

"I hope that you will continue to lay special emphasis upon the need of psychopathic hospitals and wards in connection with general hospitals, and especially with the university medical school. The greatest need is for improved care and treatment of early and curable cases of mental derangement and for border-land cases which can be prevented from passing into the insane state; also for better instruction of students and physicians in psychiatry. These needs will be better met by psychiatric institutions in connection with general hospitals and university clinics than by the familiar type of hospitals for the insane existing in this country."

On July 10th, 1908, Dr. Welch sent me another letter telling me that my book had played a part in the negotiations with Mr. Henry Phipps that led to the establishing of a Psychiatric Clinic at The Johns Hopkins Hospital. Thus I had the satisfaction of knowing that another of my objectives, as presented in the first edition of my autobiography, was being achieved. The letter read in part as follows:

"I knew that none would rejoice more than you at the good news, and you may look upon the benefaction as one of the fruits of your efforts. Mr. Phipps became interested in the subject as the result of some remarks which I made at the time of a visit in May to see the workings of the dispensary for tuberculous patients which he has established in connection with The Johns Hopkins Hospital. These remarks were incidental and without thought of making an appeal to him. Shortly after his return to New York I received a letter saying that he was interested in what I had said about the need of improved care of the insane and desired further information. I then wrote him rather fully about the need of an institution such as those known in Germany as psychiatric clinics, and it will interest you to know that among other pamphlets, etc., I sent him my copy of your book, in which I marked many passages. His son, Mr. John S. Phipps, who was in his father's councils in this matter, also procured a copy of your book.

"When I told Mr. Phipps later how pleased you would be with his gift, especially as I could say that your book had influenced him, he himself expressed his pleasure at this. I told the reporters also about this feature, and mention of you and the book was made in the Baltimore papers, although not with as much detail as should have been the case, if they had reported my remarks more fully and accurately.

"I want you to know these facts, as they must be a great encouragement and gratification to you. The Phipps Psychiatric Clinic will, I think, be in a measure a fulfillment of your dreams."

As Mr. Phipps had shown so convincingly that he was interested in improving the treatment of mental diseases, he was invited to become a member of The National Committee for Mental Hygiene, which invitation he readily accepted. Here at last was a man who, when he understood the needs of the organization, would, I believed, give financial as well as moral support. Of moral support, the National Committee had a great deal; of financial support it had very little. Indeed, its only financial support was that which I gave it indirectly through loans made to me, personally. Though I could ill afford to assume these obligations, the fact that the National Committee was not yet organized and had no funds for preliminary expenses made it necessary for me to do so. There was one loan, however, made to me by Professor William James which he converted into a contribution toward the initial expenses of organization. I had written Mr. James for advice regarding the advisability of asking Mr. Phipps to "take over" the debts I had incurred in organizing the National Committee and to trust me or the organization to repay him later. In giving my reasons for wishing to appeal to Mr. Phipps for assistance, I had unwittingly appealed to Mr. James, who, until now, had not been told of my debts. As I was innocent of any intention of securing help from Mr. James—one does not think of a university professor as being in a position to play the rôle of philanthropist—I found it possible to accept his gift, so generously offered in the following letter:

London, England.

August 16, 1908.

DEAR BEERS:

You seem to be doing splendidly, and I should be a caitiff not to chip in to the taxes which you have so nobly piled upon your head. So I enclose to you an order on Lee Higginson & Co. of Boston for $1,000 to which extent I am only too willing to bleed for the cause. So you need not think of paying me till you become a millionaire yourself! I wish I could contribute more to relieve you of your indebtedness. I can easily contribute this. In October I shall be home and glad to perform whatever duties my place as committeeman of the National Society may call for.

Sincerely yours,

WILLIAM JAMES.

807 St. Paul Street
Baltimore.

November 27, 1908.

To HIS EMINENCE, JAMES, CARDINAL GIBBONS,
DEAR CARDINAL GIBBONS:

I am writing this line in the hope that you may become sufficiently interested in Mr. Clifford W. Beers and his remarkable book to be willing to encourage the national movement in behalf of improved care and treatment of the insane, and of better mental hygiene in general.

Mr. Beers's book, "A Mind That Found Itself," has made a profound impression upon the medical profession as well as upon the general public.

You will observe that Mr. Beers has secured the support of eminent men in the movement which he has initiated. I feel confident that you would do a great service toward better care of the mentally afflicted, if you should be willing to lend your name in support of the national society to effect this purpose.

With the highest respect, I am

Faithfully yours,

WILLIAM H. WELCH.

ARCHDIOCESE OF MARYLAND
Chancery Office
408 North Charles Street,
Baltimore, Maryland.

November 18, 1909.

MY DEAR MR. BEERS:

Some months ago your work, "A Mind That Found Itself," fell into my hands. I read it with profound interest. To me it is a wonderful book. I scarcely remember ever having read anything which stirred me so deeply, or left upon my memory stronger or more vivid impressions. Its revelations of the sufferings and the tortures which the mentally afflicted have been doomed to undergo must touch even the hardest nature, and arouse compassion in every breast. Its purpose therefore is a noble one, and I have not the slightest hesitation in accepting your invitation to enroll my name among the members of The National Committee for Mental Hygiene, which is at present being organized.

Indeed this movement to mitigate the sufferings and agonies of this class of unfortunates commands my highest admiration and merits my heartiest support.

With sentiments of great esteem, I am

Yours very sincerely,

JAMES, CARD. GIBBONS.

As the pioneer State Society for Mental Hygiene (organized by me in Connecticut in May, 1908) had proved successful, plans for completing the organization of the

National Committee were now decided upon. The formal founding occurred at a meeting held in New York City on February 19th, 1909. At this meeting, plans for work which had been formulated with great care during the preceding year and a half were adopted. To formulate these plans had not been an easy task, as there was no society in existence whose plan of work was sufficiently comprehensive to serve as a model for the work of the National Committee, nor, indeed, of the pioneer State Society of Connecticut, whose plans, by the way, were also made by the group that organized the National Committee. Work previously done, however, in behalf of the insane in New York by the State Charities Aid Association had made it easier to formulate part of the plans of the National Committee, namely, those features relating to State care and to after-care of the insane, in both of which fields the New York State Charities Aid Association had done the pioneer work so far as this country is concerned.

Again Dr. Welch played a vital part in the work, as the following letter indicates:

1063 Fifth Avenue
New York City.

November 4, 1911.

DEAR DR. WELCH:

For some time past I have been thinking of what I could do toward ameliorating the condition of the insane in public and private institutions and I shall be very glad, as mentioned to you this morning, if you will accept Fifty

Thousand Dollars ($50,000) and appoint suitable parties to carry out such views as you may have on the subject. I will send you a check whenever it is required.

Sincerely yours,

HENRY PHIPPS.

Though Mr. Phipps at this time was a member of The National Committee for Mental Hygiene he, like most other members, did not know much about its work—for the simple reason that it had done no active work. But he had read my story and I have reason to believe that its effect upon him, of which he spoke to others later, perhaps inspired this gift. His desire, as stated in his letter, was "to ameliorate conditions among the insane in public and private institutions," which was one of the chief purposes of The National Committee for Mental Hygiene. As might have been expected, Dr. Welch recommended that the $50,000 be given to that organization, which was soon done.

Shortly after the announcement of Mr. Phipps's gift to the National Committee, I received from him a note in which he said: "I should like to take you motoring when you can find time to call, giving me notice of a day or two. We could have an interesting talk."

A week later I spent an afternoon with Mr. Phipps. While motoring he talked about my book and showed lively appreciation of the service I had rendered in publishing it and in organizing The National Committee for Mental Hygiene. Evidently my story had given Mr. Phipps the impression that one who had once suffered a mental breakdown should not, after recovery, work too hard and, above all, should not be subjected to worries. I assured him that I had proved that I had a high degree of resistance both to the strain of work and to such worries as had been involved in carrying my project forward. But Mr. Phipps seemed not to be convinced, for he said, "How much would it take to keep you from worrying?" This was indeed a baffling question put to a man in debt on account of the work—by a man of great wealth, famous for his generosity, who had already shown interest in the project. I told Mr. Phipps that as I was his guest it hardly seemed proper for me to discuss my personal affairs and needs. "I had you come to see me for the purpose of discussing them," he said. "Would five thousand dollars be of use? I want you to have it as a buttress—for a 'rainy day.'" As the period from January 1st, 1907, when I abandoned my business career and an assured salary to give my whole time to the publishing of my book and the organizing of the National Committee, had, in a financial sense, been one continuous "rainy day," I at once accepted this golden bolt from the blue that cleared my financial skies. The next day I received the following note from Mr. Phipps:

> 1063 Fifth Avenue
> New York City.
>
> December 12, 1911.

DEAR MR. BEERS:

It gives me much pleasure to ask you to accept the enclosed check for Five Thousand Dollars ($5,000), to be exclusively for your own use: nothing to do with The National Committee for Mental Hygiene.

Trusting it may add to your pleasure,

Yours sincerely,

HENRY PHIPPS.

This was, indeed, a timely gift, for I had expended more than ten thousand dollars in publishing my book and organizing the National Committee, eight thousand of which represented money borrowed of banks, and of a few individuals who believed in my ultimate success. Through a partial reimbursement secured by the National Committee for the specific purpose and previously voted me by it on account of expenses incurred in its behalf, both before and while serving as its temporary secretary, I had already paid three thousand dollars of my debts. With Mr. Phipps's unexpected gift I was now able to pay all other debts. For the first time in nearly five years, I owed no one a dollar on account of my work. I also had the satisfaction of knowing that my judgment regarding the feasibility of my project had at last been vindicated, for not only was I out of debt, but the National Committee had funds sufficient for at least three years of active work. Soon afterwards I was appointed Secretary with a real, if modest, salary.

Many fortunate occurrences have contributed to the success of The National Committee for Mental Hygiene, chief among them being the securing of Dr. Thomas W. Salmon as its Medical Director when the active work was begun in March, 1912. Having been an officer of the

United States Public Health Service in charge of the mental examination of immigrants at Ellis Island for several years, and a member of the medical staff of a State Hospital and later Chairman of the Board of Alienists of the New York State Hospital Commission, Dr. Salmon was able to place the work of the National Committee on an effective basis within a short time. During the ten years that he served as Medical Director, virtually all of the important plans for work were visioned, formulated and directed by him, especially with reference to special studies, surveys and war and reconstruction work, the most difficult of the many activities of the organization. Fortunate, too, has the National Committee been in having among its most active members leaders in psychiatry, neurology, psychology, general medicine, education, finance and social work in this country, who have given generously of their time in serving as members of its inner committees.

The National Committee was now a going concern. The tendency of the work to find itself occupying a wider and wider field is illustrated by an address delivered in September, 1912, by Dr. Lewellys F. Barker, former Professor of Medicine at Johns Hopkins University, who for several years served as President of the National Committee. To quote in part:

"By a campaign for mental hygiene is meant a continuous effort directed toward conserving and improving the minds of the people, in other words, a systematic attempt to secure human brains, so naturally endowed and so nurtured, that people will think better, feel better, and act better, than they do now. Such a campaign was not to be expected before the rise of modern medicine. For only with this rise have we come to look upon states of mind as directly related to states of brain, to view insanity as disordered brain-function, and to recognize in imbecility, and in crime, the evidences of brain-defect. The imbecile, the hysterical, the epileptic, the insane, and the criminal, were formerly regarded sometimes as saints or prophets, sometimes as wizards or witches, often as the victims of demoniac possession, on the one hand to be revered or worshipped, or, on the other, to be burned or otherwise tortured. Now, such unfortunates are looked upon as patients with disordered or defective nervous systems, proper subjects of medical care; some of them are curable; some are incurable, but still educable to social usefulness; a part of them are socially so worthless, harmful or dangerous as to make their exclusion from general society necessary, or desirable. It is but a short step from such a reformation of ideas to the realization that less marked deviations from normal thought, feeling, or behavior, are also evidences either of brains defective from the start, or made abnormal in function by bad surroundings or by bodily disease. As examples of such marked abnormalities may be mentioned those met with in children who are difficult to educate, in young people arraigned in the Juvenile Courts, in adults, who, inadequate to the strains of life, crowd our hospitals or sanitaria on account of 'nervous' or 'mental' breakdown, or who, owing to anomalies of character and conduct, provide material for the news columns of the sensational press.

"Modern medicine has taught us to recognize that the conditions necessary for a good mind include, first, the inheritance of such germ-plasm from one's progenitors as will yield a brain capable of a high grade of development to individual and social usefulness, and, secondly, the protection of that brain from injury and the submission of it to influences favorable to the development of its powers. Now if these doctrines of modern medicine be true, the general problems of mental hygiene become obvious; broadly conceived, they consist, first, in providing for the birth of children endowed with good brains, denying, as far as possible, the privilege of parenthood to the manifestly unfit who are almost certain to transmit bad nervous systems to their offspring—that is to say, the problem of eugenics; and second, in supplying all individuals, from the moment of fusion of the parental germ-cells onward, and whether ancestrally well begun or not, with the environment best suited for the welfare of their mentality.

"The natural sciences are built up by the gradual discovery of causal relationships; and physicians and psychologists have, since the time of Pinel, gone far in the establishment of the laws underlying normal and abnormal phenomena of mind. From the conviction that a proper application of the facts already discovered can vastly improve the mental powers of our people, decreasing to a large extent the prevalence of mental defect and mental disease, has come the impulse to arouse public opinion in favor of a definite plan for mental hygiene. This impulse, thanks to the initiative of a layman, Clifford W. Beers (now Secretary of the National Committee), author of 'A Mind That Found Itself,' whose personal sufferings led him on recovery to devote himself to the cause of mental hygiene, and who enlisted the cooperation of a group of representative men and women, has found expression in the voluntary formation of a National Committee for Mental Hygiene."

As pointed out by Dr. Barker, we immediately found that the usefulness of such an auxiliary organization was bound to spread from fields mapped out to new fields not originally included in the scope of the work. Though written much later, a letter from Dr. Walter E. Fernald, Superintendent of The Massachusetts School for Feebleminded at Waverley (the recognized leader in the field of mental deficiency in this country), shows how we had all builded better than we knew. Under date of November 27th, 1916, Dr. Fernald said:

"Had you begun your work with the express purpose of rendering help to the mentally defective, instead of to the insane, you could not have planned an agency better fitted to cope with the difficulties of the problem of mental deficiency than is The National Committee for Mental Hygiene.

"It has been my privilege to witness and, in various ways, to participate in the growth of the now widespread movement in behalf of the mentally defective. At first this was a slow growth, but during the past ten years— and especially during the past five—it has been one of the most striking social developments of the day. Many individuals, groups and forces have contributed to this fortunate result. The National Committee for Mental Hygiene felt the force of this movement within one year of the time it began its active work in 1912 and wisely began then to bring into its membership physicians who had special knowledge of the problem of mental deficiency. As in all new fields—when pioneer work is done by many unrelated groups and by zealous individuals—there was great danger that propaganda might outrun dependable data and that unwise plans, policies and laws relating to State care of the mentally defective might be hastily adopted in many States. This danger, however, has been averted, and I believe that The National Committee for Mental Hygiene and its affiliated State Societies are destined to continue to influence, along wise and effective lines, the management of all phases of the great problem of mental deficiency."

So many people fail to appreciate that the mental hygiene movement is of vital concern to *everybody* that it seems advisable to present an excerpt from an article that appeared in *Mental Hygiene* (July, 1921), by Dr. C. Macfie Campbell, Professor of Psychiatry at Harvard University. To quote:

"Mental hygiene is not concerned merely with those serious forms of mental disorder which require treatment in State hospitals; it is concerned with those other forms of mental disorders which do not necessarily mean the removal of the individual from his ordinary social environment. A disorder is a mental disorder if its roots are mental. A headache indicates a mental disorder if it comes because one is dodging something disagreeable. A pain in the back is a mental disorder if its persistence is due to discouragement and a feeling of uncertainty and a desire to have sick benefit, rather than to put one's back into one's work. Sleeplessness is a mental disorder if its basis lies in personal worries and emotional tangles. Many mental reactions are indications of poor mental health, although they are not usually classified as mental disorders. Discontent with one's environment may be a mental disorder, if its cause lie, not in some external situation, but in personal failure to deal with one's emotional problems. Suspicion, distrust, misinterpretation, are mental disorders when they are the disguised expression of repressed longings, into which the patient has no clear insight. Stealing sometimes indicates a mental disorder, the odd expression of underlying conflicts in the patient's nature. The feeling of fatigue sometimes represents, not overwork, but discouragement, inability to meet situations, lack of interest in the opportunities available. Unsociability, marital incompatibility, alcoholism, an aggressive and embittered social attitude, may all indicate a disorder of the mental balance, which may be open to modification. Acute phenomena characterized by unreasoning emotional reactions, such as lynching and other mob reactions, waves of popular suspicion sweeping over a country, may be looked upon as transitory disorders. The same factors that are involved in these familiar reactions play an important part in the development of insanity."

The gift of $50,000 from Mr. Henry Phipps financed the first three years of the National Committee's active work. Then came recurrent deficits, when financial resources failed to keep pace with the ever-growing demands made upon the National Committee for advice and assistance. These crises were met, however, through securing substantial gifts from persons of wealth and vision, among them being Mrs. William K. Vanderbilt, Sr., Mrs. Elizabeth Milbank Anderson, Mr. V. Everit Macy, Mr. Payne Whitney, Mrs. E. H. Harriman, the McCormick family of Chicago, Mr. Harry Payne Whitney, Mrs. Joseph H. Choate, Mr. George F. Baker, Jr., Mrs. John Wood Blodgett, Mr. Charles A. Stone, Mr. Marshall Field III, and, during later years, Mr. and Mrs. Henry Walters and Mrs. Edward W. Bok; and the Hon. Calvin Coolidge, Hon. Alfred E. Smith and Mr. Julius Rosenwald, acting for the Estate of Conrad Hubert. To this roll of honor should be added the names of the following funds and foundations: the Rockefeller Foundation, Commonwealth Fund, Milbank Memorial Fund, New York Foundation, General Education Board, Julius Rosenwald Fund, and the Carnegie Corporation of New York. Without this support, neither the National Committee nor the movement could have attained the high degree of success already achieved in what is still a difficult and relatively undeveloped field of endeavor.

The support of the few, rather than that of the many, during the formative years of the National Committee's existence was perhaps desirable. But the time has now come when a wider basis of support is not only

desirable, but indispensable to the healthy growth of
the work.

During the past few years efforts have been made to
secure nominal contributions (of five, ten, twenty-five,
fifty or one hundred dollars), through letters of appeal,
sent to a large number of persons known to contribute to
one good cause or another. As a result, the nucleus of a
supporting membership has been created. But only a
small proportion of the tens of thousands who have become interested in one phase or another of mental hygiene work seem to appreciate that The National Committee for Mental Hygiene, which started the movement,
has worked continuously for twenty-five years under
the handicap of an uncertain and inadequate annual income for the maintenance of its general work. It is
known that many persons have assumed that the National Committee has had no difficulty in financing its
work because of the large gifts and grants made to it by
Foundations, Funds and by a few individuals. To correct this misleading impression of affluence, it should be
said that crisis after crisis in the financial affairs of the
National Committee has occurred and, even now, with its
work a proved success, its budget for each new year is
only partially covered.

To end for all time these recurrent and hampering
crises, an organized effort to secure a large fund to be
used as working capital by the National Committee is
now under way. With such a fund to draw upon, the
work can be developed in keeping with the needs, and
continuous efforts to secure many thousands of contribut-

ing members who will give nominal amounts annually can also be made.

As a further source of strength to the National Committee and security to the movement as a whole, The American Foundation for Mental Hygiene, of which the National Committee is, as it were, a working arm, is seeking a large fund, the interest on which and the principal if necessary (except such part of it as may be given for endowment), will be expended in aiding not only the National Committee, but other agencies and activities in the field of mental hygiene.

The following representative opinions will serve to indicate the recognized need for this Foundation, and the steps that led to its establishment.

THE JOHNS HOPKINS UNIVERSITY
SCHOOL OF HYGIENE AND PUBLIC HEALTH
Baltimore, Maryland.

Office of the Director

December 21, 1926.

DEAR MR. BEERS:

I have been greatly interested in what I have read and what you have told me concerning the proposed American Foundation for Mental Hygiene. It is evident that the project both in its broader aspects and in its details has received the most careful consideration, and I am glad of the opportunity to add my hearty approval and support to this proposal.

For nearly two decades The National Committee for

Mental Hygiene has occupied a field which it has made peculiarly its own.   It has become the most authoritative source of information and has achieved results in mental hygiene which have attracted world-wide attention.

The appeal now made emanates largely from this Committee, which gives assurance that funds donated to the Foundation will yield results in the prevention and cure of mental disorders, in improved care of the mentally afflicted and in the advancement of knowledge by research of the utmost value to mankind.

My attention has recently been called to the appeal made by Dr. Frederick P. Keppel, President of the Carnegie Corporation of New York, for the establishment of smaller Foundations of definite although limited scope.   The American Foundation for Mental Hygiene would be in line with this suggestion and would furnish us an example which might well serve as a model.

I do not know what could make a stronger appeal to public-spirited philanthropy than contributions to a cause so full of promise in results of the highest importance in protecting the mental health of the members of the community.

With best wishes for the success of your efforts in a field to which you have devoted your life work, I am

Very sincerely yours,

WILLIAM H. WELCH.

DIOCESE OF MASSACHUSETTS
1 Joy Street, Boston.

Office of the Bishop   September 17, 1925.

DEAR MR. BEERS:

In planning for "The American Foundation for Mental Hygiene," you may, I believe, do so with confident hope of support; for it has elements which will appeal to the good sense and generosity of the American people, provided you can get concrete facts before them.

The bare statement of the numbers of children and adults who are mentally hampered is startling. The immense and preventable wastage of life and efficiency in relation to the home, to industry and national defense is enough to arouse the Nation.

The heavy load laid upon the sympathies of fathers and mothers in every walk of life through the presence of a mentally hampered child is sometimes beyond endurance.

What are straight limbs, clear eyesight, sound teeth and physical vigor good for if our lives and those of our children are dogged by fears, delusions and evil habits? Happiness is the soul of true civilization and the purpose of Mental Hygiene is to help people to be happy.

You have a great cause. Your first problem is to give to the people the facts and some definite results. Then they will come forward with support. My own experience in helping to secure large gifts for various purposes in which I have been interested, makes me feel that an initial fund of from at least one to five millions of dollars should be your objective.   The income from such a fund would help meet present needs, give financial stability to the movement as a whole, and open ways to secure added resources for new developments and the needs of the future.

Wishing you and your associates complete and early success in your search for the donor or donors who will finance this great project,

Yours sincerely,
WILLIAM LAWRENCE.

Northeast Harbor, Maine.
June 22, 1925.

DEAR MR. BEERS:

The stress of modern life which began about a hundred years ago has already reached a high intensity, and is sure to rise higher in the future as means of communication by land and water, by air, ether, wireless and radio become available in business of all sorts, in the trades and professions, and in social and family life.

The subject of Mental Hygiene will become more and more important as the decades and generations move on; so that the new Foundation you propose to establish will have an ever-widening field.   Hence, its policies should be preventive in large measure, and also flexible and adjustable to the new needs of the future.

Therefore, the work of The National Committee for

Mental Hygiene should be broadened and be made permanent by establishing an independent "American Foundation for Mental Hygiene" with a large income of its own to be dispensed by a carefully selected Board of Trustees. The object of the Foundation should, of course, include scientific research and inquiry into new industrial, social and family conditions.

Sincerely yours,

CHARLES W. ELIOT.

20 West 50th Street
New York City.

February 16, 1926.

DEAR MR. BEERS:

In the proposed "American Foundation for Mental Hygiene," with your usual vision you have outlined a great plan for the further advancement of mankind. With the introduction of health education into all of our public and private schools during the last five years, the physical health of the people is being cared for as never before. The next step should be a corresponding solicitude for the mental health of the growing generations, the training of the children in right-thinking and behavior and in all that conduces to the prevention of mental disorder. Since the children are the race, I do not know of any more magnificent program than one that will insure to them strong bodies and sound and able minds. Where we have so many generous givers to hospitals, colleges, museums and the like, you should be able to

lead someone to see the opportunity for something fundamental and far-seeing and far-reaching in your plan for a
Foundation to deal with the mind.

Yours very truly,

FREDERICK PETERSON.

YALE UNIVERSITY

New Haven, Connecticut.

Office of the President

November 10, 1925.

DEAR MR. BEERS:

The proposal to establish The American Foundation
for Mental Hygiene has my very warm sympathy and
support. It would be difficult to name any other health
field in which preventive and curative work is so impera-
tively needed. Such an organization as the Foundation,
if properly endowed, would serve a highly useful function
in promoting coördination of the efforts now being put
forth to deal with this problem by various individuals
and agencies and would also serve to promote public
knowledge of the needs and the possibilities of successful
attack upon it. No one familiar with the conditions in
our American communities can possibly question the demand for an effective organization of this kind.

Yours very truly,

JAMES R. ANGELL.

BROWN UNIVERSITY
Providence, Rhode Island.

President's Office

May 21, 1926.

DEAR MR. BEERS:

The Foundation proposed may bring relief to millions of persons now in difficulty or wretchedness. For the last half century we have been studying problems of public health, and have made remarkable progress in the conquest of physical disease. Meanwhile all around are many persons who are unhappy, inefficient, or in positive distress, whose troubles lie too deep for ordinary medical practice.

Especially is this true in our schools and colleges, where young people are often blamed, disciplined, or expelled, when the one thing they need is to be understood. The obscure region of mental hygiene is still to most teachers a *terra incognita*. Those who do enter it are usually poorly trained and may do much harm. Every large school should command the services of some physician who is trained to deal with the manifold problems of adolescence and can rescue boys and girls from their fears and repressions and despairs. I wish all success to this great enterprise.

Sincerely yours,

W. H. P. FAUNCE.

SEAWOOD
Kennebunkport, Maine.

July 28, 1926.

DEAR MR. BEERS:

I believe that no thoughtful person can remain indifferent to the project for a Foundation for Mental Hygiene. You are fighting a danger that at one time or another threatens almost every large family group with distress, and often agony, through the seizure of some member of it. We cannot *afford* to fail to coöperate with you.

With best wishes always,

Yours heartily,

BOOTH TARKINGTON.

Envisaging a world-wide movement, as I did even before I began to collaborate with those who later became my advisers, it was logical that I should begin to make the work international in scope at the first opportunity. This came soon after The Canadian National Committee for Mental Hygiene, founded by Dr. Clarence M. Hincks, had been successfully launched in 1918, following the initial meeting held in the home of Mrs. David A. Dunlap in Toronto. At a meeting held in New York City on February 4th, 1919, I outlined a plan for holding an International Congress on Mental Hygiene and creating an International Committee and this resulted in the appointment of an Organizing Committee, with power to proceed.

One of the many letters received from various countries in support of the plan was sent by Sir Maurice Craig,

Consulting Physician in Psychological Medicine at Guy's Hospital, London, and Chairman of the National Council for Mental Hygiene. It read as follows:

87 Harley Street
London, w. 1.

October 27, 1923.

DEAR MR. BEERS:

I am glad to hear that you are able to report a very definite move towards an International Congress. I am certain that nothing but good can come of such a conference. From the medical standpoint and also from that of the lay public, you could not have selected a more fortunate time to hold such a meeting. Much of the knowledge that was collected during the war has now been sifted, and the way is prepared for a very real advance in mental hygiene.

Thirty years of work in psychological medicine have proved to me that by prophylactic measures we can hope greatly to lessen the incidence of mental disorder. I feel that if only we used to the full our present knowledge, a very large number of persons could be saved from breaking down.

The proposed Congress would be very helpful in allowing men interested in the subject to meet and discuss measures which would result in a common line of action in their respective countries, while the papers that such a Congress would be able to issue would be of no small value in setting forth the various ways in which the mental hygiene problem should be handled.

I gladly accept the honor you offer me of becoming a member of the Organizing Committee of The International Committee for Mental Hygiene which is to arrange for the Congress.

Sincerely yours,

MAURICE CRAIG.

Under the auspices of the Organizing Committee, plans for holding in this country the First International Congress on Mental Hygiene gradually took form, in the interest of which I made two trips abroad. It was hoped that this Congress could be held in 1924 or the year following, but not until 1928 was it possible to finance the basic expenses, at which time The American Foundation for Mental Hygiene appropriated the money needed for the purpose. With this guarantee, it was possible to announce that the International Congress would be held in Washington in May, 1930, and that The International Committee for Mental Hygiene would be formally founded at that time. Though it took eleven years to bring these projects to fruition, the unavoidable delay proved to be advantageous as is shown by the representation of virtually all important countries at the First International Congress.

As the reader may have sensed from the foregoing account, my work has had in it the quality of romance. Difficult situations, successfully overcome, have given added zest to it. Unexpected satisfactions have more than offset, and have practically erased, memories of my unhappy and, at times, distressing years as a mental patient. And now, in the 25th Anniversary year of my work, just passed, there was conferred upon me as gratifying an honor as can come to anyone during his lifetime. In response to the request of Dr. William H. Welch, acting as chairman of a Tribute Committee, several hundred 25th Anniversary letters were presented to me, in appreciation of my part in inaugurating the Mental Hygiene Movement. The American Foundation for Mental Hygiene has published them, together with other information about the movement, in a book entitled, "Twenty-Five Years After—Sidelights on the Mental Hygiene Movement and Its Founder,"* as a tribute to the pioneer National Committee for Mental Hygiene upon the completion of its first quarter century.

Dr. Wilbur L. Cross, in his Editor's Preface to the book, writes as follows: "Originally designed as a tribute to Mr. Beers on the occasion of the twenty-fifth anniversary of his founding of the Mental Hygiene Movement, these letters have turned out to be not merely personal tributes but something of much more enduring value. They represent an interesting and authoritative collection of opinions from many parts of the world on the fundamental significance, in nearly every field of human activity, of the movement which received its first impulse from Mr. Beers." Dr. William H. Welch, in his Introduction to the book, says: "Many of the letters from leaders in various fields describe so vividly one phase or another of the movement that the distribution of this

*Doubleday, Doran & Company, Garden City, N. Y.

book, as widely as possible, will aid in its further progress.   Incidentally, the tributes which follow add a new and dramatic chapter to Mr. Beers's autobiography."

It now seems not amiss for me to express approval of the wider use that will be made of the anniversary tributes, though I was at first reluctant to consent to their publication in book form.   Having undergone a period of embarrassment when I gave to the world the intimate account of my experiences while a patient in various public and private hospitals for the insane, and at a time when it was generally believed that "to be once insane was to be always insane," I am human enough to enjoy having in existence a book which shows that my early sacrifice of privacy in the interest of the cause was not made in vain.

It is my hope that those who have done me the honor of reading this summary of developments will read, in the Supplement, the interesting résumé of progress of the Mental Hygiene Movement.

SUPPLEMENT

I

THE MENTAL HYGIENE MOVEMENT
(1908–33) AND ITS FOUNDER

C.-E. A. WINSLOW, Dr.P.H.*

Professor of Public Health, Yale University; President, Connecticut Society for Mental Hygiene

NEARLY thirty years ago a young man—a citizen of Connecticut and a graduate of Yale—was discharged after three years of institutional life in various hospitals for the care of the insane. Twenty-five years ago to a day, this young man, Clifford Beers, with thirteen other men and women, met in the residence of the Rev. Anson Phelps Stokes (now the Faculty Club of Yale University) and founded The Connecticut Society for Mental Hygiene under a plan formulated by Mr. Beers and members of the group that later founded the National Committee. From this tiny seed has grown one of the most notable social achievements of the modern world.

What really happened on May 6, 1908? What was the true significance of this movement? What is mental hygiene?

Mental disease and mental health are fundamentally

---

*Pages 303–17 are an address delivered at Sprague Hall, Yale University, New Haven, Connecticut, at the 25th Anniversary Meeting on May 6, 1933. Other significant honors, selected from the many received, follow, pages 318–24.

medical problems; and the branch of medicine that deals with them is known as psychiatry. Now psychiatry was not born on May 6, 1908. Its history goes back to the dawn of medicine, with roots deep in the soil of folklore. Pinel in France at the end of the eighteenth century introduced the modern humane treatment of the mentally diseased. Fifty years later, a notable reform in the field of institutional care was initiated in this country by Dorothea Dix, and no less than thirty-two new institutions were established for the insane as a result. By the end of the nineteenth century, thanks to Conolly and to the Tukes, to Griesinger, Meynert, Wernicke, Kraepelin, Bleuler, and Krafft-Ebing, a true science of psychiatry was in being.

Yet something wholly new was born in New Haven, on May 6, 1908. Let me read the objectives of the Connecticut Society and ask you to consider their significance. They run as follows:

"The chief purpose of this Society shall be to work for the conservation of mental health; to help prevent nervous and mental disorders and mental defects; to help raise the standards of care for those suffering from any of these disorders or defects; to secure and disseminate reliable information on these subjects; to coöperate with federal, state, and local agencies or officials and with public and private agencies whose work is in any way related to that of a society for mental hygiene."

The psychiatrist—and the physician in general—deals with a single patient and usually with a single temporary state of that patient. The group that met in New

Haven extended their vision both in space and time. They visualized, not a single patient, but a whole community; and they considered each member of that community as an individual whose mental and emotional status was determined by definite causative factors and whose compelling need was for prevention rather than cure.

The Mental Hygiene Movement, then, bears the same relation to psychiatry that the public-health movement, of which it forms a part, bears to medicine in general. It is an organized community response to a recognized community need; and it lays its prime emphasis on the detection and the control of those incipient maladjustments with which the physician *qua* physician never comes into contact, unless specific community machinery and far-flung educational facilities are provided for the purpose.

There have been times and seasons when the fact that psychiatry and mental hygiene are not identical has been made obvious by distinct differences of attitude on the part of their respective exponents. The psychiatrist in his hospital world, face to face with the enormous complexities of advanced mental disease, is deeply conscious of the fact that his science has in many respects scarcely progressed beyond the descriptive stage. It is almost inevitable that he should be alarmed by the growing demand of the public for results beyond the bounds of present knowledge and that he should deprecate what appear to be extravagant claims for its possibilities. On the other hand, the mental hygienist is continually aware of the urgency of the problems pressing for solution and his experience with incipient deviations from normal behavior in the child-guidance clinic or elsewhere gives him concrete evidence that mental hygiene in such early cases does yield positive and concrete results.   It is natural that he should be at times impatient with the conservatism of his colleague.

Fortunately, the Mental Hygiene Movement has, from the first, had the support and guidance of such psychiatrists as Adolf Meyer, William L. Russell, and Thomas W. Salmon.   At the present time both psychiatrists and mental hygienists are more than ever conscious that their objectives are in fact identical and that each group needs the other for the fulfilment of their common task.   Within the past month a committee of our Connecticut Society has laid down our essential objectives in the following words: "To prevent nervous and mental diseases through lay coöperation with the neuro-psychiatric profession in the community."   The essentials of our relationship could not be better stated than in this phrase.

The psychiatrist must furnish the scientific basis on which the whole movement rests.   He must conduct or direct the treatment of the individual.   He must be referee on programs and censor on educational propaganda. (The mental hygiene society has the task of securing state legislation and appropriations, of developing coördinated local programs and securing support for them, of impregnating the schools and the courts with the mental hygiene point of view, and of disseminating sound attitudes toward mental and emotional problems throughout the community as a whole.

On such a basis as this the fourteen pioneers builded at the founding meeting twenty-five years ago. Their names should be recalled with honor to-day. They were, in addition to Clifford Beers himself, Robert A. Beers (his father), George M. Beers (his brother), Miss Rebekah Bacon, James Kingsley Blake, Frederick S. Curtis, Dr. Allen R. Diefendorf, Dr. Gustavus Eliot, Everett G. Hill, William J. Hoggson, Judge A. McC. Mathewson, Dr. Elizabeth Spencer McCall, Dr. Henry W. Ring, and the Rev. Anson Phelps Stokes, Jr. It was significant of the breadth of the movement that this group, small as it was, included representatives of the church, the school, the university, the bench, the bar, the hospital, and the fields of general medicine, psychiatry and social work, as well as a former mental patient and members of his family.

Things moved rapidly thereafter. In 1909 Clifford Beers organized The National Committee for Mental Hygiene. For the first eight years of its existence, the major objective of the National Committee was the accumulation of a solid factual basis for its community program. This was the period of local and state and national surveys, under liberal grants from the Rockefeller Foundation, in which for the first time data were made available as to the actual resources for the care and treatment of mental disease and defect and clear and sound programs were formulated—and in large measure carried out—for better institutional facilities. In the prosecution of this first task, a second need became obvious—the crying need for more specially trained psychiatrists and psychiatric social workers to meet the growing demands of the time; and the National Committee applied itself to this task also, and with notable success.

In 1917 came the war, and the National Committee for a time devoted its entire energies to applying the principles of psychiatry and mental hygiene to the men who formed the armed forces of the nation. The machinery created under its guidance for the detection and treatment of emotional disturbances among the soldiers attracted world-wide attention and made a record in regard to "shell shock" which was astonishing in comparison with that of other countries.

After the war, the scope of the work of the National Committee was gradually and substantially broadened. It did not lose sight of its primary objectives—humane and scientific institutional care of mental disease—but it directed a part of its attention (with the aid of the Commonwealth Fund in 1921) to the subtler and less obvious indications of emotional maladjustment. Steadily and inevitably, like light spreading from a focus to illumine an ever wider territory, the field broadened to include the early but obvious forms of disease that come to the psychiatric ward of the general hospital or the mental hygiene clinic, and to a group of maladjustments that are sufficiently serious to bring the child into conflict with the machinery of the law. Finally, we envisage those still slighter deviations from perfect harmony with the environment which manifest themselves in maladjustment to the social world of the school and the nursery. At each step we go deeper toward the roots of ultimate difficulties. At each step we find the prospect of success more hopeful.

No one is more conscious than the speaker of the degree to which we still fall short of our goals, even with respect to the basic essentials of good institutional care. On the whole, however, no one can look back on the quarter century that has passed without a profound sense of the magnitude of accomplishment. The humanization of legislation, the improvement of institutional facilities, the development of mental hygiene clinic services have made more progress since 1908 than in the nineteen centuries that went before. And this is only a small part of what has been accomplished. The really great thing, as I see it, is that the Mental Hygiene Movement has given us an altogether new attitude toward mental disease and a new comprehension of human personality.

Clifford Beers and his colleagues have taught us, first of all, that the old distinction between the sane and the insane belongs to those "categories which have nuclei, but no boundaries." He has in his own person crossed the border line between violent insanity and a position of unique leadership in the world of men and affairs. He has shown that the doors of a hospital for the insane swing out as well as in.

The second principle which we have grasped is that the varying degree of internal harmony within the individual and the varying degree of accuracy with which that individual responds to stimuli from his environment are determined not by accident or by intention, but by definite laws of cause and effect. Manifestations of emotional maladjustment to society, as has been said, are "not sins, but symptoms." And finally we have learned that the causes that lead to these symptoms can frequently be controlled if they are recognized in time.

There is, of course, in mental disease as in other forms of disease, a definite and sometimes a determining factor of heredity which is beyond our control. In most instances, however, the reaction of any one of us to a given situation is the resultant of a whole series of life experiences reacting upon a primal personality.

We are beginning to understand a little how such life experiences affect the personality and how their influences can be guided and controlled. The child is born with a libido, a will-to-live, which is the source of all human achievement, the *"élan vital"* which drives the race forward. Napoleon said, "I was born to rule"; and we are all born that way. Most of us are not Napoleons, however, and soon the budding life force meets irresistible obstacles. If the conflict that ensues be too severe, the emotional self receives wounds that may never heal. If the nature be pliant, it may yield so completely as to drain all its future of any freedom and initiative. This is perhaps the most hopeless of the possible outcomes of the emotional war of the nursery. If the child is stronger and fights back, there may develop the "no-no" child, the temperamental "anti," the revolutionary. Or the child, too persistent to yield and too pliant to fight, may evade the issue and take refuge in a world of imaginative illusion. All these reactions are in some degree natural and inevitable and useful. The first gives us our solid citizens, the second our prophets and reformers, the third our poets and artists. If any of these reactions goes too far, however, we have a loss of contact with reality, an emotional reaction that is too weak or too strong to meet aptly the situations that elicit it, or one that bears no true relation at all to such situations.

In the home of a Spanish peasant, one may find a pot of what is called "olla podrida." Each day this pot receives contributions from the food uneaten at meals, and each day it is brought to a boil and used as a source for savory, if ambiguous, soup. The pot is never emptied, and if stirred incautiously, it reveals strange and disturbing relics of the past. Such an olla podrida is the subconscious mind. If we once grasp the conception that it is the shadow of this subconscious mind which largely determines our actions and not the cold, clear light of reason, our entire attitude toward ourselves and toward others will become at once more realistic and more tolerant.

The treatment of crime and delinquency, for example, must be transformed—as it is here and there beginning to be transformed—by a new understanding of human nature. Altogether sane human selfishness is a real problem, and deterrents of the conventional type will always have their place in its control. To influence human behavior by seeing to it that social conduct rather than antisocial conduct is rewarded is perfectly good mental hygiene. Yet the motivation of crime, and particularly of juvenile delinquency, is often far more complex than this; and our legal machinery will function with real effectiveness only when it takes this fact into account. Ex-Governor Alfred Smith's suggestion that judges and juries should determine whether a given individual did or did not commit a given antisocial act, and that a special commission of experts, including one or more psychiatrists, should then prescribe the proper treatment, indicates a really sound line of approach.

Most important of all are the influences that mental hygiene must ultimately exert upon the care and training of children in the home and in the school. Our traditional theory of education has been implicitly based on the assumption that man is a rational animal whose conduct can be directed by logical perception of the laws of cause and effect. We know to-day that this view is largely erroneous and that very frequently the methods used to influence conduct on the assumption of the directive force of reason produce effects exactly opposite to those that we intend. Gradually an understanding of the true subconscious emotional sources of motivation is spreading among teachers and parents. Perhaps we do not yet know enough to accomplish much positive good, but at least we know enough to avoid much negative harm. I believe that in the homes of to-day children are exposed in far less degree to the emotional wounds that produce lasting scars than was the case a quarter of a century ago; but the task of remoulding educational procedure to conform to a true knowledge of human personality and the springs of human conduct has only just begun.

It is not easy to exaggerate the importance of the problems that were placed before the world by Clifford Beers on May 6, 1908. As I have elsewhere suggested, "If we attempt to weigh justly the burden laid upon the shoulders of mankind by mental diseases and mental defects, we shall find, I think, that this burden is equivalent to that of all other types of physical disease and defect taken together. We know that the provision of institutional facilities for the care of mental disease and mental defects, even to-day, is approximately equal to the total of hospital beds required for all other conditions; and we know that such facilities are grossly inadequate to meet existing needs. . . . It is the testimony of social workers and nurses, throughout the land, that in the average family the disability due to mental disease and mental defect is fully equal in extent to that caused by diseases of all the other organs of the body put together.

"Nor is this all. The cases of mental disease and mental defect, so pronounced as to require institutional care, are serious enough. Yet if we could really measure all the effects involved, the burden laid upon society by such conditions as these is far less than that created by more widely prevalent, though less extreme, deviations from the normal. It is the innumerable minor emotional maladjustments, hampering us all in our daily lives, which constitute the real burden.   The thousand petty fears, jealousies, prejudices, and inhibitions which keep us, hour by hour, from complete internal harmony, and from a just and perfect reaction to the persons and conditions that surround us—here is the supreme problem of mental hygiene."

In the whole field of human relationships the new science of the mind must furnish the ultimate key.   We are realizing that "it is in mental hygiene thus widely interpreted that the basis of a new industrial order must be found.   There are few disputes between capital and labor that could survive a discussion about the same table by employers and employees, both free from inferiority complexes and defense reactions.   In international affairs the same thing holds true.   We have overstressed economics and ignored psychology as the cause of class struggles and of wars between nations.   It is a supreme value of the League of Nations that it constitutes a great experiment in mental hygiene.   Geneva is no superstate; it is an atmosphere in which straight and honest thinking about international relationships, by men who stand face to face with each other in the public eye, is easier than such thinking has ever been before."

The really significant thread in the history of the human race is the progressive conquest of the forces of nature by the powers of invention and experimentation, beginning with the first use of a stick or a stone as a weapon by our simian ancestor and ending—perhaps— in the far future.   The exciting moments in this history have been those in which a new field of phenomena has been transferred from the region of dark and uncontrollable fate to that of courageous and purposeful scientific experimentation.

I never look at the tower of the Empire State Building without a thrill of pride in the mastery of the laws of mechanics and of æsthetics that made its glories possible. If the human race had lived only to create a thing of such power and beauty, it would not have lived in vain. As we gaze at it, however, and think of the world crisis that coincided with its completion, the contrast between our mastery of engineering materials and our helplessness before economic forces comes irresistibly to mind. During the past two months we have seen for the first time a courageous and purposeful attempt on a grand scale to control those forces by intelligent planning. Some of the methods may fail, some may succeed; but we shall learn in the process. The main thing is that we have taken the first great step; we have abandoned the fatalistic attitude of *laissez-faire;* we have begun to assert the mastery of the scientific method in the economic field.

It was this first great step that was taken in the field of human behavior twenty-five years ago.

We pass next to the crowning event of this anniversary celebration—the presentation of "Exhibit A." Rarely has a great movement been so truly the shadow of a single creative spirit as in this instance. Clifford Beers, the man "who lost his mind and found it again," has been its prime mover from the first. He wrote the book that outlined the problem so clearly as to catch the vision of the human race. He planned the little gathering in New Haven twenty-five years ago. He saw the movement grow—he made it grow—from that little room in the house at 149 Elm Street, to cover the state of Connecticut, the United States, the whole world; and in 1930 fifty nations were represented at Washington, D. C., in the First International Congress on Mental Hygiene which he planned and carried into execution, just as he planned the gathering of those fourteen persons on May 6, 1908. In the present anniversary year he has been showered with tributes and congratulations from psychiatrists, and other physicians, university presidents, lawyers, clergymen, educators, social workers, and sociologists. They furnish impressive evidence that some prophets are not without honor and—what is more important to Clifford Beers—that the Mental Hygiene Movement has indeed come of age. In comment on "A Mind That Found Itself," William James wrote to its author: "Your tenacity of purpose, foresight, tact, temper, discretion, and patience are beyond all praise, and I esteem it an honor to have been in any way associated with you. Your name will loom big hereafter, for your movement must prosper." That judgment has been justified and that prophecy fulfilled.

The objective of psychiatry and mental hygiene is the study of human personality. Could the importance of that study be better exemplified than in this story of what one human personality has accomplished for the welfare of the human race—the personality of Clifford Whittingham Beers—the Founder of the Mental Hygiene Movement?

OTHER ESTIMATES OF THE MENTAL HYGIENE MOVEMENT AND ITS FOUNDER

"A Mind That Found Itself" is one of the most remarkable autobiographies ever written. Its author, Clifford Whittingham Beers, in telling frankly the story of his experiences while mentally ill some thirty years ago, has shown high moral courage, unusual vision and great tenacity of purpose under difficult circumstances. To convert what at one time seemed a wrecked career into one so useful that thousands have already benefited is indeed a rare achievement, made possible through the enthusiastic interest and support which he has secured from neuro-psychiatrists, educators and psychologists of this and other countries.

A prophet not without honor in his own country—since Yale University, his Alma Mater, conferred upon him in 1922 an honorary degree—Mr. Beers, during the summer of 1923, was signally honored abroad.   In Belgium he was received in private audience by King Albert at the Royal Palace in Brussels, and by Cardinal Mercier at Malines; and later, while in France and England, through interviews and addresses, he enlisted the interest of various leaders in the international phases of the Mental Hygiene Movement.   At a meeting in Paris, held in the Great Amphitheatre of the Sorbonne, filled to overflowing, Mr. Beers, who was the guest of honor, was given an ovation after his address.

It is not only as a writer and a constructive force in humane endeavors that Mr. Beers has won recognition. Though his autobiography was first published in 1908, when he was only thirty-two, he has won an international reputation as the founder and accredited leader of the Mental Hygiene Movement. As a result of his efforts, the First International Congress on Mental Hygiene was held in Washington in 1930, with fifty countries participating, at which an International Committee, to coördinate the work of mental organizations throughout the world and to arrange for future Congresses, was established. Following his third visit abroad, in 1932, in the interests of the Second International Congress to be held in Paris, the French Government conferred upon Mr. Beers the Cross of Knight of the Legion of Honor; and in May, 1933, the Gold Medal of the National Institute of Social Sciences was awarded him in recognition of his services to humanity.

WILLIAM H. WELCH

BALTIMORE, MARYLAND

"You have handled a difficult theme with great skill, and produced a narrative of absorbing interest to scientist as well as layman. It reads like fiction, but it is not fiction; and this I state emphatically, knowing how prone the uninitiated are to doubt the truthfulness of descriptions of abnormal mental processes. I think that your tenacity of purpose, foresight, tact, temper, discretion and patience are beyond all praise, and I esteem it an

honor to have been in any way associated with you.
Your name will loom big hereafter, for your movement
must prosper." *William James**

"Among your friends and supporters, the most interesting and remarkable personage, to my thinking, was
William James. His letters to you about your work,
and his gift of a thousand dollars to your cause—for him
a very large gift—must have been very delightful to you,
and helpful also. They moved me very much as I read
them last evening; and I hope that they will move to aid
you some among his numerous friends and admirers
who can afford the luxury and enjoy the privilege of
liberally endowing worthy and competent agencies for
promoting human welfare." *Charles W. Eliot*

"Dr. Philippe Pinel, during the French Revolution,
risked his life and liberty when he insisted that the insane were sick human beings, and pleaded for, and
secured, official permission to unshackle the so-called
maniacs in the asylums of Paris. Clifford W. Beers,
through the imperilment of his life and an actual deprivation of liberty, has transformed our ideas concerning the management of the mentally diseased. His
personal message has created a new understanding of
the mentally afflicted. Through finding his own mind,
he was enabled to awaken and foster a public conscience
against the incompetence, abuse, and injustice so preva-

*It was William James who wrote the Introduction to the first
edition of "A Mind That Found Itself," published in 1908.

lent in institutions for the mentally ill. . . . The world may celebrate the tercentenary of Shakespeare's folio edition, but its social value has been inconsequential compared with this autobiography. Disregard its really literary excellence, ignore its merit as a psychological document, cast aside its historical values, still one cannot escape its inspirational character, or fail to recognize its power as a social instrument for promoting human welfare."

Survey Graphic, New York City

A similar estimate of the value of Mr. Beers's services was given at the 16th Annual Meeting of The National Committee for Mental Hygiene, when Dr. Bedford Pierce, for thirty years Medical Superintendent of the York Retreat in England, where William Tuke in 1795, without ever having heard of the work of Dr. Pinel in Paris, instituted humane care and treatment for the insane, said that "the name of Mr. Beers will go down to posterity with those of Tuke and Pinel as one of the great benefactors of humanity."

Yale University, in June, 1922, conferred upon Mr. Beers, himself a graduate of Yale, the honorary degree of Master of Arts. "His life," Professor William Lyon Phelps said upon that occasion, "has been filled with spiritual adventures. He is the author of a book apparently destined to become a classic, 'A Mind That Found Itself.' In this, with unmatched eloquence of sincerity, he has described his terrific experiences in that obscure border-land beyond the bounds of sanity. On his return to the world of causation, instead of trying to forget his sufferings, he determined to use them for the benefit of mankind. Besides the extraordinary influence of his book, both in the field of literature and human helpfulness, Mr. Beers has labored incessantly for the cause of mental hygiene. No explorer on land or sea has shown more inflexible courage than has Mr. Beers in penetrating beyond the frontiers of orderly thought." When President Angell conferred the honorary degree, he said it was "for indomitable courage and devotion in turning to the enduring benefit of mankind experiences that have driven most sufferers to silence and seclusion."

At the dinner held in New York City in November, 1929, in celebration of the Twentieth Anniversary of The National Committee for Mental Hygiene, Dr. William H. Welch spoke as follows:

"The history of great movements, like that of Mental Hygiene, is often very obscure. It is often a difficult thing to disentangle all the threads which lead to some great movement. In the tuberculosis movement, it is a rather complicated story before you come to the actual conception of the movement as we recognize it to-day. But the historian will have a very easy task when he inquires into the origin of this movement. I don't know any kindred movement where the story can be told in so few words, so directly. It is one man, Clifford W. Beers, and it is one book, 'A Mind That Found Itself.'

Other books have been written by those who have gone through mental disturbances, but no book in any way, in my judgment, is comparable to his. It is of interest to psychologists, of interest to psychiatrists, of interest to humanitarians—to all who are interested in great social movements.

"We recognize, dangerous as judgments of one's contemporaries may be as to the historical niche which one may occupy, that Clifford Beers's name is imperishable in connection with the launching of this great movement."

The American Psychiatric Association, the oldest national medical society in the United States, which, in all its history, has admitted to membership only a few laymen, elected Mr. Beers an honorary member at its 80th Annual Meeting, in recognition of what he, his book and The National Committee for Mental Hygiene had done toward bringing about a better understanding on the part of the public regarding problems of institutional management and the nature, treatment, and prevention of mental disorders.

II

THE MENTAL HYGIENE MOVEMENT—
MORE RECENT DEVELOPMENTS

LUTHER E. WOODWARD, PH.D.

Field Consultant, National Committee for Mental Hygiene

WITH full faith in the dynamic nature of the Mental Hygiene Movement which he started, Mr. Beers stipulated in his will that all editions of his autobiography shall include a record of the continuing progress of the movement. Dr. Winslow has well described the originality of the mental hygiene viewpoint and its significance during the first twenty-five years. It remains to add the high lights and trace the major trends of the movement since 1933. This can be only an account of high lights and trends. A complete history of the movement would require a volume of several hundred pages rather than a chapter.

A brief account of developments in this field is difficult because mental hygiene affects every department of human activity. The basic institutions, namely, home, school, and church, are vitally concerned with it. And there have been stirrings of interest in all our other institutions. Organized efforts have been made to apply the mental hygiene viewpoint in medicine, the law, education, criminology, social work, economics, industry, and even in international relations.   The movement which Mr. Beers started to secure better treatment of the mentally ill, without losing that interest, has become more and more concerned with the mental health of all the people—with preventing illness and unhappiness and with insuring opportunities for healthy personality development and the achievement of a full and satisfying life.

Moreover, because the mental and emotional life of people is peculiarly susceptible to tensions arising from social changes, such as prosperity and depression, war and reconstruction, and the atomic bomb and its challenge to peace building, the major focus of the mental hygiene movement changes accordingly.   Because attention is given currently to problems of greatest concern and emphasis is shifted as needs change, mental hygiene work has sometimes appeared opportunistic and its major long-term goals have not always been clear. Yet even a cursory study of its history to date reveals that certain goals have been pursued steadily, although more popular attention has been given to the more dramatic projects which change with the times.

THE CARE OF THE MENTALLY ILL

Recent exposés by novels and by magazines and newspaper stories have given graphic evidence that the United States and its forty-eight sovereign states have not properly provided for the care of their mentally ill.   Yet substantial efforts have been made every year since the beginning of the Mental Hygiene Movement. Following the first publication of Mr. Beers's autobiography surveys were made in practically every state of the Union, with the result that additional hospitals for the care of the mentally ill were established. Virtually every year some additional studies were made, architectural plans for proper buildings have been supplied to the appropriate divisions of state government, professional standards for psychiatry, general medicine, psychiatric social work, and other services have been set up, and information has been given to all inquirers who have had interest in or responsibility for such services. Notwithstanding all this and the much-extended hospital building program of the Public Works Administration during depression years it became increasingly apparent that services were not at all keeping pace with psychiatric and general medical advances. As compared with the jails and almshouses of the pre-Dorothea Dix era, the so-called hospitals for the mentally ill were an improvement. But compared with the best of care which people ill from other diseases receive in general hospitals throughout the country, the treatment of the mentally ill has left much to be desired.

In the late thirties there was a growing conviction in professional circles that the situation was unhealthy. Consequently under liberal grants from the Rockefeller Foundation the National Committee for Mental Hygiene, American Psychiatric Association, United States Public Health Service, and several other professional organizations combined in a nation-wide mental hospital survey under the direction of Dr. Samuel W. Hamilton. This survey revealed some bright spots, but in the main the picture was one of inadequacy if not neglect.   Studies of 169 hospitals in forty states were made by the Survey Committee Field Staff over a three-year period. Reports of these surveys were made available, in so far as officialdom permitted, to legislators, governors, and other public officials and to citizen groups interested in raising the standards of service.

The survey revealed that most hospitals were understaffed with regard to medical, nursing and other personnel.   In only two of the forty states were mental hospitals free from overcrowding, and some states had four times as many hospital beds in relation to population as others.   Political interference in hospital management and particularly in the appointment of personnel was rife in fourteen states and it sometimes occurred in eight more.   Only fourteen states had legal specifications regarding requirements of psychiatric training and experience for hospital superintendents, and only eight states had a department or a division of a department with a qualified psychiatrist as administrator in charge of the state's mental institutions.   In only fifteen states were the hospitals engaged in any out-patient clinical or social services or other community mental health work.

That was the situation in 1940.   Naturally, during the war which soon followed, many psychiatrists and other physicians, nurses, and social workers were drawn into the armed forces, the Red Cross, or other war-related services, thus depleting still further the professional personnel to serve the civilian mentally ill. This dearth of personnel combined with the increased demand by relatives and communities that more of the mentally ill be cared for in the state hospitals truly led to deplorable conditions, such as have been depicted in magazines and newspapers.

There are many reasons for the stubbornness of this mental health problem. For one thing, statistically it is our major national health problem with a little more than 50 per cent of all patients in our hospitals and institutions consisting of the mentally ill and feeble-minded. But the problem is not alone one of size and cost. Primarily it seems to be a psychological one. Illness of the mind offers to the average individual a much more severe threat than even the most serious and most loathed diseases of the body. Because of the close linking of the mind and the self people do not want to think anything could go wrong with their minds. Consequently they do not want the reminders of seeing mentally ill people, and because mental illness has tended to stigmatize whole families it has been popular "to put away" those who have become mentally ill. Almost universally states have erected their mental hospitals well outside urban centers, partly because land is cheap there but also so that patients will not be so much in evidence.

It was logical enough that the National Committee for Mental Hygiene and other professional organizations sought to get the facts and bring about results by bringing the facts to the attention of professional groups and divisions of government which shared responsibility for our mentally ill. That that approach was not adequate is now clear. It still remains to be seen whether the recent wave of exposés which has brought the horrible conditions involved in the care of the mentally ill to the attention of the masses will bring about desired results or not. The people must do more than cry, "How terrible!" In the few places where there has been recent improvement in provisions for the treatment of the mentally ill, this has come about through dynamic leadership in the state government and insistent demand on the part of the people that their legislators make adequate provisions for decent care of the mentally ill. The spread of information regarding mental illness which occurred during the war has also made a difference. Psychiatric rejections for military service and discharge of large numbers of men who broke down under combat or other military conditions brought home to every community the fact that even outstanding and seemingly stable men may become mentally ill under sufficient stress. This has helped greatly to remove the age-old stigma and to bring the mentally ill within the pale of respectability, sufficiently like ourselves to be worthy of adequate care and treatment. This partial loss of stigma which for generations was attached to mental illness and the increased interest on the part of rank and file citizens offer new hope.

There is now, too, a different viewpoint among professional groups. For the first time the problems of the mentally ill are being seen in proper perspective. There is a new demand that psychiatric services be organized on a community or area basis rather than by isolating those who are so ill that they have to be hospitalized and dealing with them in a sort of social vacuum which takes too little into account, both the environment from which they have come and that into which they hopefully will return. As Preston,[1] Stevenson,[2] and others[3] have pointed out, the psychiatric function of society must be brought nearer to the community and the centers of research and learning. Those who are administratively responsible for the treatment of seriously ill should also have responsibility for the care and treatment of psychoneurotic patients, the care and guidance of behavior problems especially in children, give consultation to teachers, social workers, nurses, ministers, general practicing doctors, and others in the community who deal with people in trouble. The psychiatric leadership responsible for all of these functions should also aid in ferreting out and correcting defects in the community which contribute to mental disorders and breakdowns. With such a reorientation procurement of staff and the maintenance of staff morale would be much easier, for the work would be dynamic and the job challenging.

[1]Preston, George H., "The New Public Psychiatry," *Mental Hygiene,* Vol. 31, No. 2, April 1947, pages 177–84.

[2]Stevenson, George H., "Needed A Plan for the Mentally Ill." New York *Times Magazine,* July 27, 1947.

[3]Memorandum on the Future Organization of the Psychiatric Services, prepared jointly by the Royal College of Physicians, British Medical Association, and the Royal Medical Psychological Association. Supplement to the *British Medical Journal,* London, June 16, 1945.

CHILD GUIDANCE AND COMMUNITY CLINICS

After the first wave of concentrated attention to the treatment of the adult mentally ill, consistent efforts have been made on the preventive side, especially by way of developing child guidance and other community psychiatric clinics. (As the treatment of psychotic patients was put on a more scientific basis, as the psychoanalytic view became more prevalent in this country and more attention was given to the psychiatric treatment of psychoneurotic persons, and again as studies were made of children and youth who were involved in delinquency or whose behavior problems made home and school adjustment difficult, child guidance and other community clinics seemed to offer increasing hope.) The demonstration work carried on originally by the National Committee for Mental Hygiene, by the Bureau of Children's Guidance in New York City under the direction of Dr. Bernard Glueck and Dr. Marion Kenworthy and continued by the Institute for Child Guidance under the direction of Dr. Lawson Lowrey, and by a few community clinics in other major cities, gave proof that the community clinic is a most helpful tool for early treatment and for prevention of more serious disorders. This led to the establishment in the National Committee for Mental Hygiene of a Division on Community Clinics which has operated since 1927. Most of these efforts until very recently have been directed toward the establishment of child guidance clinics on a sound, professional, and community basis. In 1946 the work of the

Division was broadened to include the establishment of clinics to serve adults as well as children, partly with a view to establishing a pattern which may be used in setting up all-purpose clinics under provisions of the National Mental Health Act.

Through the years the Community Clinics Division has surveyed many communities both as to the need for child guidance service and the readiness of the community for it in terms of the adequacy of other health and social service provisions. At all times it has upheld high standards in planning and organization. The Division staff has visited the clinics, met with clinical representatives at headquarters and at medical and scientific gatherings, has influenced the training and selection of personnel, promoted central and uniform statistical recording, and has maintained close working relationships with other national agencies and leaders in other fields which impinge on child guidance work. Except during the worst phases of the depression there has been steady growth of child guidance clinics throughout the country, and the amount of service during the first ten years of the work of the Division of Community Clinics was doubled. In 1937 there were 631 clinics giving general community service. There were then fourteen states without any type of psychiatric clinic. It was then true and still is that community clinic services are largely concentrated in large cities, and that there are still many cities between 100,000 and 250,000 population which have no standard type of child guidance service.

In the last few years the need for out-patient clinical services in the rehabilitation of veterans who had suffered some degree of mental or emotional breakdown has added some thirty mental hygiene clinics administered by the Veterans Administration and additional services for adults by other community agencies. In a few states there has been substantial growth of clinics under the direction of the state bureau or division of mental hygiene, such as in Connecticut, Washington, and Michigan, which bring clinical services to some of the smaller urban centers and to some extent even in rural areas. But it is still true for the most part that rural areas and urban centers of less than 100,000 population are largely without child guidance or other community clinics services. This is a major task still to be done, and its accomplishment awaits, among other things, the availability of larger numbers of well trained psychiatrists, clinical psychologists, and psychiatric social workers.

Since 1935 the Division of Community Clinics of the National Committee with the financial assistance of the Commonwealth Fund has made fellowships available for the training of child psychiatrists to serve as physicians and administrators in community child guidance clinics. This, in fact, has been the chief source of supply since the Institute for Child Guidance closed in 1933. It is expected that training of specialists for child guidance work will be further promoted now under the provisions of the National Mental Health Act.

It has long been conceded that the three-man team

of psychiatrist, clinical psychologist, and psychiatric social worker can give the best service in child guidance. In the early days of the child guidance movement there was a tendency toward rather rigid and somewhat arbitrary division of labor between the several members of the team. During the war, when many staffs were partially depleted and there was unusual pressure for service, a much smaller percentage of the children received all three forms of study. Psychiatric social workers and psychologists have participated more largely in treatment functions, and in other ways the work has been characterized by greater flexibility and more economical use of staff. A corollary to this trend is the demand that all members of the team be very adequately trained so that they can assume independent responsibilities and work effectively without the kind of close supervision which was given ten or fifteen years ago.

During the war years particularly it was impossible to make an adequate survey of the clinics of the country. The best that could be done was to compile a listing of the agencies available for service. A more adequate survey of the situation is now in progress and a directory containing the results of this should be available early in 1948. It is hoped through this study to get a better sense of the variety and quality of work being done as well as the volume of it.

RESEARCH

The Mental Hygiene Movement from its beginning has been most concerned with the education of professional groups and the general public with regard to the mental hygiene viewpoint and with the planning and operation of services that would insure maximal mental health. Far from attempting to do the whole job the National Committee for Mental Hygiene has always encouraged other groups and organizations to extend their activities. This has been especially true in reference to research. Research into the causes of mental illness and psychoneurosis, delinquency, and behavior problems has been carried on independently by many persons and organizations. The professions of psychiatry, clinical psychology, and social research have made numerous studies of research value.

In 1936, for the first time, an important fraternal organization assumed financial responsibility for a major research effort in psychiatry and mental hygiene. Each year since 1936 forty to fifty thousand dollars has been made available to the National Committee for research into the causes and treatment of schizophrenia, through the Supreme Council, Thirty-Third Degree, Ancient Accepted Scottish Rites, Northern Masonic Jurisdiction, U.S.A. Each year, for more than a decade, various projects, usually twelve to eighteen in number, have been aided by the fund, under the direction of Dr. Nolan D. C. Lewis. In the first year, thirteen main research problems were taken up by seventeen of the country's leading investigators and their staffs. Research has embraced the whole life span and covered practically every aspect of the individual accessible to observation and experimentation. For example, in the first year one of the projects dealt with the study of physical and mental behavior differences in newborn babies in a maternity ward. In another center autopsies on deceased dementia praecox patients were made for a comparison of tissue reactions with those found in other, better-known diseases.

A summary of the many research projects and their findings during the first decade of the National Committee's Division of Research is now in the process of preparation, and is expected to be available soon. While our knowledge of the nature and cause of this baffling disease of the mind is still incomplete, the history of the research done thus far shows very substantial progress both in our understanding of the nature of the illness and the development of more effective methods of treatment.

With increasing awareness that many of the physical symptoms of illness have partly if not wholly a psychological basis, an additional fund of ten thousand dollars was secured by Mrs. Edward Lasker for research in psychosomatic medicine. Various additions have been made to the fund. This work is directed by Dr. Edward W. Weiss of Philadelphia. Gratifying progress is being made in the study of arthritis, peptic ulcer, and the psychosomatic aspects of hypertension. Dr. Weiss has also set up several post-graduate courses in psychosomatic medicine, and training in psychosomatic medicine is now accepted by the American Board of Internal Medicine, the Council of Medical Education, and hospitals of the American Association as a most desirable part of the training for certification in internal medicine. Brief psychotherapy for patients with psychosomatic symptoms is being carried on experimentally by the Chicago Psychoanalytic Institute. These are representative of many projects carried on in this field by various groups.

MEETING THE NEED FOR TRAINED PERSONNEL

The promotion of mental health depends largely on the provision of sufficient numbers of well-trained personnel. As Preston pointed out at the annual meeting of the National Committee in 1946, "No building ever cured a patient. Patients can be cured only by trained people. They can be cured at home or in tents or on farms or crowded wards, if there are enough trained people to spend enough time with each patient." And what is true of therapy is equally true of the preventive aspects of mental hygiene. It requires thoroughly trained people to carry on mental hygiene education and to work effectively with children who have primary behavior disorders or show signs of neurosis.

This truth has been recognized almost from the beginning of the mental hygiene movement, notwithstanding the fact that states and municipalities have often made much more adequate provision by way of buildings and grounds than they have for trained personnel. Very early in the movement it was recognized that psychiatric training was pretty much a hit-or-miss proposition, with the widest variations existing among the sixty-eight medical schools in this country. Before the problem could be attacked at its roots, namely at the level of the training institutions, it was necessary to develop some standards of training and experience for the profession. Accordingly, in 1934, on the initiation of the National Committee for Mental Hygiene and with the coöperation of the American Psychiatric Association, the American Neurological Association and the American Medical Association, the American Board of Neurology and Psychiatry was set up to develop standards of training and practice in the professions of psychiatry and neurology and to institute examination procedures whereby qualified practitioners in these fields could be certified. The National Committee has always maintained a complete and current file of all physicians who have thus been certified and has made extensive use of this file in informing inquirers regarding qualified people in their communities.

With standards thus set up it was then possible to move into the field of medical education in general and psychiatric education more specifically. As early as 1920 Dr. Salmon, the first medical director of the National Committee, noted, "No very lasting reform, no very essential change in the treatment of mental diseases will occur until physicians generally are better educated in these matters and have something of the same standards in the care of mental illness that they have in the care of general illness. The education of doctors without clinical material, of course, is nothing but preaching. It is impossible to train physicians to recognize mild and borderland types of mental disease except with rich clinical material. This is best provided for in the university phychiatric clinic. The National Committee has therefore decided to make a drive on this particular subject and try to build up public support of the university psychiatric clinic and try to secure from one source and another some substantial financial aid for the dozen universities which are willing to establish a university psychiatric clinic as soon as reasonable expectation of support is assured."

During the next decade some progress was made in establishing additional clinics in connection with teaching institutions and in improving the quality of psychiatric instruction, both for the general medical practitioner and for those specializing in psychiatry. This occurred, however, only in a limited number of the medical schools of the country.

In 1932 the National Committee of Mental Hygiene set up a division on Psychiatric Education under the leadership of Dr. Franklin G. Ebaugh. During the next eight years this division actively promoted the inclusion of psychiatric instruction in all three years of the medical school curriculum and aided medical schools in arranging for more adequate clinical experience which had long been accepted in other medical specialties but was still being largely neglected in psychiatric education. An extensive volume on the work of the division and in its many surveys and recommendations regarding general medical education and psychiatric education in particular was published in 1942.[4] A follow-up study of the development of psychiatric departments in 1940 revealed radical departure from the traditional isolation of psychiatry in the medical curriculum. In 1932, when the psychiatric education program was launched, there were still sixteen medical schools that taught psychiatry only in the senior year. In 1940 there were only two such schools. In 1940 nearly all grade-A schools handled the subject in the lower years and most of them were approaching high standards of teaching, including fairly adequate provision for clinical experience and training.

During the war years of World War II little organized attention was given to improving the standard in psychiatric education, but with the greatly expanded need for a trained psychiatrist to serve in the armed forces and subsequently in the work of rehabilitation high priority was given to psychiatric educators, and many medical schools thus included more psychiatry in their curriculum than previously. By the end of the war eighteen or nineteen of the sixty-eight schools were providing very adequate psychiatric education, comparable to the education provided in other medical specialties such as surgery and internal medicine. An additional eighteen or nineteen had made fair provision but were still lacking somewhat in adequate provision for clinical training. In the remaining thirty or more medical schools psychiatric education is still decidedly lacking,

[4]Ebaugh, Franklin G., and Rymer, Charles A., "Psychiatry in Medical Education," Commonwealth Fund, 1942.

often poorly integrated with the rest of the curriculum, and limited largely to lectures on acute pathology with little attention to dynamic psychiatry that has its root in the psycho-social development of the individual and the community forces that impinge upon the individual.

Since World War II the Veterans Administration has given decided emphasis to psychiatric education, and of course the in-service training of psychiatrists within the armed forces during the war greatly extended the interest in psychiatry on the part of medical practitioners generally. The Veterans Administration had made fairly liberal provision by way of fellowships and arrangements for half-time study and half-time service. Since its hospitals and out-patient clinics are scattered throughout the country, it has actively promoted some centers which previously had given it little attention. A few schools have for the first time set up regular departments of psychiatry and are including more psychiatric instruction in all three years.

Another influence stemming indirectly from the war which further promotes psychiatric education was the wartime discovery of the prevalence of emotional disorders of the general population. This has greatly increased the need among general practitioners for further orientation in psychiatry and has also increased the demands made by social and health agencies for psychiatric consultation and treatment. Some of this interest is being caught up in medical schools in efforts to train more men for the psychiatric specialty and to give all their graduates some worth-while orientation in the field.

This has led to a greatly stimulated interest on the part of practicing physicians in taking post-graduate study that will increase their understanding of psychoneuroses and psychosomatic disorders and give them some skill in treating these conditions. The National Committee for Mental Hygiene has accordingly held conferences on this subject financed by the Commonwealth Fund which set up special training courses at the University of Minnesota in 1946. This course was enthusiastically received by all who attended and a follow-up study indicates that it yielded genuine results.

From the time of World War I other efforts have been directed to the training of psychiatric social workers. The need for such a group of trained people became acute at the end of World War I, when it became clear that many men returning from the armed forces had suffered some degree of mental and emotional breakdown and would need the aid of specially trained social workers to help them in their family and community adjustments. This led to the provision of professional training initially at the Smith College School of Social Work and a year or two later at the New York School of Social Work. The National Committee staff took a major part in planning this curriculum and participated during the first two years at Smith College, and since that time has usually had on the staff one or more psychiatric social workers who among other things have promoted the professional training for this specialty. Following the organization of the American Association of Psychiatric Social Workers, that organization took over largely the matter of accrediting schools of social work for training in this specialty, but to a large degree education in this field has been promoted by the Division of Community Clinics in setting up standard clinical training programs and in acquainting employing agencies with these standards and in making information available to them.

With the greatly increased demand for psychiatric social workers since World War II and with the prospect of substantial developments in several governmental agencies as well as in many communities, utilizing private voluntary facilities, the National Committee has taken on for at least a three-year project a full-time psychiatric social work consultant, and recently the American Association of Psychiatric Social Workers, under a grant from the Commonwealth Fund, has employed an educational secretary, likewise on a three-year project, to advise the many schools of social work that wish to establish standard training for the specialty of psychiatric social work and to insure that formal instruction and clinical practice are adequate.

The training of psychologists has been less closely associated with the mental hygiene movement per se. University schools of education have largely trained psychologists for use directly in school systems and in the instruction of teachers. Generally the standards of such training vary very widely and in many instances there has been little tie-up with the clinical approach. The result is that many people who receive the doctorate in psychology have not really been adequately trained for clinical work. Recently a joint committee of the American Psychiatric Association and the American Psychological Association has been working on this problem and has recommended to its parent bodies a plan which would remedy this long-standing defect in the training of psychologists, and which, if accepted, would incidentally correct what has often been a defect in the training of psychiatrists. In brief, the plan calls for a doctor's degree in psychology and at least one full year of clinical experience in conjunction with the psychiatrist and psychiatric social worker, and in turn requires that no training institution in psychiatry would be considered adequate unless it also provides for a full-time psychologist who shall have some part in the training of psychiatrists in reference to psychological tests and measurements.

Both after World War I and World War II the National Committee for Mental Hygiene maintained an active personnel service particularly for psychiatrists coming out of the armed forces and seeking either further training or a new civilian position. For a number of years pretty much the same kind of service was given to psychiatric social workers. But the conduct of a full placement and advisory service for professional personnel on a nation-wide basis has not been considered an appropriate service of the National Committee. The Social Work Vocational Bureau has largely performed this function for psychiatric social workers.

The Division of Psychiatric Personnel of the National Committee for Mental Hygiene was organized in

1940 to serve as the clearing house of information on all aspects of personnel work in mental hygiene and related fields. It compiled a Directory of Psychiatrists engaged in institutional, clinical, and private practice, including some 3,500 biographical records, and used it helpfully in reference to inquiries about candidates for positions, personal psychiatric advice, and other purposes. During the war much of this information was used in aiding the armed forces to procure and best place the limited numbers of well-trained psychiatrists available. After the war special attention was given to the training and employment needs of men coming out of the armed forces seeking new positions or training opportunities. Continuously through the years there has rarely been a week in which there were not at least a few professional people who sought information regarding opportunities for training and employment or in which educational and training agencies have not sought information regarding possible personnel.

SCHOOL STUDIES AND THE EDUCATION OF TEACHERS

As has already been indicated, the first movement in the direction of prevention was in the field of delinquency. The very earliest demonstration child guidance clinics were set up specifically to show that the child guidance clinic is a helpful means of preventing a substantial amount of delinquency. It was very soon found, however, that prevention could not be done in relation to the courts alone but inevitably led to all aspects of community life and especially to the school and the home. In the early years of child guidance work considerable attention was therefore given to the school life of children, particularly to the study and treatment of those who showed difficulty in school. It was recognized at once that the teacher is the key person in the school, as she is the one who has the continuous contact with the children. She largely determines the atmosphere and spirit of the classroom, and her ability to wield a hygienic influence on the children depends largely on her personality make-up and her ability to maintain interest, secure coöperation, and give children a sense of security in their relationships within the class.

In 1935, under a grant from the Carnegie Corporation, a series of school studies were undertaken under the supervision of Dr. George S. Stevenson, Director of the Division of Community Clinics. The approach initially was from three angles: (1) A survey was made of thirteen representative teacher training colleges and normal schools in ten states; (2) problems of psychopathology among teachers were studied by direct observation and classroom work in a large city public school system; (3) a study was made of teacher attitudes toward the behavior of children and the reporting and dealing with behavior problems, capacity to secure home coöperation, and other phases of teacher-pupil relationships involving mental hygiene.

During the second year a canvass was made of the methods of selection used in one hundred fifty teachers' colleges, normal schools, and departments of education.

During this year also (1937) the National Committee began the publication of *Understanding the Child,* a 32-page quarterly magazine designed for the special instruction of teachers in mental health principles and practice. Also a number of regional conferences were held on mental health and education to promote mutual interest and understanding and action among educators and mental health workers throughout the country.

In 1939 case conferences were conducted in twenty teachers' colleges in five eastern states to determine the personality factors, undiscernible in students on admission, that are considered significant from the standpoint of mental health, and to develop and refine methods of selection and effective training procedures along mental hygiene lines. Subsequently over a two-year period psychiatric consultation was made available to three teachers' colleges, namely, in New Haven, Connecticut, Trenton, New Jersey, and San Diego, California. The task of these consulting psychiatrists was to determine from observation of students, case studies, faculty opinion, and other means, what are the chief qualities to be looked for in prospective students. In San Diego special attention was given to adverse personality factors that should have excluded candidates in the beginning. In Trenton, attention was centered on the more positive aspects of the study, that is, discovery of personality traits that are the marks of a good teacher. Unfortunately, with the advent of World War II and the exodus of thousands of teachers from their classroom to the armed forces, war plants, and other more remunerative work, standards of teacher selection inevitably slumped, and in many states have not yet been restored to where they were before the war. Follow-up studies of the hundreds of students in training of whom case studies were made about ten years ago should be done in order to determine the actual effectiveness of the standards of selection which were then set up in a number of training institutions.

Two other special school projects are worthy of mention. Under the aegis of the National Committee for Mental Hygiene in the late 1930s educational experiments were initiated in Delaware to demonstrate the feasibility of imparting a knowledge of mental hygiene principles to pupils and teachers, through the medium of normal classroom activity in which excerpts from selected films were presented, as a stimulus to discussion concerning child development and human motivation in general. Later a special film was produced for this purpose. More recently the Delaware Society for Mental Hygiene has sponsored classes in "human relations" in the normal classroom study. With the aid of story-telling and playlets presented by the children themselves they are encouraged to talk about their experiences and their relationships with others. The discussions are directed in such a way as to throw light on the springs of human conduct. This work was extended to sections of New York State and sample materials have been prepared for use in every grade from kindergarten through senior high school. These experiments have been the subject of popular articles which have resulted in hundreds of inquiries coming to the Delaware Society from all parts of the country. There is little doubt that human relations and psychological principles can be taught to children.

Another project in which the National Committee has engaged has been a special kindergarten project conducted in Public School 33 in New York City, as a part of an all-day neighborhood demonstration. In this project very small groups of kindergarten children are drawn from their usual classes to a special room where they are guided and observed by a psychological counselor who has had much work with young children. In the separate room equipped with toys, books, blocks, art material, etc., a small group of children has a chance to select the toys they want and can play with them as they like. Informal talk and play acting help to enrich the information the children have already had in kindergarten. Two regular kindergarten teachers take turns at sitting in in order to observe individual differences in their pupils such as attention span, adaptability, choice and handling of toy materials, etc. Those children are selected for special work who are somewhat shy and withdrawn, who come from homes where little English is spoken, or who give other evidences of special needs.

"Mental Hygiene in the Classroom," a primer for teachers prepared by the National Committee for Mental Hygiene and issued by the National Education Association and the American Medical Association, which presents the principles of mental hygiene in relation to children's problems in a simple, interesting, and novel way, has been used extensively by teacher training schools and especially in in-service courses for employed teachers. This pamphlet sold 5,000 copies during its first year and has had considerable demand through the years since. Books by Ryan[5] and Prescot[6] have served a similar function.

MENTAL HYGIENE ORGANIZATION

Organized efforts to promote mental health have assumed various forms. National leadership in the United States has been given by the National Committee for Mental Hygiene and in Canada by the Mental Hygiene Society of Canada. As was already indicated, the first state society in the United States was the Connecticut Society, which was founded one year before the National Committee. A number of other states organized societies soon after the National Committee was established. At the present time they number thirty-four. A few additional ones were organized but fell apart for lack of an adequate, continuing program and a paid staff. Several societies organized more recently hold promise of being more permanent. Each year the January issue of *Mental Hygiene* carries a complete list of state societies.

The state societies, while maintaining a close working relationship with the National Committee, have been

[5]Ryan, Carson W., "Mental Health Through Education," Commonwealth Fund, 1939.

[6]Prescot, Daniel A., "Helping Teachers to Understand Children," American Council on Education, 1946.

really quite independent. They have not had the kind of organic relationship which has prevailed between the National Tuberculosis and Health Association and the State Associations devoted to anti-tuberculosis work. Objection has been made repeatedly that there should be a closer relationship between the various state societies and the National Committee. At the present time there is a strong sentiment in favor of that. Some things can be done best at the national level, others at the state level, but even in such a problem as obtaining desired federal legislation the state societies are very necessary to acquaint the people of the various states with the need for such legislation and to carry on an educational program which will inform the public and secure the support of the states' representatives in Congress. The procurement of state legislation for the care of its own mentally ill and the inculcation of the mental hygiene viewpoint in the educational system of the state are clearly functions to be performed by a state-wide organization. There is no tendency whatever to take from the state societies any of these very necessary functions. Requests of state societies for closer affiliation with the National Committee take the form of wanting more field service in connection with organizational procedures, program building, and the preparation of basic materials which can be used in the education of the public or of specific professional groups.

To meet some of the requests that were coming to the National Committee for help in organizing state societies, in 1945 two additional field representatives were taken on to give such service. Major assistance was given to Ohio and Oklahoma in organizing new state societies, and some assistance has been given in Kentucky, West Virginia, Florida, and other states that are now requesting help.

In the states which have recently been organizing societies more attention is given to developing a broad membership base and in utilizing existing organizations such as farmer organizations, labor unions, coöperatives, and other citizen groups which have a natural interest in the promotion of the mental health of the people. This trend seems to be all to the good but does require added staff and funds for the development and maintenance of adequate programs that will serve the needs of all the diverse groups.

Through the years there has been considerable growth of local mental hygiene societies. This growth has been very uneven, many states having no such organization, but certain other states, such as Connecticut and Michigan, have for many years had active organizations in many urban centers and in a few rural counties. Local organizations, if they have proper leadership, can be very effective in carrying forward the education of the public and promoting the development of adequate community resources for the discovery and early treatment of people who have problems in mental health.

At the opposite extreme there has been considerable effort along international lines. In 1930 an outstanding International Conference on Mental Hygiene was held in Washington, with an attendance of four thousand, including representatives from fifty countries or more, and another was held in Paris in 1937. Through the years definite national committees or associations have been formed in several South American and European countries and in a few countries in the Far East as well. Some of these inevitably were quiescent during the war period but efforts are now being made to revive them.

The International Committee for Mental Hygiene, which sponsored the first two International Congresses, has recently been reactivated and is sponsoring an "International Conference on Mental Hygiene" which is part of the International Congress on Mental Health to be held in London in August 1948. The Conference is unique in its emphasis on inter-disciplinary group thinking. The program will be built around the reports of small inter-disciplinary discussion groups, called "Preparatory Commissions," which are being established throughout countries represented on the International Committee.

The International Committee is also in the process of organizing a "World Federation for Mental Health" which will take over the present functions of the International Committee and greatly enlarge the program. It is anticipated that the new World Federation will work closely with UNESCO and with the World Health Organization of the United Nations as soon as this organization is properly ratified. Emphasis throughout will be on positive and preventive aspects of mental health, rather than on mental illness.

The President of the International Committee and

Chairman of the Congress is Dr. J. R. Rees of London.
Dr. Frank Fremont-Smith is Vice-President for the
United States and Chairman of the Executive Commit-
tee. Dr. Nina Ridenour is on leave from the New
York City Committee on Mental Hygiene for a year
in order to serve as Executive Officer of the Committee.

MEETING THE SPECIAL NEEDS OF CRITICAL PERIODS

As was noted at the beginning of this chapter, the
emotions and mental attitudes of people are largely influenced by the social tensions of a given period. This
has meant that in every period of stress certain needs
have risen to the surface with such force that special
attention had to be given to them.

This has been especially true during the two world
wars which the present generation has experienced. In
World War I both the Director and the Assistant Director played leading roles in developing the neuro-
psychiatric services in the Army. This was a task for
which there had been virtually no precedent, so that the
work had to be organized from the beginning. While
the selection of men for the armed forces in World War
I was far from what was desired, substantial efforts
were made, and many thousands of the mentally unfit
were eliminated, and with the appointment of divisional
psychiatrists as members of the army divisions, those
men who experienced breakdown in battle were discovered early and treated promptly in field hospital units
behind the front lines and in neurological hospitals far-

ther back in the zone of the advance. Many a neurosis was thus "nipped in the bud." The work of the psychiatrists in the A.E.F. effectively contributed to the fighting efficiency of our troops and to the conservation of man power to such an extent as to earn a personal message of thanks from Dr. Salmon and from General Pershing.

Following World War I there was great need for the development of psychiatric facilities for the treatment of servicemen who had suffered mental breakdown during military service and others who became ill after discharge. The Federal Government was slow in meeting this need, but after some controversy with the administration and considerable agitation by the National Committee and the American Legion, a chain of veterans' psychiatric hospitals was established.

The period immediately following World War I also resulted in the development of psychiatric social work as a major specialty within the social work profession. Reference has already been made to the role of the National Committee for Mental Hygiene in this development.

During the depression years of the early thirties there also were special needs which had to be cared for. While there was no general rise in mental disease in its more serious form, there was substantial increase in milder types of mental and nervous disturbances, behavior disorders, and personality maladjustments, particularly among the unemployed. Psychiatric hospitals reported increasing difficulty in returning patients to the community because of unemployment. There was more overcrowding and it was impossible to secure legislative appropriations for institutional expansion. In many communities budgets for child guidance and other community clinics were cut, and while this resulted in real loss in some communities the pressure of the times did require a careful evaluation of all health and social services and in many instances resulted in the elimination of overlapping and better integration of the various services. With the assumption by the Government of full responsibility for public assistance to those in economic need, family agencies and mental hygiene clinics were left freer to devote their time and energy to problems of human relationship and mental hygiene.

The depression years also brought about a closer association of various national agencies having somewhat kindred interests. During this period the National Committee collaborated more closely with the National Congress of Parents and Teachers in the coördination of mental hygiene with parent-teacher education. The coöperation of national agencies was extended to the field of recreation. Moreover, as the depression wore on and the problems of students completing their formal education obviously became acute, the National Committee for Mental Hygiene and the various national recreation, health, social service, and educational agencies united in study of the needs of youth, the findings of which were of real value to the Government in its establishment of the National Youth Administration.

The National Committee for Mental Hygiene also interceded in Washington on behalf of the various state hospital commissions in obtaining Public Works Administration funds for the building of additional hospitals for the care of the mentally ill.   At least $10,000,-000 was obtained and used in this way.   Other projects of the depression years were concerned to provide employment for unemployed teachers and other groups which were particularly hard hit.   A number of mental hygiene projects were also carried on as a part of the Civil Works Administration.   One such project of importance was a study, state by state, of the Commitment laws in use throughout the nation.   This resulted in recommendation for new legislation that would facilitate early discovery and commitment of patients in need of hospital care without the cumbersome routine of court trials, lunacy commissions, and other awkward residuals of the earlier period when the mentally ill were considered a legal problem rather than a medical one.

MENTAL HYGIENE IN WORLD WAR II AND THE FOLLOWING PERIOD OF RECONSTRUCTION

Only the briefest account of developments during this period is given here since these have been more adequately described elsewhere.[7]   There doubtless has been no period in American history when so much attention was given to problems of mental hygiene.   The National Committee for Mental Hygiene, the American

[7]See Rennie, T. A. C., and Woodward, L. E., "Mental Health in Modern Society," chapters 1–4. Commonwealth Fund. 1948.

Psychiatric Association, and other professional groups were naturally interested to see adequate standards of selection established for men to be taken into the Army and Navy. Aid was given to the Division of Procurement and Assignment in the finding of well-qualified psychiatrists and other auxiliary personnel for assignment to key posts in all branches of the armed forces.

Much special attention was given to the development of procedures for the selection of men to serve in the armed forces so that those likely to break down under stress of military training or active combat could be eliminated as far as possible. Through stimulation by the National Committee for Mental Hygiene in coöperation with various state and local groups, early experimental work was done in compiling social and health history information which was made available to medical examiners and local draft boards. Such work carried on especially in Connecticut, New York, and a few other selected places revealed rather clearly that while it is difficult and in some instances impossible to discover less obvious psychiatric conditions in a brief interview, these conditions are mirrored in the social, health, and work history of men. Studies of several groups of men discharged early from the Army or Navy for psychiatric disabilities revealed that a high percentage of these men were suffering from psychoneurosis or other forms of mental or emotional illness prior to their induction into the armed forces, and almost without exception these conditions would have been revealed by adequate pre-induction history. In the state of New Jersey a follow-up study was being made of 1,200 former schizophrenic patients who had been treated in the hospitals of that state. A few score of these men had found their way into the armed forces. The National Committee secured the coöperation of the various branches of the armed forces in obtaining reports of the military experience of these men and found that a high percentage of them suffered relapse and were discharged after a few months' service. A number of others, particularly those whose illness was of a paranoid nature, had completed military training and had done combat duty for long periods of time. These men were considered, however, to be a hazard to their unit, for although they made violent fighters they sometimes used poor judgment, which endangered their entire units.

In early 1943 the writer was employed by the National Committee to serve in a liaison capacity between the National Committee for Mental Hygiene and National Headquarters of Selective Service in the interest of developing more adequate history-taking procedures to aid in the proper selection. The results of earlier study and experimentation were compiled, and with the coöperation of National Headquarters of Selective Service numerous state headquarters were visited in the interest of developing plans which would be practical for each state in question. Because states differ widely in their organization of health and welfare work and in the availability of significant data, plans had to vary somewhat state by state. Tentative plans for developing history-taking procedures nationally were discussed very early with the heads of the leading national health and welfare organizations, both those that operate services and those that are concerned with professional standards. All of these bodies offered full coöperation and made available information which they possessed regarding resources.

On October 18, 1943, the National Headquarters of Selective Service adopted the medical survey which made provision for the appointment of trained social workers and public health nurses as medical field agents to be attached to local boards and whose work would be to compile social and health information regarding men about to be examined for service in the armed forces. Plans provided for the clearance of all potential inductees against institutional files, for the obtaining of health, family, and work history information from local sources, the record of school achievement and behavior from the secondary schools, and for forwarding this information to the armed forces induction stations immediately prior to the arrival of men for their pre-induction examination.

For various reasons this system did not work perfectly by any means. In the first year of its operation there were no federal funds to defray costs and the examiners at the armed forces induction stations, who were not responsible to Selective Service, ofttimes were not adequately informed about the operation of the medical survey. More supervision, at both state and local levels, of the medical field agents compiling the histories would have been desirable, but notwithstanding these various defects approximately 10,000 social workers and public health nurses were recruited, appointed, and assigned to most of the 6,400 local boards throughout the country. In the fiscal year of 1944–45, when $1,000,000 of federal money was made available, histories were compiled on upward of one million men. The highest percentages of histories and the better histories were compiled in places where there were sufficient numbers of well-trained field agents and where it was the accepted policy to go beyond clearance against institutional and agency files by interviewing registrants, members of their families, employers, family physician, and others who were in a position to know well the individual registrant.

Another mental hygiene project carried on actively during the war, with the aid of the Josiah Macy, Jr., Foundation, was the republication and free distribution to professional men in the armed forces of carefully selected professional articles dealing with psychiatry and mental hygiene, social service, and related topics. More than a million such articles were distributed to medical personnel in the armed forces. A similar project carried on by the National Committee for Mental Hygiene and the Federal Council of Churches involved the republication and distribution of appropriate material to chaplains serving in the armed forces.

In 1943 it became clear that the problem of psychiatric rehabilitation arising from the war would be stupendous. In order to meet some of this need a Division on Rehabilitation of the National Committee for Mental Hygiene was set up under the direction of Dr. T. A. C.

Rennie, who was already conducting an experimental rehabilitation clinic at the Payne Whitney Clinic of New York Hospital under a grant from the Commonwealth Fund. Early in 1944 the writer became Field Consultant of the Division and has continued in this capacity to date. The objectives of the Division's work have been as follows:

1. To encourage and assist communities in extending or establishing psychiatric facilities for the proper care of veterans and others who have psychiatric handicaps;

2. To obtain the inclusion of the mentally handicapped in the plans of the State Vocational Rehabilitation Bureaus;

3. To assist industry in fitting the mentally handicapped veterans into gainful and productive employment;

4. To assemble facts showing the need of psychiatric rehabilitation;

5. To suggest specific methods of providing such rehabilitation;

6. To be in constant communication with the appropriate division of the Federal Government in reference to further legislation and the improvement of existing services;

7. To give field service to states and communities with special reference to points 1, 2, and 3.

This Division was extremely active during the latter part of the war period and the first two postwar years. An early pamphlet, prepared on the basis of the experience of the New York Hospital Rehabilitation Clinic and a few other clinics which were established early, entitled, *A Plan for the Organization of Psychiatric Rehabilitation Clinics,* was widely used and gave impetus to the organization of many special clinics for the study and treatment of men returned from the armed forces with some psychiatric disability.   Through numerous articles and addresses by the Director and Field Consultant, through press releases regarding the work of the Division, and especially through the publication of a pamphlet *When He Comes Back* and *If He Comes Back Nervous,* two talks to families of returning servicemen, much was accomplished in educating the public in regard to the adjustments that had to be made by men returning from the armed forces and by the families awaiting their return.   This pamphlet was widely distributed, selling more than 80,000 copies without special advertising efforts.   The Federal Council of Churches of Christ in America, the National Lutheran Council, and the General Federation of Women's Clubs coöperated in bulk distribution, suggesting to their constituency methods for the effective use of this pamphlet.

Later a handbook entitled, "Jobs and the Man," by the same authors, was published in response to requests from labor and management groups.   The material of this handbook was based upon the experience of the Rehabilitation Clinic of the New York Hospital and upon consultations with professional personnel working in industry, service centers, and rehabilitation clinics. It was designed to serve employers, supervisors, interviewers, foremen, and shop stewards as a guide in their relations with workers, veteran or civilian, with special reference to those who were employing, counseling, or supervising individuals with emotional problems.

Currently, the Division of Rehabilitation is carrying on a project in the vocational rehabilitation of the psychiatrically handicapped in the civilian population. This is designed to bring to the attention of medical and psychiatric agencies the need for attention to appropriate vocational training and employment as a part of the rehabilitation process. The major objective is to work out experimentally effective procedures of case selection, referral, and coöperative relationships between medical and psychiatric agencies on the one hand and the various state bureaus of vocational rehabilitation on the other. Because of wide differences both in the various state bureaus and in psychiatric agencies procedures have to vary somewhat from place to place. It is expected that over a two- or three-year period procedures can be worked out experimentally with such flexibility as may be needed to suit prevailing conditions in the various states. Effort is being made also to determine the size of the vocational rehabilitation job that needs to be done with persons who have had a mental or other psychiatric disability which constitutes something of a vocational handicap. It is hoped to determine also the extent to which vocational rehabilitation should enter into the plans and methods of psychiatric therapy and follow-up.

THE MENTAL HYGIENE MOVEMENT TODAY

Mental hygiene is in the air today as it has never been in the past. There have been previous waves of popular interest in mental hygiene, but the present wave assumes larger proportions. This is borne out by the greatly increased numbers of people from magazines, newspapers, and radio who have sought consultation at the office of the National Committee within the last two or three years, and it is further borne out in the greatly increased number of articles, in professional and lay magazines, which deal with mental hygiene in one or another of its aspects.

Because of this decided wave of popular interest and the greater awareness of mental health needs which has grown out of the war, the demands being made on the mental hygiene organizations are greater than they have ever been. The demands to include the general public on the mental hygiene team are particularly pressing. Through the years substantial efforts have been made to educate the public regarding the principles of mental health and the proper care of those who become mentally ill, but it appears to the writer that throughout most of the history of the mental hygiene movement insufficiently consistent efforts have been made to keep the public informed. It would, of course, have been an equally serious, if not more serious, mistake to have stressed the education of the public to the neglect of training professional personnel to carry on educational programs and to give clinical and hospital services. It is essential that balance be maintained between the various aspects of mental hygiene education. As early as 1920 the late Frankwood Williams stated well this need for balance. "Most educational campaigns in the field of public health—tuberculosis, venereal disease, prenatal care—have a clear, single purpose. Mental hygiene likewise has a single objective but that objective is so comprehensive and is capable of so many important subdivisions and touches with its numerous facets so many major divisions of human activities that it can scarcely be considered pragmatically. It must depend for its attainment upon a forward movement of all of its parts. Balance and proportion as between parts therefore become unusually significant. Balance in stress and emphasis may well be considered as between various major divisions—mental hygiene in education, criminology, the public care of the mentally ill, the mental defective—but decision in such considerations must be left somewhat to circumstances. There is yet a finer consideration and one not dependent upon opportunism—a balance in effort that will lead to the simultaneous preparation, so far as is possible, of the fields represented by the different professional and lay groups concerned in any one of these major activities. A few illustrations may make the point clearer.

"Only unfortunate results could come of a popular campaign for mental hygiene in the field of education if that campaign did not carry with it a campaign among psychiatrists to arouse their interest and coöperation and a campaign among normal schools to equip teachers to meet the new demand. Conversely, a campaign would be fruitless if directed at psychiatrists or the normal schools without the preparation of a general interest on the part of the public and the school authorities so that psychiatrists and specially trained teachers when ready might find a market for their special preparation. An educational campaign among the workers and agencies of the country urging more attention to the mental hygiene side of social problems, or the special preparation of psychiatric social workers, will react harmfully in the end unless at the same time an effort is made to educate institutions and psychiatrists to the benefits to be derived from expert social work. It would not be difficult to arouse the general public in any state to demand an increase in the number of public psychiatric clinics to meet the needs of the community, but such an aroused public interest would eventually turn upon those who had stimulated it unless an equally spirited and successful campaign were carried on among medical schools and elsewhere to prepare physicians capable of meeting the demand anticipated from the coördinated campaign. To be sure, as singly directed campaigns progress, they serve as a challenge to members of coördinated groups and are helpful only if not permitted to get out of bounds.

"Local agencies and organizations interested in a single field may well give their strength to that particular phase of mental hygiene that for the time seems opportune or in which the group is primarily interested, but it is of the greatest importance that the National

Committee in its educational work shall view the field broadly, shall see clearly the relation of the parts to the whole, and shall so direct, advise, and stimulate that no part shall unwisely outrun too far but that the entire front shall move forward. It may happen more slowly but with greater assurance of success."

The wisdom of this policy has been borne out through the experience of the years. The demand to-day is not that the various educational programs should get out of balance but rather that the base of operations should be broadened. Since the war it has become generally recognized that additional members must and can be added to the mental hygiene team. The general physician with adequate orientation in psychiatry and mental hygiene can do much to alleviate the less acute mental and emotional problems of people who seek his help. The same is true of the social worker, the psychologist, the clergyman, the industrial counselor, the educator, the teacher, and the public health nurse. If we can bring about the adequate orientation of all of these groups and increase their skill in guiding and counseling with those who naturally come to their attention in the course of their professional work, we will do much to broaden the base of operation.

A corollary to this is the need to educate our citizens generally in regard to mental hygiene principles and methods of improving our interpersonal relationships. Such education is of equal help to parents, husbands and wives, employers, and to people generally in their social relationships. Such education can be carried on effectively only by much more extensive use of the mass media for education; namely, magazines, newspapers, radio, and films. Mental hygienists as a rule have not had much experience with such mass media and, vice versa, those versed in the techniques of such communication have seldom been adequately informed regarding the facts and principles of mental hygiene. In short, the larger educational job calls for a new kind of close coöperation between the mental hygienists and those who are expert in informing the public.

It has become clear to how great an extent the happiness and satisfaction of the individual are dependent on his basic feelings and attitudes toward himself and his fellow men. Thus sound education of both youth and adults along mental hygiene lines becomes of great importance. Likewise, it is extremely important that sufficient numbers of psychiatrists, psychologists, social workers, nurses, and other professional persons be trained to meet the numerous demands for consultation and the treatment of those who are ill or in trouble, and in so far as added facilities in the form of hospitals, clinics, research centers, etc., are required, those, too, must be provided.

That all of these needs have come to be better appreciated by large numbers of people is clear from the extent to which psychiatric services and mental hygiene have been taken up by public, governmentally financed agencies. The treatment of the severely mentally ill has always been largely a state function, but it is only very recently that extended provisions have been made by governmental agencies for the development of mental hygiene community clinics and other facilities for the study and treatment of the less severely ill and the socially maladjusted. Several federal agencies are now engaged in such a program. The Veterans Administration has set up thirty or more out-patient clinics to serve veterans who need professional guidance and treatment but do not require hospital care. The National Mental Health Act, which became a law in 1946 and for which substantial provision has been made in the 1947–48 budget of the United States Government, calls for the active promotion of research into the causes and treatment of mental illness and makes provision for grants-in-aid to states in the development of all-purpose mental hygiene clinics and in the training of psychiatrists, psychologists, psychiatric social workers, and psychiatric nurses.

The Children's Bureau has been moved from the Department of Labor to the Social Security Administration of the Federal Security Agency with the special function of safeguarding the interests of children, including opportunities to develop sound physical and mental health. Consequently this agency, too, is promoting the development of mental hygiene facilities in especially needy communities.

The Barden LaFollette Act of July 1943 broadened the provisions for vocational rehabilitation to include those with a mental or emotional handicap and made it possible for the state bureaus of vocational rehabilitation to purchase psychiatric treatment and social services as well as to provide training, guidance and placement. This makes vocational rehabilitation service as readily available to the mentally handicapped as to the physically handicapped.

The recently enacted Hospital Construction Act makes provisions for federal aid in constructing hospitals in communities lacking adequate hospital facilities. Federal aid may be given for the construction of hospitals for the treatment of mental or nervous disorders as well as for general medical care.

Moreover, an increasing number of states are establishing active mental hygiene bureaus or departments to provide clinical services for both children and adults in their various communities. In the state of Connecticut funds are now available for the development of psychiatric services in general voluntary hospitals. At last the right to mental health, long recognized as a legal right, is being implemented sufficiently to provide hope that it will be a reality and not merely a legal fiction.

The field of international relations is another new field in which mental hygiene seems about to come into its own. The preamble to the Constitution of UNESCO states: "Since wars are first made in the minds of men, it is in the minds of men also that the defenses of peace must be constructed." While our own Congress seems to be somewhat slow in approving the participation of the United States in a world health organization, it is of interest to note that the problem of peace building is recognized as basically a mental hygiene project. In the various divisions and studies within the UNESCO program outstanding interest has been shown in the section concerned with the study of social tensions that tend to war. Through these means and the World Federation of Mental Health which is being organized there is promise of bringing forcefully to the attention of national and international leaders the significant roles which fear and hostility play in the psychology of war and the corresponding consistency with which personal satisfaction and security tend toward peace.

In summary, the mental hygiene movement is one of the most alive movements of the present time, with no less a goal than the development and maintenance of the mental, emotional, and social health of all the people. It is confronted with tremendous tasks yet to be accomplished, tasks of public education, of professional training, of community organization, of industrial harmony, and of international statesmanship. These are tasks which will require more personnel, more participation by the public, and more adequate financing than the movement has had to date. (In proportion to the number of persons involved in the illness, mental health work has been supported only about one six hundredth as much as has work for the prevention and treatment of poliomyelitis.) It is hoped that the popular interest in mental hygiene and the public demand for education and services will, with proper planning and organization, provide the necessary facilities with which the movement can be carried forward.

III

THE MENTAL HYGIENE MOVEMENT
1948 through 1952
Nina Ridenour, Ph.D.[1]

THE story of the mental hygiene movement from its inception through World War II has been well told by Dr. Winslow and Dr. Woodward in the preceding sections. Under the arrangement that Clifford Beers himself planned, the story is now carried through the postwar years to the beginning of 1953.

THE NATIONAL COMMITTEE FOR MENTAL HYGIENE REORGANIZES

As the mental hygiene movement grew and spread, it was perhaps inevitable that other organizations should spring up with purposes similar to those of the National Committee for Mental Hygiene. By the late 1940s there were two such organizations. One was the Psychiatric Foundation, which had been established as a fund-raising arm of the American Psychiatric Association to do a special job of inspecting and rating mental hospitals. The other was the National Mental Health Foundation, organized in Philadelphia in 1946 by a group of conscientious objectors who had been assigned to

[1]Director, Division of Education, The National Committee for Mental Hygiene, and its successor, The National Association for Mental Health, February 1949 to September 1952; for the year and a half prior to that, Executive Officer, International Committee for Mental Hygiene.

work in mental hospitals during World War II. Although their purposes covered the whole gamut of what needs to be done for the mentally ill and for the promotion of mental health, they concentrated on two particular efforts: education of the public and improvement of the care given mental patients by hospital attendants.

To win broad public support for their common interests it seemed clearly to the advantage of all concerned for these three organizations to combine their energies. Accordingly, in September 1950 a merger was effected and the new organization was called The National Association for Mental Health. The statement of purposes in the by-laws has a familiar ring: "To promote mental health and to work toward the prevention of mental handicap and toward improved care and treatment of persons suffering from such handicap."

Although often in the past good working relations had existed between the former National Committee for Mental Hygiene and the various state and local associations, there had never been a systematic structure of national-state-local relationship. The state and local associations were highly autonomous. No two programs were alike except by coincidence and none of them stood in any defined relation to the program of the national office. This fact had long complicated the problem of providing impetus for a nationwide citizens' movement and that of raising the funds the mental hygiene movement so grievously needed. Consequently the new Association was particularly charged to build a broad base of citizen support—in the tangible form of money and in the form of concerted citizen action. To this end, a membership and affiliation plan was developed. By mid-1952, twenty-seven state mental health associations had become member organizations of the National Association, bringing into the network some two hundred and fifty local associations. For the first time a nationwide approach was initiated for support by Community Chests and United Funds. Simultaneously, plans were developed to launch in the spring of 1953 the most extensive financial campaign ever undertaken in the mental health field.

Although itself in the throes of reorganization during this period, the national office provided as much leadership as limited staff and funds permitted. Series of manuals or guides were prepared on such subjects as how to organize state and local associations (1),[2] how to organize community clinics (2), how to evaluate community needs (3), how to use volunteers in state hospitals (4), and how to set up education programs (5) and publicity and fund-raising campaigns (6). As the 1953 campaign approached, the field staff, which earlier had concentrated on helping state and locals with their organization problems, centered on fund raising. As this goes to press the outcome of the 1953 campaign is still in the future.

THE NATIONAL INSTITUTE OF MENTAL HEALTH

Probably the most important mental hygiene event since the founding of the National Committee for Mental Hygiene in 1909 was the National Mental Health Act, which, promoted and sponsored by the National Committee, was passed in 1946. Providing for funds to be made available on a scale far greater than ever before, backed by the prestige and facilities of the federal government, this act revitalized the entire movement. Responsibility for its administration was vested in the Public Health Service, Federal Security Agency, which in April 1949 established the National Institute of Mental Health. The program of the National Institute falls into three major categories: research; training of personnel; and community services. While the research and training programs are thought of as investments in the future, immediate benefits reach the people through the community

[2] See bibliography.

services program. For research and training, grants-in-aid are provided to appropriate institutions, hospitals, laboratories, etc., and stipends or fellowships to individuals. For community services, grants-in-aid are provided to states and territories for mental health programs outside mental hospitals; state or local funds must supply one dollar for every two supplied by federal funds. Other activities of the National Institute include surveys and biometric studies, and the production and distribution of scientific and popular material on mental health subjects. The budget for the year 1952–53 was eleven million dollars.

ACTIVITIES FOR THE MENTALLY ILL

In the fifty years since Clifford Beers came out of a mental hospital, progress toward better care for mental patients has of course been steady. But no thinking person can feel any real glow of pride in the achievements of the country as a whole. There are too many places where the same evils that Clifford Beers fought against all his life still exist. In assessing the situation one must recognize both the progress and the lack of it. *"Better"* care for mental patients we now have; *"good"* care for all who need it is still far in the future.

One of the weak links in the long chain of proper care is faulty legislation. As a step toward strengthening this link the Federal Security Agency, in collaboration with a number of other organizations, has prepared a "Draft Act Governing Hospitalization of the Mentally Ill" (14). This important document is meant to be used by states as a model statute. Its basic philosophy is that a mental patient is ill, not criminal, and that he needs treatment, not punishment. It protects him against improper commitment or confinement; protects his civil rights and his property; and protects him against such harmful and degrading experiences as the exposure of his private troubles in court. At the same time it also protects the community against persons whose mental conditions do not warrant their living at liberty.

But legislation is only one segment of the total problem. Often it is easier to get good statutes on the books than it is to put them into effect. How are the laws used? What interferes with effective administration? Many groups, both voluntary and official, are concerning themselves with these questions.

For instance, an extensive Study of the Administration of State Psychiatric Services is now being conducted by the National Association for Mental Health and financed by the National Institute of Mental Health. An experienced field staff is analyzing the relation between legal structure and administrative practices. The study will help administrators and legislators recognize the questions they should ask themselves about their own state structures.

Other instances of joint voluntary-official collaboration are found in some of the activities of the American Psychiatric Association. At its annual Mental Hospital Institutes, hospital administrators meet to discuss mutual interests and share the experience of leaders in the field. Any state mental hospital system may request inspection by the American Psychiatric Association's Central Inspection Board as an aid in planning how to improve its own services. About one third of the country's state hospital systems have been inspected and rated, and there is a long waiting list.

At many different places in government there is evidence of a new ferment of interest in the mentally ill and of increasing co-operation between different levels of government and different governmental agencies. One example is the way in which the Veterans' Administration and state hospitals are now beginning to work together, each utilizing the facilities of the other to mutual advantage. Another example is the amount of time devoted to mental illness at the annual meetings of the Council of State Governments. In 1949 a voluminous and impressively documented report entitled "The Mental Health Programs of the 48 States" was prepared in connection with these meetings (15). All the old perennial problems and a few new ones were analyzed: overcrowding, personnel shortages, commitment procedures, operation of clinics, community relations, and so forth.

It does not happen very often in legislation that so simple a device as the omission of a single word in a statute benefits a whole segment of the population. The Barden-LaFollette Act, which for years had provided for the rehabilitation of the physically handicapped, was revised in 1943 so that the word "physically" was omitted. This meant that federal funds for rehabilitation were now available for the mentally handicapped. It was several years before states began to take full advantage of this opportunity but now more and more states are establishing rehabilitation programs for the mentally ill and the mentally deficient. Practical and constructive planning for rehabilitation has been spurred on by three recent studies. Two of these, conducted by the National Committee for Mental Hygiene and the National Association for Mental Health, concerned the vocational rehabilitation of psychiatric patients (16, 17); the third (18), prepared in the Office of Vocational Rehabilitation, Federal Security Agency, concerned the vocational rehabilitation of the mentally retarded.

Everybody who has had firsthand experience with mental patients knows that the hospital attendant is a key person in their treatment. He is closest to the patients and can speed or block their recovery. And yet, until recent years the hospital attendant has been the forgotten member of the psychiatric team. For the most part attendants have been casually selected, ill paid, untrained, unrecognized, and lacking in professional status. With convictions growing out of their own experiences, the founders of the former National Mental Health Foundation set about improving this situation. One of the first things they undertook was to change the name from "attendant" to "psychiatric aide." This name is now widely used; in some places the term is "psychiatric technician." The activities initiated by the National Mental Health Foundation were continued by the National Association for Mental Health and are still moving vigorously forward in collaboration with many voluntary and government agencies. Three "workshops" under the joint sponsorship of the National Association and the American Psychiatric Association have attempted to define the role of the psychiatric aide and to develop standards for selection and training. Since 1947, annual awards have been offered to outstanding psychiatric aides. Their chief purpose is to attract the attention of the public and to endow the position of psychiatric aide with more dignity. That this purpose has been well served is attested by the impressive amount of publicity the awards have obtained, and by the fact that over a hundred mental hospitals and schools for the mentally deficient now participate in the annual nominations. Each nomination is accompanied by a statement about the candidate's ability, often including graphic descriptions of ways in which he has helped patients. An interesting by-product of the entire award project has been the accumulation of this scientifically significant human material showing how important the aide is to the patient. In fact scientific interest in this exact point is growing and the Russell Sage Foundation has recently initiated two studies of the functions and interrelations of personnel on psychiatric wards.

Publications for aides include a handbook (7) distributed by the National Association for Mental Health and a book *Psychiatric Aide Education* (19) which reports the results of a three-year experiment in aide training conducted by the Menninger Foundation in co-operation with the Topeka State Hospital. Several states now have aide training programs, and for the first time a national professional association for aides is being organized.

THE MULTI-PROFESSIONAL PUSH

A few years back, one of the accusations leveled against mental health specialists was their isolation. Now just the opposite is true. Co-operation is everywhere. Trained mental health workers are working more and more closely with people in other professions, and those people are reaching out eagerly for mental health concepts to apply to their own work. One consequence of this conscious effort at cross-fertilization has been a truly astonishing array of important conferences and reports in the last five years. Sometimes these are described as "inter-discipline," or "multi-professional," and sometimes they are unlabeled but just proceed along those lines. Typical examples are the Milbank Memorial Fund conference and subsequent report on "Epidemiology of Mental Disorder" (20) in 1949, and the Jackson Memorial Laboratory (Bar Harbor, Maine) conference on "Effects of Early Experience on Mental Health" (21) in 1951. The Josiah Macy Jr. Foundation's "Conference Program" (22) has included more than a score of conferences on a wide range of mental health subjects, such as "Training in Clinical Psychology," "Problems of Aging," "Problems of Infancy and Childhood," and several on "Personality Development in Childhood." Three Macy conferences on "Health and Human Relations in Germany" were co-sponsored by the World Federation for Mental Health and approved by the U. S. High Commission for Germany.

The Commonwealth Fund, which in the twenties and thirties put the child guidance clinic movement on its feet, has in more recent years tackled basic problems of how to incorporate mental health concepts into pediatrics, public health, and general medicine. A notable series of institutes since 1946 has set patterns which are being widely copied and which are influencing medical education and in-service training everywhere. Several outstanding books have appeared such as the widely used *Teaching Psychotherapeutic Medicine* (23) and *Public Health Is People* (24).

Another lively series of conferences are the semi-annual meetings of the Group for the Advancement of Psychiatry, also started in 1946. This organization set itself to bring psychiatry out of the clinic and into the world of real life, to grapple with practical problems on a wide front. Although some of its committee reports (25) have dealt with technical subjects, such as shock therapy, lobotomy, and statistics, others have studied professional and community problems and branched out into such diverse subjects as psychiatry in industry, in civil defense, in international relations, and in academic education. Practically all reports propose specific recommendations and lines of action.

One other important conference should be noted because it not only cut across professional lines but involved extensive collaboration between professional and citizen groups. This was the Mid-Century White House Conference on Children and Youth, in December 1950, which was attended by more than five thousand people. Its theme—"a fair chance for every child to achieve a healthy personality"—placed it squarely in the middle of the mental health field. It was preceded by a fabulous amount of preparation, with an estimated hundred thousand individuals working on hundreds of agency and committee reports. The factual material (26) assembled for the conference is an impressive contribution to the field.

THE INTERNATIONAL SCENE

Clifford Beers worked long and hard for international mental health. He would have been gratified to know all that has happened internationally in the last five years. The third International Congress on Mental Health (27) held in London in August 1948 was acclaimed highly successful. More than two thousand people attended from nearly fifty countries. Distinctive features were the several hundred small "preparatory commissions" which worked in different countries in advance of the congress, and the excellent statement on "Mental Health and World Citizenship" (8) of the International Preparatory Commission which met at Roffey Park in Sussex, England, for two weeks. The most important event of the congress was the formation of the World Federation for Mental Health, with member societies from twenty-one countries. Each winter since 1948 the executive committee of the Federation has met and there has been an annual summer meeting attended by several hundred people. A fourth International Congress was held in Mexico City in December 1951, and a fifth is planned for Toronto, Canada, in the summer of 1954.

Soon after it was organized, the World Federation was given official consultative status by UNESCO and the World Health Organization, specialized agencies of the United Nations. The relation between the World Federation and the World Health Organization continues to be particularly fortunate because they are able to support each other in the furtherance of their common goals. A single example is a three-week seminar on "Mental Health and Infant Development" held in Chichester, England, in the summer of 1952. The Federation selected the international faculty and ran the conference, while the World Health Organization issued invitations to thirty European governments and paid the traveling expenses of the public health officials who were selected to attend.

In addition to its joint projects with the World Federation, the World Health Organization has itself done some outstanding work in mental health. Its Expert Committee on Mental Health has produced two farseeing reports (28) which are likely to modify public health practices throughout the world. It has also initiated a series of monographs, at least one of which deserves particular mention: Bowlby's

"Maternal Care and Mental Health" (29). This remarkable piece of work, which is both a practicum for present workers and a stimulating guide for future investigators, is already influencing policies both voluntary and governmental in a number of different countries, especially in those agencies responsible for the care of young children who must be placed outside their own homes.

INTERPRETATION TO THE PUBLIC

When in 1949 the Junior Chamber of Commerce announced the first National Mental Health Week, no one foresaw the mammoth operation into which "the Week" would grow in three short years. The first two annual Mental Health Weeks occurred before the merger which brought the National Association for Mental Health into being and soon after the National Institute of Mental Health was established. Beginning in 1951, the National Association undertook the major responsibility for co-ordinating the activities of the large number of organizations participating in Mental Health Week. By 1952 more than five thousand organizations were working with the National Association in carrying the message of mental health to tens of millions of people—through meetings, conferences, forums, lectures, radio and television broadcasts, films and dramatic presentations, magazines and newspapers. It is safe to say that there was hardly a community in the entire country which was not reached by one or another of these means.

Mental Health Week was popular from its inception. For organized mental health groups at all levels—national, state and local, voluntary and governmental—it provided a focus for their year-round educational activities and a peg on which to hang expanded publicity. The National Association planned the major portion of its stepped-up education and public relations activities around Mental Health Week. From the time of the merger in September 1950 through 1952 (at which time this account ends) an estimated eight million pieces of educational and publicity material and audio-visual aids went out from that office.

The way Mental Health Week took hold was a tribute to the hard work and imagination of staffs and boards of the natonal office, the state and local associations, and the many other participating groups, but it was also a sign of public readiness to hear about mental health, evidenced by the avidity with which they reached out for materials. Conscious of the public's readiness and operating on the premise that a major obstacle to mental health progress has been the lack of public understanding, the Division of Education of the National Association developed a philosophy of education to guide both its educational and its public relations activities. Experience has shown that it is important for any organized mental health group to have a clear philosophy of education, particularly in that area where education and publicity overlap. The newly formulated philosophy stated that mental health education includes education *about* mental health and education *for* mental health. The purpose of education *about* mental health (including mental illness) is to inform people of the facts so that they will act as intelligent and socially responsible citizens in providing and supporting adequate community health services. The purpose of education *for* mental health is to bring about understanding of mental health ideas in order to help people get along better with themselves and each other.

It is a phenomenon of the field of mental health that it often gets its best publicity, not from the kinds of events and activities which seem to be regarded as news in other fields, but from *mental health ideas*—in other words, from materials intended as education *for* mental health.

Any number of examples could be cited from the experience of the National Association. For instance, in 1951 the

Association prepared a leaflet entitled "Mental Health Is . . . 1, 2, 3," (9) describing the characteristics of people with good mental health. ("1. They feel comfortable about themselves; 2. they feel right about other people; 3. they are able to meet the demands of life.") The leaflet not only sold two and a quarter million copies in a little over a year but was copied in a large number of other publications and was used again and again by reporters as a peg on which to hang news stories. Thus this leaflet, intended as straight education *for* mental health, provided an extraordinary amount of publicity for the Association. Another pamphlet, entitled "Some Special Problems of Children: Aged 2–5 years," (10) sold over six hundred thousand copies and was widely quoted by press and radio. When the famous cartoon strip "Blondie" (11) was adapted to mental health and produced in a booklet by the State of New York Department of Mental Hygiene, the Department distributed half a million copies and the National Association sold another half million.

Thanks to the pioneering efforts of the National Association, the National Institute, and any number of other organizations, an impressive quantity of new educational material was produced during this period. An unpretentious but notable "first" was a little pamphlet prepared by the National Association: "Facts and Figures about Mental Illness and Other Personality Disturbances" (12). Although there had been numerous "Fact Sheets" released by many groups in previous years, this was the first one based on accurate statistical analysis and precise definition of terms; it has settled many statistical controversies and become a standard reference from which other popularly styled publicity pieces are derived. The *Psychiatric Bulletin* (30) was the first psychiatric periodical directed to the general medical practitioner. The Mental Health Film Board, initiated by the National Institute, sponsored by the National Association, and financed by pooled grant-in-aid funds from several states, produced seven mental health films (31). Except for the popular Mental Mechanism Series of the National Film Board of Canada, this was the first series of its kind.

Another successful pioneering venture was the use of drama for mental health education, which started in 1942 when the American Theatre Wing Community Plays, Inc. (then called Victory Players), and the New York State Committee on Mental Hygiene worked together to develop short dramatic sketches for mental health education (13). In 1951, Community Plays in collaboration with the National Association produced an excellent series: *Temperate Zone: Three Plays for Parents about the Climate of the Home,* followed the next year by two others . . . *And You Never Know* and *The Case of the Missing Handshake.* Played without scenery or properties, on a bare stage with small casts, these sketches have been widely used by amateur groups throughout the country and have been translated into a number of foreign languages. They are examples of a desirable kind of collaboration between groups with different kinds of skills: the mental hygiene group, with their understanding of behavior, and the theatre group, with their skill in getting across ideas.

Utilizing this same dramatic technique, the National Association and the American Theatre Wing Community Plays jointly produced *My Name Is Legion.* This hour-long dramatization is based on Clifford Beers' autobiography, *A Mind That Found Itself.* The first fifty minutes dramatizes Beers' story, just as he told it in this book, and attempts to convey an impression of what mental illness is like and the dreadful suffering of the mentally ill. The last ten minutes tells about the mental hygiene movement and tries to present a balanced picture of what has been accomplished for the better care of the mentally ill, though stressing how much still remains to be done. The sketch was conceived as fulfilling three purposes: straight education about mental illness, publicity for the mental health movement, and a focus for fund-raising efforts.

The first seven productions with a Broadway cast were in New York and neighboring cities in the spring of 1952. In the fall the Broadway cast, sponsored by state and local mental health associations in thirty-six cities, toured fourteen states for six weeks. As this goes to press a ten-week tour of some twenty-five or so states is being arranged for the spring of 1953. Reception by the public, the professional field, and the theatrical world has been enthusiastic. The script will in time be available for amateur production.

THE BROAD SWEEP

At the time of Clifford Beers' death[3] in 1943 some of the trends, which in the decade since have become so clearly defined, were only beginning to be apparent.

In his section Dr. Woodward has already commented on the great wave of public interest during the period 1933-47. This has been enormously accelerated in the last five years. As mental health specialists learn more about the mass media they become more skillful in utilizing these techniques to get their materials to the public. Concurrently, as workers in the mass media learn more about mental health they reach out for more and more material. Behind both, of course, are the readiness and avidity of the public which have already been commented on in this section. Evidence is so extensive on this point that it needs no further belaboring. However, it is worth noting that the public's eagerness for ideas about mental health exists side by side with its inertia toward improving conditions for the mentally ill.

Parallel to the accelerated wave of interest on the part of the lay public is a similar acceleration of interest on the part

[3]Clifford Beers died on July 9, 1943. In the few years following his death, the mental hygiene movement lost several more of its loyal pioneers: Samuel W. Hamilton, M.D., Paul O. Komora, Adolf Meyer, M.D., James Plant, M.D., and William L. Russell, M.D.

of a large number of professional groups. Every professional association, every professional meeting these days seems to include mental health on its agenda, and the number of mental health articles in other professional journals is striking.

Dr. Woodward has also commented on the way in which the mental health movement has, without losing interest in the mentally ill, become increasingly concerned with the mental health of all the people. It may be this broader interest in mental health that accounts for the unpopularity of the phrase "mental hygiene," which is now seldom heard. Practically all new organizations in the field prefer "mental health," and many old ones which originally had "mental hygiene" in their titles have changed to "mental health."

Apparent in both Dr. Woodward's account and this one is the fact that government is concerning itself with many more mental health areas than in earlier years. Government at the state level long ago assumed responsibility for the care of the mentally ill. But now government at all levels, from local to international, is concerning itself with the whole broad field of mental illness and mental health. Whatever government concerns itself with is by implication a responsibility of all the people. Therefore it is evident that there is growing recognition of the fact that *the mental health of all the people is properly a concern of all the people.*

The above trends were all apparent earlier, although they have accelerated in the last five years, some to an extreme degree. A more recent trend has taken shape and moved ahead so rapidly that it can be considered a phenomenon of the postwar years.

There is no single word or phrase to describe this phenomenon. It is a sort of dynamic synthesizing process, a cross-fertilization, a breaking down of psychiatric isolation, a new give and take between mental health and other professions, and between mental health and community groups. Characteristic of it is the new willingness of mental health specialists to examine their own work critically and to try to assess their own role in solving real-life problems and their relation to others who are trying to solve the same problems.

Examples of this phenomenon are all around. It is, for instance, surely no mere coincidence that the year 1946 ushered in the Commonwealth Fund institutes, the Macy conferences, the group for the Advancement of Psychiatry, the National Mental Health Foundation, the Central Inspection Board, the National Mental Health Act, the advanced program of the Veterans Administration, and the initial planning of the third International Congress on Mental Health. All of these are outstanding examples of co-operative effort between different groups. Psychiatrically oriented workers everywhere are integrating their clinical and their educational activities and collaborating with more different professional and community groups than ever before. Clinics, hitherto well satisfied to keep to themselves, now regard it as their duty to reach out into the community and to develop with others broad but integrated community programs. Government, with its wider responsibilities for health, welfare, and education, and voluntary agencies, with theirs, are redefining and enlarging the concept of mental health. Many of the most frequently used words and phrases, such as "co-ordination," "integration," "community planning," "citizen responsibility," "multidiscipline collaboration," seem to embody the central idea of the postwar years in mental health.

Unhappily, it is not yet possible to announce definitive progress in the understanding of the basic causes of mental disease. Many competent scientists are laboring. Little by little a significant body of knowledge is being accumulated. But prediction, control, prevention are still out of grasp. It is to be hoped that, when the time comes for the next report on the mental health movement for this volume, progress toward prevention will be the trend which can be acclaimed with certainty.

BIBLIOGRAPHY

Publications referred to in the text available from the National Association for Mental Hygiene, 1790 Broadway, New York 19 N.Y.

1. Manual for Organizing State and Local Mental Hygiene Societies, by Marian McBee and Marjorie Frank. 1949. 36pp.
2. The Organization and Function of the Community Psychiatric Clinic, by A. Z. Barhash, Mary Bentley, Milton E. Kirkpatrick, and Helen Sanders. 1952. 105pp.
3. Evaluation of Community Needs and Resources for Mental Health, by Marian McBee and Marjorie Frank. 1950. 50pp.
4. Volunteer Participation in Psychiatric Hospital Services, by Marian McBee and Marjorie Frank. 1950. 110pp.
5. Planning a Mental Health Education Program; Working with Key Groups, by Division of Education. 1952.
6. Interpreting Mental Health through Public Relations, by Lynn Stratton. 1950. 37pp.
7. Handbook for Psychiatric Aides. Section I, 1946, 58pp.; Section II, 1950, 101pp.
8. Mental Health and World Citizenship. Statement prepared for the International Congress on Mental Health, London, 1948. 47pp.
9. Mental Health Is . . . 1, 2, 3. Leaflet.
10. Some Special Problems of Children: Aged 2–5 Years, by Nina Ridenour and Isabel Johnson. 1949. 72pp.
11. Blondie. Comic strip by Chic Young, adapted by Joe Musial. 1950. 16pp.
12. Facts and Figures about Mental Illness and Other Personality Disturbances. 1952. 9pp.
13. Dramatic Sketches of the American Theatre Wing Community Plays. FOR HIGH SCHOOLS: *The Ins and Outs,* by Nora Stirling. FOR PARENT EDUCATION: *Temperate Zone: Three Plays for Parents about the Climate of the Home,* by Nora Stirling: *Scattered Showers; Fresh Variable Winds; High Pressure Area. . . . And You Never Know,* by Nora Stirling. *The Case of the Missing Handshake,* by Nora Stirling. FOR COMMUNITY GROUPS: *My Name Is Legion,* by Nora Stirling and Nina Ridenour.

OTHER PUBLICATIONS MENTIONED IN THE TEXT

14. A Draft Act Governing Hospitalization of the Mentally Ill. Public Health Service, Federal Security Agency. 1951.

15. The Mental Health Programs of the 48 States; A Report to the Governors' Conference. Council of State Governments. 1949.

16. Vocational Rehabilitation of Psychiatric Patients, by T. A. C. Rennie, Temple Burling, and Luther E. Woodward. New York: Commonwealth Fund. 1950.

17. Vocational Services for Psychiatric Clinic Patients, by T. A. C. Rennie and Mary Bozeman. Published for the Commonwealth Fund, Harvard University Press. 1952. 100pp.

18. Vocational Rehabilitation of the Mentally Retarded, ed. by Salvatore G. DiMichael. Office of Vocational Rehabilitation, Federal Security Agency. 1950. 184pp.

19. Psychiatric Aide Education, by Bernard Hall and Associates. Grune and Stratton. 1952.

20. Epidemiology of Mental Disorder. Milbank Memorial Fund. 1950. 198pp.

21. Minutes of the Conference on the Effects of Early Experience on Mental Health. Jackson Memorial Laboratory, Bar Harbor, Maine. 1951.

22. Josiah Macy Jr. Foundation Reports: Training in Clinical Psychology, 1947; Problems of Infancy and Childhood, Series of 4, 1948–50; Problems of Aging, Series 4, 1948–51; Health and Human Relations in Germany, 2 reports, 1950 and 1951; Healthy Personality Development in Children: As Related to the Federal Government, 1952; and other reports.

23. Teaching Psychotherapeutic Medicine, by Helen L. Witmer. Commonwealth Fund. 1947.

24. Public Health Is People: an institute on mental health in public health held at Berkeley, California, 1948, by Ethel L. Ginsburg. Commonwealth Fund. 1950.

25. Published Reports of the Group for the Advancement of Psychiatry. 3617 West 6th Ave., Topeka, Kans. 2 volumes. 1949–52.

26. Children and Youth at the Mid-Century, Preliminary Reports for the Mid-Century White House Conference on Children and Youth, Washington, D.C., December 1950: Fact Finding

Report; A Digest, 170pp.; Report on State and Local Action, 61pp.; Report on Youth, National Organizations, and Federal Government. 122pp.

27. Proceedings of the International Congress on Mental Health, London, 1948. 4 vols. New York: Columbia University Press.

28. Reports of the Expert Committees on Mental Health, 1950 and 1951. Technical Report Series. World Health Organization, Geneva, Switzerland.

29. Maternal Care and Mental Health; a report prepared on behalf of the World Health Organization as a contribution to the United Nations program for the welfare of homeless children, by John Bowlby. World Health Organization Monograph Series, No. 2. New York: Columbia University Press. 1952. 194pp.

30. Psychiatric Bulletin (a quarterly for physicians in general practice). Medical Arts Foundation, 2310 Baldwin St., Houston, Tex.

31. Mental Health Film Board: The Emotions of Everyday Living, series of seven films: *Angry Boy; The Steps of Age; Fears of Children; The Lonely Night; Roots of Happiness; Farewell to Childhood; First Lessons.* Distributed by International Film Bureau, 57 East Jackson Blvd., Chicago 4, Ill.

IV

THE AMERICAN FOUNDATION FOR
MENTAL HYGIENE

The American Foundation for Mental Hygiene, Incorporated, was established on May 24, 1928, under the laws of the State of Delaware, and later was officially approved by the proper authorities of the State of New York. It is located at 1790 Broadway, New York 19, N.Y., in the offices of the National Association for Mental Health.

The Foundation was originally established as a financing agency; its purpose was to give financial aid to work and research in the whole broad field of mental illness and mental health. The first gift in 1928 was an amount of fifty thousand dollars from the estate of the late Mrs. Annie C. Kane of New York City. This gift was used to finance the basic expenses of the First International Congress of Mental Hygiene, held in Washington, D.C., May 5–10, 1930, and made it possible to hold the Congress and later publish its Proceedings.

The Foundation holds the copyright on *A Mind That Found Itself* and on *The Mentally Ill in America*, by Albert Deutsch, and also certain rights in the literary estate of the late Clifford W. Beers. It is governed by a Board of Trustees. Because of shifting emphases and broadening functions of the National Committee for Mental Hygiene and later the National Association for Mental Health, the Foundation has not in recent years been active in fund raising. It continues to exist as a non-profit corporation, however, and is desirous of receiving bequests which will be devoted to mental hygiene work.

SHORT FORMS OF BEQUEST AND DEVISE IN A WILL

1. ABSOLUTE BEQUEST OF PERSONAL PROPERTY

I hereby give and bequeath to The American Foundation for Mental Hygiene, Incorporated, and its successors forever, the sum of .... Dollars (or otherwise describe the gift) to be used in the furtherance of its general corporate purposes (or name of specific purpose or activity within the Foundation's field of work).

2. ABSOLUTE DEVISE OF REAL PROPERTY

I hereby give and devise to The American Foundation for Mental Hygiene, Incorporated, and its successors forever, the following described real estate: (describe the real estate particularly) to be used in the furtherance of its general corporate purposes (or name a specific purpose or activity within the Foundation's field of work).

3. BEQUEST FOR ENDOWMENT TO THE FOUNDATION AS TRUSTEE FOR ITSELF

I hereby give and bequeath to The American Foundation for Mental Hygiene, Incorporated, and its successors forever, the sum of .... Dollars (or otherwise describe the gift), in trust, nevertheless to be held as endowment (if as a memorial, add "in memory of ....
............, by whose name the fund shall be known in the records of the Foundation") and administered as a charitable trust; to invest, reinvest and keep the same invested, and to collect and apply the income arising therefrom to its own use and in furtherance of its general corporate purposes (or name a specific purpose or activity within the Foundation's field of work).

4. BEQUEST TO A BANK OR TRUST COMPANY AS TRUSTEE FOR THE FOUNDATION

I hereby give to the (here insert name of bank or trust company) and its successors forever, the sum of ....
.... Dollars (or otherwise describe the gift, and inserting, if it is given as a memorial, "in memory of ...., by whose name the fund shall be known in the records of the bank or trust company and of the Foundation") to be held, invested, reinvested, kept invested and administered by it as a charitable trust, and to collect the income arising therefrom and pay the same to The American Foundation for Mental Hygiene, Incorporated, at such times as it shall specify, for use in the furtherance of its general corporate purposes (or name a specific purpose or activity within the Foundation's field of work).